The Army and Its Air Corps
Army Policy toward Aviation
1919–1941

Dr. James P. Tate
Lt Col, USAF, Retired

Air University Press
Maxwell Air Force Base, Alabama

July 1998

Library of Congress Cataloging-in-Publication Data

Tate, James P.
   The Army and its air corps : Army policy toward aviation, 1919–1941 / James P. Tate.
      p. cm.
   Includes bibliographical references and index.
   1. United States. Army. Air Corps—History. 2. Air power—United States—History. I. Title.
   UG633.T35   1998
   358.4'00973—dc21

98-28888
CIP

ISBN 1-58566-059-0

First Printing July 1998
Second Printing March 2005

Disclaimer

Opinions, conclusions, and recommendations expressed or implied within are solely those of the author and do not necessarily represent the views of Air University, the United States Air Force, the Department of Defense, or any other US government agency. Cleared for public release: distribution unlimited.

Cover: Far right, Brig Gen William "Billy" Mitchell with other flyers by his aircraft. Second from left, Clayton L. Bissell, later an Air Force general, led the flight that sank the Ostfriesland.

Air University Press
131 West Shumacher Avenue
Maxwell AFB AL 36112-6615
http://aupress.maxwell.af.mil

Contents

Chapter		Page
	DISCLAIMER	ii
	FOREWORD	v
	ABOUT THE AUTHOR	vii
1	THE RETURN TO PEACE: VISIONARIES AND REALISTS	1
	The Uncertainty of Its Future	5
	A Very Unfortunate and Critical Situation	15
	Notes	20
2	CREATION OF THE ARMY AIR CORPS	27
	Business Methods in the War Department	28
	"Almost Treasonable Administration of the National Defense"	34
	A "Bolshevik Bug in the Air"	39
	Notes	48
3	AT WAR WITH THE NAVY	59
	Warning from the Air Corps: The Navy Is Coming Ashore!	61
	Not a Matter of Law	66
	The MacArthur–Pratt Agreement	71
	Notes	79
4	THE GREAT DEPRESSION	83
	Hoover Orders an Economic Survey of the War Department	84
	"Just Hog-tied a Mississippi Cracker"	89
	That Same Old Chestnut	98
	Notes	105
	PHOTO SECTION	111
5	THE AIRMAIL CRISIS AND THE CREATION OF THE GHQ AIR FORCE	131
	"The Army Has Lost the Art of Flying"	131
	An "Air Plan for the Defense of the United States"	134

Chapter		Page
	The GHQ Air Force Becomes a Reality	143
	Notes	151
6	PREPARATION FOR WAR	157
	The Heavy Bomber	157
	The Army Air Force	170
	Notes	180
7	CONCLUSION	185
	Notes	192
	BIBLIOGRAPHY	195
	INDEX	205

Illustrations

Figure		
1	Cost of the Army Air Corps by Fiscal Years	86
2	Annual Strength of the Air Corps	103
3	Reduction in Other Arms to Permit Increases in Air Corps under Five-Year Plan	104

Foreword

The Army and Its Air Corps was James P. Tate's doctoral dissertation at Indiana University in 1976. During the past 22 years, Tate's remarkable work has gained wide acceptance among scholars for its authoritative and well-documented treatment of the formative years of what eventually became the United States Air Force.

Thoroughly researched but bearing its scholarship lightly, Tate's narrative moves swiftly as it describes the ambitions, the frustrations, and the excruciatingly slow march to final success that never deterred the early airmen.

The Army and Its Air Corps is one in a series of airpower history classics that the Air University Press is pleased to bring before a wider audience.

ROBERT B. LANE
Director
Air University Press

About the Author

Dr. James P. Tate (Lieutenant Colonel, USAF, Retired) is a 1963 graduate of the US Air Force Academy. During his 20 years of active service, he flew a wide variety of aircraft, including the Navy F9F, in which he was carrier qualified. In his first tour in Vietnam, he flew 73 combat missions in the F-105; in his second tour, he served as operations inspector on the Inspector General team. Colonel Tate subsequently returned to the Air Force Academy to teach history. He continued his studies in that discipline, earning his master's and doctorate degrees from the University of Indiana. This book is based on his doctoral dissertation, which has been widely used and cited by scholars.

After his retirement from the Air Force in 1983, Colonel Tate continued his studies, earning a doctorate in jurisprudence from the University of Texas at Austin. He now practices law in Colorado Springs, Colorado.

Chapter 1

The Return to Peace: Visionaries and Realists

I guess we considered ourselves a different breed of cat, right in the beginning. We flew through the air and the other people walked on the ground; it was as simple as that!

—Gen Carl A. Spaatz

    The development of the Army Air Corps was a history of struggle and compromise between realists and visionaries, in which neither side was always fair or even wise. The adherents of both looked as best they could to the security of their country. The airmen of the First World War who carried their heady ideas into the years after 1918, were dashing, romantic, and heroic. They were challenging the future; they had wings and could soar; they had no patience with any hesitation their countrymen might have had about the airplane as the mainstay of America's defense. The young visionaries wanted to see the country airborne. The years after the Great War, however, were hard years for the United States Army (USA) and even for the Navy, and not everyone shared the dreams of the flyers. The leadership of the Army and Navy lived with ever dwindling appropriations from Congress and was responsible for America's defense on land and sea as well as in the air. Of what avail, said the generals and admirals, was defense of the country only in the air?

    The problem of money for the Army and Navy had arisen almost with the very end of the war. Only hours after the guns had fallen silent, while cheering crowds were filling the boulevards of Paris, Edward R. Stettinius, who was in France representing the United States on the Inter-Allied Munitions Council, read a cablegram from the War Department instructing him to "cut down expenses as rapidly as possible."[1] At Chaumont, France, headquarters of the American Expeditionary Force (AEF), a War Department cable informed Gen John J. Pershing that "all draft calls and special inductions into the service have been canceled," and that "Sunday work and overtime work in production for the Army, Navy, and shipping contracts have been stopped."[2]

    America had enthusiastically sent men to war at a rate of over 250,000 a month and was about to show its willingness to pursue peace with equal enthusiasm.[3] The problem would be how much money to spend on national defense. Could Americans return to their peacetime tradition of ignoring military questions except those related to the defense of the national borders? Or had the responsibilities of world power along with technological advances in the war, particularly the introduction of the airplane, so changed the world military balance as to demand a change in the cost of defense—perhaps by expenditure of several hundred millions of dollars to acquire the newest airplanes and to train men to fly them?

During the next years, indeed the next two decades, almost until the United States prepared to enter the Second World War, much of the debate on peacetime priorities would center on airpower, its definition, and its effect on military policy. In the postwar American army, where money was short, and during the Depression, desperately short, the question of technological change and combat readiness came to revolve around expenditures demanded by proponents of airpower—for the airplane was the most revolutionary weapon of the new military technology.

While there was differing opinion as to where the airplane should fit in peacetime military policy, realists and visionaries typified the positions in the controversy. The visionaries dealt with what they sensed to be the future; the realists dealt with what they knew to be the present.

In the grand argument of what to do about technological change—or what to do about airpower—Brig Gen William "Billy" Mitchell was of course the leading visionary. During the war, Mitchell had seen an awesome potential for airpower as distinct from land and sea power, but the war ended before he could demonstrate it. The airplane had excelled at patrol, reconnaissance, and artillery directing. There had been epic "dog fights" with German pursuit formations, and the exploits of Edward V. "Eddie" Rickenbacker, Raoul Lufbery, and other American aces captured the imagination of young men for years to come. The record in independent operations of the sort Mitchell envisioned as the essence of airpower was unimpressive. By the end of the war, the pilots of the Air Service dropped only 138 tons of bombs; their deepest penetration of enemy territory had been 160 miles.[4] There were plans for strategic bombing units in the Air Service, a long-range inter-Allied bombing force, and even an airborne operation dropping paratroopers behind German lines. None of these plans had been carried out.[5]

Years later, Mitchell's friend and follower, Henry H. "Hap" Arnold, reflected on Mitchell's frustration. "In a sense," he wrote, "for Billy, the Armistice was an untimely interruption—as if the whistle had ended the game just as he was about to go over the goal line."[6] But Mitchell was not to be deterred. Lacking proof for the potential of airpower in war, he offered his vision as testimony and his good faith as guarantee of the truth of his argument. Having revealed the truth about airpower, he became increasingly impatient with those who would compromise that truth. In his mind, he was "righter than hell and he knew it, and whoever wasn't with him a hundred percent was against him."[7] As his battle for airpower intensified, he came to consider those who opposed him as stupid or immoral. In the case of antagonists in the Army bureaucracy, he suspected the latter. They feared innovation, he contended, because it might curtail "their ancient prerogatives, privileges, and authority." Mitchell never admitted that the austerities of peace were as much to blame for blocking the development of airpower as any conspiracy of admirals and old-fashioned generals. He was a prophet absolutely sure of his truth. This self-confident, self-righteous attitude was perhaps Mitchell's chief legacy to the Air Corps. It intensified the partisan aspect of the airpower controversy, conditioning his followers and those they would later indoctrinate never to be satisfied with anything short of independence from the Army.[8]

Mitchell's first antagonist after he returned from France proved to be Secretary of War Newton D. Baker, a moderate on the aviation issue, who saw himself as a realist with a healthy civilian perspective toward military affairs. A thin wisp of a man in his early forties, with a "whimsical eye" and quick step, Baker had become a familiar sight in the tiled halls of the old State, War, and Navy Building, but—and one might suspect he wanted it that way—he never quite seemed to fit the surroundings.[9] Secretary of the Treasury William G. McAdoo wrote of him:

> Baker used to sit at his desk at the War Department with one leg curled up under him on the cushion of his chair. On his desk there was always a fresh pansy, and he continually smoked a pipe. A small man physically, Baker looked boyish in the company of the tall and bulky generals who were usually around him.[10]

A civilian's civilian, Baker saw the military as a necessity, but he had no awe of people in uniform, no romantic feelings toward them, and no dreams of glory. Before he came to Washington in 1916, his closest brush with military service had been during the Spanish–American War when he volunteered but was rejected because of poor eyesight.[11] On the day President Woodrow Wilson announced Baker's appointment as secretary of war, he admitted his ignorance of military matters. "I am an innocent," he told reporters, "I do not know anything about this job." But he had a sharp, analytical mind and considerable skill at administration. He quickly learned the job, and as he had pointed out to the reporters on that first day, he was unencumbered with "obsessions or prejudices about policies."[12] During his term in office, he became reasonably informed in military matters but not expert. For decisions of policy, he remained reliant upon his military advisers but exerted his powers of logic and his understanding of human nature from the perspective of his military innocence.[13]

Baker understood the airmen's frustration. "We were dealing with a miracle," he explained in 1919. "The airplane itself was too wonderful and too new, too positive a denial of previous experience to brook the application of any prudential restraints which wise people know to apply to ordinary industrial and military developments."[14] The young men closest to the miracle were awed by it, taken in by the "desperate, daredevil, hazardous" experience of pioneering in flight. Even before their exhilarating work in the First World War, he had seen in them a "disposition to chafe at the restraint and discipline which was made for more normal kinds of service, feeling that they were not adapted to the regulation and restrictions of men who were not engaged in so unusual an occupation."[15]

During the war, as Baker well understood, the War Department had contributed to the elitist attitude of the airmen. Flyers were selected by a careful process for what was considered the most perilous duty in the military. "You scour the United States and get 5,000 of the most daring youths you can possibly find," Baker pointed out to congressmen questioning alleged prejudice against the Air Service within the Army:

> You train them in almost nursery methods. A man is trained a certain way, and the doctors examine his nerves; they make a prima donna of him, and he has a prima donna's job to do. They are a very highly specialized and a most carefully selected crowd of men. You send them out into the Army; or you send them anywhere; they have a class feeling; a feeling of superiority, which is a thing altogether natural. They can not help feeling it.[16]

But Baker knew that in the final analysis victory went to the men on the ground, even though it was tempting for the airman, high above the mud and grime that infantrymen lived in, to feel he could accomplish more than the foot soldier could and do it faster.

The flyers themselves seemed to verify Baker's analysis, as Gen Carl A. "Tooey" Spaatz observed many years later when he said they considered themselves a different breed of cat.[17] And the most unique cat of all was Billy Mitchell, the man who was to become the air enthusiasts' spokesman. In France he had been the Prince of the Air, holding court in his headquarters at Souilly. Wearing a distinctive, nonregulation uniform and speeding through the French countryside in a Mercedes, allegedly the fastest car in France, he was almost the caricature of an airman.[18] General Pershing, looking for an airman with leadership qualities, put up with Mitchell while the AEF was in France. After the war, Mitchell's flamboyance and that of his followers irritated conservative Army brass. To them it appeared that airmen needed discipline rather than independence.

Baker agreed with his commanders that the airmen deserved some sort of comeuppance, but not because the airmen themselves had irritated him. "The art itself," he wrote in his annual report in 1919, "is so new and so fascinating, and the men in it have so taken on the character of supermen, that it is difficult to reason coldly, and perhaps dangerous to attempt any limitation upon the future based even upon the most favorable view of present attainments." Nevertheless, he felt that one must reason coldly and that the airmen's perspectives were narrow and their "youthful" exuberance needed supervision. Aerial bombing of military targets had not as yet proved effective. "Back areas and inland cities," the kinds of targets that strategic bombing would likely be directed against, "should plainly be excluded upon the most elemental ethical and humanitarian grounds." He mentioned the airplane's high cost, its fragile nature, and its vulnerability to antiaircraft artillery—the technology of which also was advancing very rapidly. He concluded that aviation's young supermen should not be given their head, that "the time has not come to set up an independent department of the air," and that "as yet, the infantry is the backbone of military effort, and all other arms on land, on the sea, and in the air, are mere aids to its advance and protection to it while it is performing its functions of advance and occupation."[19]

The caution in Baker's attitude was typical of most War Department leaders in the years following the First World War. Their sense of responsibility for a practical military policy made them wary of proposals that would put too much of the defense establishment's resources into the development of airpower. There would be no hedge against changing circumstances. Since they had to be concerned with the worst, as well as the best possible outcome of their decision, they could not accept such risk.[20]

The Uncertainty of Its Future

It was hardly surprising that Mitchell was not chosen as postwar leader of the Air Service, though he was undoubtedly the choice of many airmen who had served with him in France and of some who had not. Hap Arnold claimed that on an inspection trip in France shortly after the Armistice he had asked Mitchell to get the appointment by using his influence with General Pershing. Arnold had spent the war in Washington. To fight postwar battles for funds, Arnold concluded that the "Air Service needed Billy home fast." Although Mitchell's first reaction to Arnold's suggestion was a firm "No," he soon changed his mind and returned to Washington as rapidly as possible.21 It was to no avail. He received the subordinate post of director of military aeronautics, while Maj Gen Charles T. Menoher, known as a strict disciplinarian, was appointed director of the Air Service.

Menoher was a good choice. A classmate of Pershing at West Point and a veteran of 31 years, he was perhaps proudest of his record as commander of the 42d (Rainbow) Division from Château-Thierry to the conclusion of the Meuse-Argonne offensive. "The division was not out of the sound of German guns for nine months," he told the Frear Committee after the war, "and for 188 days of that time we were in contact with the enemy."22 Years later, Gen Douglas MacArthur, who served under Menoher in the Rainbow Division, remembered him as "an able officer, an efficient administrator. . . . He preferred to supervise operations from his command headquarters, where he could keep in constant touch with the corps and army, relying upon me to handle the battle line."23 Taking into account MacArthur's vanity, it is probably safe to conclude that Menoher was indeed an efficient administrator. That was also the opinion of Father Francis P. Duffy, the well-known chaplain of Menoher's division: "If he were not [in] uniform he would impress one as a successful businessman—one of the kind that can carry responsibility, give orders affecting large affairs with calmness and certainty, and still find time to be human. He is entirely devoid of posing, of vanity, or of jealousy. His only desire is to see results."24 On most Air Service issues Menoher represented the point of view of the War Department and the General Staff. Wartime experience had convinced him that the air arm should support ground forces. During the Aisne-Marne campaign he had seen his division's progress measurably slowed by lack of support from the air. After the battle his headquarters commented, "The fact that the enemy had practically complete control of the air not only prevented our troops from receiving adequate information but enabled the enemy to adopt a very aggressive attitude in the way of firing on our troops with machine guns and bombs."25

The radical airmen resented Menoher. In the words of Arnold, "Our Chief, General Menoher, was not only unable and wholly unwilling to cope with Mitchell's ideas, but he could not handle Billy Mitchell. Also to make matters worse, he did not fly much."26

Given the attitudes of Secretary Baker and the officers of the General Staff, there did not seem to be much that the airmen could do to promote their cause. In the spring of 1919 Pershing, still in France with the AEF, appointed Maj Gen Joseph T. Dickman to head a board of superior officers to determine the lessons from American participation in the war. Considered by the "Old Army" as a scholarly soldier, Dickman had read deeply on military subjects and had been an instructor at several service schools.[27] Among other members of the board were Maj Gen John L. Hines, Maj Gen William Lassiter, and Brig Gen Hugh A. Drum, all of whom would become participants in the airpower controversy of years to come. In its report the board reflected the opinion of the Army's leadership that future wars between great powers would be fought and decided by mass armies on the ground. They found nothing to indicate that "aerial activities can be carried on, independently of ground troops, to such an extent as to materially affect the conduct of the war as a whole." They unanimously agreed that the lesson of the war was that "unity of command is absolutely vital"—aviation, like the cavalry and the artillery, must remain an auxiliary, subject to authority of the principal arm, the infantry. "For the present," the report concluded, "all questions of air tactics, air strategy and the employment of aviation must be governed by the well-known and established principles of military art. Superior officers must be so thoroughly well-grounded in the fundamentals of war that this important auxiliary will be used always in pursuance of the paramount object." The Dickman Board recognized that aviation technology might change their conclusions, particularly if a large number of Americans became "air-faring." But the great cost of building a large air force could be justified only after aviation had proved itself. "If it becomes possible to use in war only aerial forces, the matter of expense is not a paramount question," the board conceded, "but if on the other hand, it is necessary to maintain ground and water forces for war, then the expense of aerial forces must be considered and the aviation must bear its proper relation to the other forces."[28]

While the Dickman Board was deliberating, the Air Service was rapidly being reduced. Of the approximately 20,000 officers assigned to the Air Service during the war, in 1919 only 220 regular officers remained detailed from other branches of the Army for temporary duty in aviation. Of the alleged billion-dollar aircraft industry created to support the war, 90 percent had been liquidated by mid-1919. With neither Army contracts nor a developed commercial market to support it, the remainder seemed destined to disappear. Even legislative authorization for the Air Service's existence was temporary, due to expire at the end of June 1920. Menoher in his report for the fiscal year from 1 July to 30 June 1920 summed up the situation: "The Air Service during the year has suffered from the uncertainty of its future."[29]

Congress, meanwhile, determined to make its own study of the American experience in the war. During the conflict, it had observed the traditional moratorium on politics and acquiesced in military policies of the executive. After the Armistice, the bars came down;

and Congress, under control of the Republican Party as a result of the elections of 1918, began a critical investigation of the conduct of the war by the Democratic administration of President Wilson. A select committee on expenditures in the War Department probed the hastily improvised mobilization. One of its subcommittees chaired by Rep. James A. Frear (R-Wisc.) investigated aviation. The subcommittee concentrated on aircraft production. After taking nearly 4,000 pages of testimony, it divided along party lines, the Republican majority declaring the aircraft program a "striking failure," while the Democratic minority emphasized "worthy" accomplishments of the Air Service. Both majority and minority reports concluded that agencies dealing with aviation should be reorganized, but differed in changes recommended. Noting that "practically every witness examined on the subject of the future of the American Air Service united in a plea for separate independent control," the majority report favored a separate department of aeronautics to control and coordinate government activities in aviation.[30] The minority report rejected a separate department but did call for a "separate Air Service, with authority to coordinate experimentation, purchase, and production." This would be a strictly civilian agency. Military aviation would remain under the War and Navy departments. Paralleling the conclusion of the Dickman Board, the minority report emphasized "unity of command" and concluded that "military aviation never can be anything other than simply an arm of the military organization and should not be a separate department."[31]

During the Frear hearings, Menoher gave his opinion on why he believed officers like Mitchell were agitating for a separate Air Service. Said he, "I think a good deal of the support of the separate Air Service plan is born of dissatisfaction. There has been a good deal of disappointment at not getting promotion, and some of it is due to a desire for more rapid advancement in the future." Identifying himself with the War Department leadership, he remarked, "We are not as temperamental as they seem to be."[32]

Maj Benjamin D. Foulois had accompanied Menoher to the committee hearing, and as soon as the general finished his testimony, Foulois asked to make a statement. Stung by Menoher's remarks, Foulois explained that flying men like himself had invaluable experience in aviation upon which to base their opinions. "In France," he said, "while I was still brigadier general I made my expressions of opinion without fear of demotion or anything else. . . . General Menoher's remarks did not apply to me, because I think he knows now of my record, and his remarks as regards promotion, I think, he did not mean to apply to me." Admitting there were "a great many officers who think of nothing but promotion," Major Foulois, who was soon to develop a reputation of being a firebrand, said, "I honestly hope that when the question of a separate air service comes up the flying men, who risked their lives for years and years in this manner, will have a right to talk and have a right to get up and express their opinions." His anger increasing, he continued, "I am prepared at any time to sit down and give my opinion as based on 21 years' service in the Army and 11 years in Aviation Service, that the General Staff in the last five or six years can not point to one instance of a General Staff Officer who has had anything constructive to do with the development of aviation today."[33]

Years later Foulois reflected on the touchy subject of rank in those days immediately following the First World War when many officers like himself were demoted. "The reduction," he wrote, "would not have been so hard to take if it had been universal, but it wasn't. Those high-ranking officers that March [Gen Peyton C. March, Army chief of staff in 1919] liked kept their ranks, and they, in turn, allowed their friends and favored subordinates to keep theirs."[34] It was galling to Foulois that Mitchell, whom Foulois disliked intensely, was allowed to keep his star as a brigadier general. It is likely that Foulois and Menoher would have agreed that Mitchell's agitation for a separate air service was moved by ambition.

The Menoher–Foulois exchange had occurred on 7 August 1919 and possibly was prompted by the congressional debate about to begin over proposals to create an air department. The previous week Rep. Charles F. Curry (R–Calif.) and Sen. Harry S. New (R–Ind.) had submitted bills, apparently in response to the recommendations of the American Aircraft Commission which had issued a report on 19 July. This group, better known as the Crowell Commission after its chairman, Assistant Secretary of War Benedict Crowell, had been appointed by Baker in May 1919 to survey aviation in Europe. Composed of representatives of the industry, as well as officers from aviation branches of the Army and Navy, the commission went to Europe and interviewed aviation leaders in Italy, France, and Great Britain. It unanimously recommended a department of aeronautics. Among its recommendations was a separate air academy similar to West Point and Annapolis.

Baker praised the commission for the thoroughness of its investigation but said it had "gone too far in suggesting a single centralized air service."[35] He did not suppress the report nor did he prevent Crowell from testifying before Congress in support of a separate department of air. He did set out an official War Department position on the commission's recommendations after the New and Curry bills appeared in Congress.[36]

On 8 August 1919, the day after Menoher's appearance before the Frear Committee hearings, Baker called on him to convene a board of general officers to report on the congressional proposals. Like Menoher, the other board members—Maj Gen William G. Haan, Maj Gen Frank W. Coe, and Maj Gen William J. Snow—were all artillery officers by training and experience. They met at frequent intervals from 12 August 1919 until 27 October 1919, when they submitted their report to the chief of staff. They examined reports of previous boards and commissions; heard testimony; and most important, conducted a telegraphic survey of the opinions of important division, corps, and Army commanders who actually took part in combat using aircraft as part of their commands. The Menoher Board dutifully appended to its report "letters from military aviators advocating a separate department . . . sent to the board by order of Brig Gen William Mitchell, Air Service, United States Army, who is, himself, an advocate of a separate aeronautical department coordinate with the Army and Navy."[37] Later describing the process, Menoher said, "We spent two months studying that question and arrived at our conclusions only after very considerable deliberation."[38]

The Menoher Board reaffirmed the principle of unity of command. "There should not be created any military air force independent of Army and Navy control." Board members were convinced the air arm could not win wars and to separate it from Army control would reduce the effectiveness of the Army, which could win wars. The argument that an independent air arm would develop more rapidly in peacetime and still be available for assignment to a unified command in wartime was not acceptable. Military forces that fight together should train together. They pointed out that the greatest deficiency of the American air force in the AEF was that it had not been trained with the other combat branches of the Army. To correct the deficiency, the "air force must be controlled in the same way, understand the same discipline, and act in accordance with the Army command under precisely the same conditions as do the other branches."[39]

Like the Dickman Board, Menoher's group emphasized the cost of an air force. Because of the "short life of aircraft and the great cost of production and maintenance," they argued that "no nation can in time of peace maintain military air fleets even approximating in size such as will be necessary in time of war." They did not mention directly, as had the Dickman Board, that the budget for aviation must be in balance with the rest of the Army, but did suggest that if emphasis was to be on aviation, Congress should make "large annual appropriations guaranteed over a period of not less than 10 years for the stimulation of commercial aeronautics." If an emergency should arise, it would be a "comparatively simple proposition" to divert production from commercial to military aircraft and select and train military aviators from the "great reservoir of commercial aviators," a healthy aviation industry would provide.[40]

Agitation for a separate department of aeronautics, according to the Menoher Board, came for the most part from the Air Service of the Army. The board asserted that the three most important reasons for dissatisfaction in the Air Service were the belief among air officers that an independent air force was essential in war, worry of air officers that no future existed for them in the Air Service as long as it remained part of the Army, and concern that "a military air force suitable to our position in the world" would not develop if Americans continued to regard aviation as an Army auxiliary. The board considered the first grievance a matter of doctrine on which it could not compromise. The other two grievances could be alleviated by providing permanency of commission for officers in the Air Service, suitable organization for the Air Service within the Army, and provision for air officers to receive the same opportunity as officers from other branches to attend service schools and be on the General Staff.[41]

Aviators were angrily critical of both the conclusions of the Menoher Board and the manner of its inquiry. Major Foulois charged that of 50 officers queried in the board's telegraphic survey, only four were Air Service officers, and that of these four, "only two are practical flying officers." He asserted that 20 flying officers who appeared to testify were not given time to present their case. All 20 were examined, he estimated, in three and a half hours.[42] Mitchell appeared before the Menoher Board early in its investigation on 14 August 1919, and afterward wrote the following:

> There was nothing in this meeting to indicate that the minds of the board were not conclusively made up ahead of time, almost to the extent of having been instructed to render a report against the bill. . . . The whole hearing impressed on me more than ever that, under the control of the Army, it will be impossible to develop an Air Service.[43]

If not true, Mitchell's suggestion that the Menoher Board had been instructed to report against the New and Curry bills was at least plausible. Baker's opposition to separating the Air Service from Army control was well established. He had expressed disapproval of findings of the Crowell Commission, and the generals of the Menoher Board must have understood, even if not told, that contrary findings would not meet the wishes of the secretary of war.[44]

Almost as if they had anticipated the airmen's charges, the generals of the board suggested in their report that military aviators who disagreed with the board's conclusions were likely suffering from "limitations of vision regarding the great problems of the combination of all arms to accomplish decisive results."[45] The airmen's perspectives were too narrow.

The Menoher Board had been charged with studying the aviation problem so as to develop War Department policy regarding aviation. By implication that meant a practical policy acceptable to the Army leadership. This the board did. Adding structure to the Dickman Board report, the Menoher Board report was for its time the most complete statement of the War Department position toward the airplane.

Armed with findings of the Menoher Board, Secretary Baker, Chief of Staff March, Pershing, and other Army leaders challenged the Air Service radicals in congressional hearings conducted on the New and Curry bills. Arrayed against the Army leadership were such men as Mitchell, Foulois, and Arnold, aided and abetted by Assistant Secretary Crowell and none other than the chairman of the investigating committee for the House of Representatives, Rep. Fiorello H. La Guardia (R-N.Y.). As a major in the Air Service during the war, La Guardia had commanded a bomber squadron on the Italian front.

During the hearings, the points of the airmen's argument emerged. The flyers argued that there were military missions for the air arm independent of the surface forces; that the airplane had an almost unlimited potential as a weapon; that the full power of the airplane could be reached only by an air arm controlled by men with knowledge and interest in aviation; that the leadership of the Army, especially the General Staff, lacked interest and knowledge in aviation and had subordinated the needs of the air arm to those of other combat arms; that a separate air service would prevent expensive duplication by concentrating the government's aviation activities under central control; that such an independent air service had been successful in Britain; and finally, that development of aviation under an independent air service would provide support, direction, and encouragement for the country's aviation industry which depended so heavily upon the military market. The best way to take advantage of the new technology in aviation was to create a new military organization.[46]

General Pershing's testimony seemingly supported some of the Air Service pilots' demands when he stated that aviation was bound to be an element of increasing importance in warfare and that America should not be allowed to lag behind other countries. Menoher, upset by the way newspapers were interpreting the testimony, asked Pershing if he would "correct this interpretation of his views" and make the War Department's position very clear in its opposition to aviators' demands for a separate organization.[47] Pershing responded that although the Air Service was essential in any future war, particularly for reconnaissance and artillery support, it could never win a war independent of ground forces. He agreed with air enthusiasts that the Air Service should be a separate arm, but it must remain within the Army, like the infantry, cavalry, and artillery. In view of the later Mitchell controversy, one of his statements to Menoher was significant: "If success is to be expected, the military air force must be controlled in the same way, understand the same discipline, and act in accordance with the Army command under the same conditions as other combat arms."[48]

The War Department's opposition to the airmen rested on the idea that the aviation technology was still in an experimental stage. While it was possible—though few Army leaders believed it probable—that wars might be fought in the air, sober assessment of present technological development in aviation did not justify an independent air service. Baker cautioned congressmen not to tamper with a proven military system. An independent air service would produce competition that could undermine cooperation among airmen and the Army and Navy. He questioned how "separate" an independent air service could be from the other branches. Being independent would imply having its own armament—bombs, machine guns, rifles, pistols, and perhaps cannons some day—even an antiaircraft defense. This would mean duplicating equipment and manpower the Army already had, or usurping much of the Army's command responsibilities.[49]

Baker typified War Department leaders who felt the best way to take advantage of aviation technology was to develop it within the established organization. Some more conservative Army leaders argued that new technology should be adapted to the established military organization.

Debate continued through the autumn and winter of 1919–20; and in the House, the results were indecisive. The Curry bill, which proposed a department of aeronautics with the secretary of aeronautics holding cabinet rank, never emerged from the House Committee on Military Affairs. In revised form, it was still before the committee in 1926.

In the Senate, there was a temporary victory for the air enthusiasts, and then the situation deteriorated. The Committee on Military Affairs reported favorably on Senator New's bill on 8 December 1919. Somewhat revised, the bill called for an executive department of aeronautics, but it differed from the Curry bill in that it proposed that the head of the new agency be a presidentially appointed director of aeronautics who would not hold cabinet rank.[50] Senator New presented his bill on 28 January 1920 for debate on the floor of the Senate and told his colleagues it was designed to change policy toward aeronautics, that up to that time had been "little short of absurd,"[51] and he forecasted a possible saving of $63 million to the government if his plan for uniting the aviation activities of the government was accepted.[52] The majority of senators remained unimpressed. Many saw no urgency in the matter, and some like Sen. William H. King (D-Utah) found it impossible to decide on the issue when there was such a "divergence of views among those who have given the subject consideration."[53] New apparently realized the bill could not pass; and on 31 January 1920, to avoid a vote, he requested unanimous consent for the bill to be resubmitted to the Committee on Military Affairs. The request was granted and the bill returned to the committee, never to emerge again. Congressional proponents of a department of air had met defeat.[54]

The following summer, Congress passed the National Defense Act of 1920, which gave permanent legislative authority to the Air Service and placed it on a par with other branches of the Army. The Air Service received authority to procure equipment. Its strength was set at 1,514 officers and 16,000 enlisted men. The act addressed specific grievances of flyers by reaffirming the principle of flight pay at a rate of an additional 50 percent of regular pay. It reaffirmed the military rating of "Airplane Pilot."

Airpower enthusiasts were disappointed. The Air Service remained under the Army, and its budget continued to be part of the War Department budget. The post of assistant chief of the Air Service was given to General Mitchell. General Menoher's title was changed from director to chief of the Air Service.[55]

The Air Service was organized into two wings, one headquartered at Kelly Field, Texas, and the other at Langley Field, Virginia. The two wings consisted of seven groups, four of which were in the continental United States. The 1st Day Bombardment Group, equipped mainly with DH-4Bs, and the 1st Pursuit Group, with SE-5As, were at Kelly Field. The 1st Army Observation Group with DH-4Bs was at Langley Field. Fort Bliss, El Paso, Texas, was headquarters of the 1st Surveillance Group. With its DH-4Bs, the 1st Surveillance Group was responsible for patrolling the Mexican border from Brownsville, Texas, to San Diego. Air border patrol and forest fire patrol over the West Coast mountain ranges were operations dreamed up by Mitchell in 1919 to keep airmen busy and to provide additional justification for a peacetime Air Service. The three groups outside the continental United States were the 1st Observation at Paranaque Field, Manila; the 2d Observation at Luke Field, Honolulu; and the 3d Observation at France Field, Canal Zone. These overseas units were equipped mostly with Curtiss Jennies and DeHavillands. Altogether, the Air Service was authorized 28 squadrons, two airpark companies, four airship companies, nine photo sections, and 28 balloon companies. For liaison between Air Service headquarters in Washington and units in the field, an air officer was assigned to each of the overseas zones and to each of the nine Army Corps areas in the United States. Supply for the Air Service was from depots at San Antonio, Fairfield (Ohio), Montgomery (Alabama), San Diego, and Middletown (Pennsylvania).

Serviceable aircraft available to the Air Service in 1921 included 1,500 Jennies; 1,100 DH-4Bs; 179 SE-5 pursuit planes; and 12 Martin MB-2 bombers. The Martins were assigned to a heavy bombardment squadron, the only one in the Air Service.[56]

A Very Unfortunate and Critical Situation

While defeat of the New bill and subsequent passage of the National Defense Act of 1920 ended the first part of the air controversy, Mitchell was just beginning his crusade for airpower. He began to campaign for public support, cleverly emphasizing the one factor about the military that concerned all Americans—cost. Tactfully directing his attack at the Navy, he argued that planes could not only defend the nation against enemy surface fleets, but do it for much less than an expensive battleship fleet. Ignoring the rapid obsolescence of airplanes and the expense of bases, he declared that the government could buy a thousand planes for the cost of one battleship. The threat of the future was from the air, not the sea; and only the airplane could defend the nation against an air attack.[57]

Central to Mitchell's case against the Navy—his larger contention, that the threat of the future would be from the air, not land or sea, was something else again—was his claim that an airplane could sink a battleship. Naval chieftains categorically stated it could not be done. Mitchell was not to be silenced by the claims of admirals whom he believed "unable to face the fact that sea power was done for."[58] Before a congressional committee in February 1920, he offered to prove his claim.[59] After trying to ignore Mitchell's challenge, the Navy, in October 1920, conducted secret bombing tests on the old battleship *Indiana*. The vessel was bombed from the air with dummy bombs, and then a live 900-pound bomb was exploded on deck. Claiming only 11 percent of dummy bombs were hits, Secretary of the Navy Josephus Daniels triumphantly made public the report of the director of naval gunnery which emphasized the "improbability of a modern battleship being either destroyed completely or put out of action by aerial bombs." Alas, the Navy's triumph was short-lived. On 11 December 1920, the *Illustrated London News* published two pictures of the battered hulk of the

Indiana extensively damaged by a single bomb. If all test bombs had been live, what would have been the devastation from 11 percent direct hits? Newspapers clamored for the answer, and Mitchell was quick to respond. "Neither coast defense guns nor a defending fleet of battleships," he said, "need fire a gun in repelling the attack of a foreign fleet if we have a properly organized Air Force." The battleship would not have had a chance.[60]

Pressure forced the Navy to conduct further tests, this time with live bombs dropped by the Army Air Service, and there followed the famous bombing tests in June and July of 1921 off the mouth of Chesapeake Bay in which the captured German dreadnought *Ostfriesland* was sent to the bottom by 2,000-pound bombs dropped from the Martin bombers of General Mitchell's 1st Provisional Air Brigade. Other smaller ships were bombed, but the sinking of the *Ostfriesland* was crucial.[61] It was sweet victory for the airmen, bitter disappointment for the Navy. Years later, Thomas D. "Tommy" Milling, who had helped plan and execute the bombing, remembered the emotions of the time.

> They had the old transport *Henderson* out there; General Pershing was aboard, and all the high-ranking officers and admirals, to watch these tests. They would go out to the vicinity of the ships where the operation was taking place, where they could see it, and then back to Norfolk at night.... We would test; then the bombing would stop, and they had a Navy board that would go over and examine the ship to see the effect of it, which was all good stuff. That procedure was followed all through, with many attacks and many examinations of the various ships that stayed afloat that way. Finally with the battleship, we reached a stage where she showed signs of sinking a bit, so we proceeded, without definite orders, to load our Martin bombers with these 2,000-pound bombs. Then we went out and made a concerted attack on it—and sank her just like that. That spelled the death-knell of the battleship as a capital ship. They tell me that old admirals, on the *Henderson*, wept like babies as she went down. Yet they would not believe that that could be done. That was the great thing, on Mitchell's part, that he pushed that to a conclusion.... They were forced into the tests. Oh, in a way I can't blame them. I don't think there's anything in the world more magnificent than those old ships at sea; a naval warship is a magnificent thing. It's a hard thing to give up. I can understand that.[62]

Reactions to the tests were quick in coming and threatening to the Navy. In the *New York Times* appeared the statement that "Brigadier General William Mitchell's dictum that the 'air force will constitute the first line of defense of the country' no longer seems fanciful to open-minded champions of the capital ship."[63] Sen. William E. Borah (R-Idaho), a leader in the fight for disarmament, declared the tests demonstrated that "the battleship is practically obsolete." Expressing the attitude of many in Congress and the country, Borah questioned the wisdom of completing the six battleships of the new *Indiana* class, then under construction at a total cost of $240 million, if "with sufficient airplane and submarine protection this country was perfectly safe from attack."[64]

Navy leaders felt a need to offset the spectacular tests. The situation was critical. The credibility of its battleship fleet was being challenged at the very moment President Warren G. Harding, on 11 August 1921, was issuing invitations to the major powers to attend the Washington Conference for the Limitation of Naval Armaments. It was no time for the Navy to appear weak. The War Department was probably concerned that the tests would revive the move for a separate department of air. The Joint Army and Navy Board, composed of the ranking active officers in the Army and Navy, studied the tests. The Joint Board Report, bearing only the signature of its senior member, Pershing, was released on 20 August 1921. The commentary was predictable: aircraft carrying bombs of sufficient size could "sink or seriously damage" any ship then in existence, but the battleship was still the "backbone" of the fleet and the "bulwark of the nation's sea defense." The airplane had added to the dangers confronting the battleship, making it necessary to improve battleship construction and also to provide the fleet with aircraft carriers for air defense. The battleship was not obsolete. Inasmuch as the airplane had made naval warfare more complicated, it had made the nation's defense more expensive, not more economical, as Mitchell claimed it would.[65]

Mitchell's report on the bombing experiment was submitted to Menoher, who, apparently, intended to pigeonhole it; but someone leaked it to the press. Of course, it contradicted Pershing and the Joint Board. According to Mitchell the problem of destroying seacraft with aircraft "has been solved and is finished." There were "no conditions in which seacraft can operate efficiently in which aircraft cannot operate efficiently."[66]

Mitchell's indiscretion, or that of his supporters, produced an unexpected result of a personal sort. Menoher was incensed. He had once before requested that Secretary of War John W. Weeks, Baker's Republican successor, relieve the undisciplined Mitchell, and the request had been denied. This was the last straw; Menoher told Weeks that either he or Mitchell must go. Weeks removed Menoher.

Resignation of the Air Service's chief came for reasons that even now, some 70 years later, seem obscure. Some writers have said it was because Menoher had been unable to "handle and discipline" Mitchell; others contended that Weeks feared tangling with the popular Mitchell; still others that the secretary chose in favor of Mitchell because he was greatly impressed with the success of the bombing tests. In the *Army and Navy Journal*, it was reported simply that Menoher had requested "duty with the troops in the field . . . for personal reasons."[67]

Whatever the reason, Menoher resigned as chief of the Air Service. Mitchell offered his resignation as well, but it was refused. Reflecting on this episode years later, Hap Arnold wrote, "If he could attack the signature of the Chief of Staff of the United States Army so bluntly, and a Chief of Staff who was General Pershing at that, it was plain it was going to take a lot to stop Billy Mitchell."[68]

The new chief of the Air Service, Maj Gen Mason M. Patrick, had no intention of stopping Mitchell, but did mean to control him. Patrick was a professional soldier in the finest sense. A master of administration, he had earned the respect of Pershing during the war by bringing order to the Air Service in France after it had become "a tangled mess" under General Foulois.[69] He was a firm disciplinarian with patience to hear subordinates out before making a decision. Fifty-nine years old when he took command of the Air Service for the second time, he set about learning to fly. After more than a year, in such time as he could spare from his command duties, he earned his rating as a qualified junior pilot. According to Maj Herbert H. Dargue, who gave the general his first flight instruction, this probably did more to raise morale of the men of the Air Service than anything else the chief of the Air Service could have done. Said Dargue, "He loves to fly like the youngest of us. He is fearless, yet conservative; his judgment of flying is of the best."[70] What Dargue recognized in Patrick's flying was characteristic of the general; he was not opposed to change but approached novelty with care, guided by judgment. Like Mitchell, he was a believer in a separate air force and the expansion of airpower. Unlike Mitchell, he was tactful and willing to compromise.[71]

From the beginning, Patrick made clear to his stormy subordinate that as commander of the Air Service he intended to command. In a brief confrontation between the two men shortly after Patrick became chief, Mitchell demanded that as the senior flying officer in the service (Patrick had not yet learned to fly) he should be given command prerogatives. Patrick listened patiently, then refused. According to Patrick's account, Mitchell threatened to resign. When Patrick raised no objection, Mitchell thought the matter over and decided to stay on as assistant chief.[72] Having established his authority, Patrick apparently realized that the best way to keep tension down in Washington was to keep Mitchell busy with projects and inspection tours elsewhere. The tactic was reasonably successful.[73]

Aside from keeping Mitchell out of trouble, General Patrick's concern was the steady deterioration of Air Service strength. Economy-minded Congresses consistently pared the defense budget to a bare minimum, which meant no funds for aircraft replacement and repeated reductions in personnel. There were fewer than 900 pilots and observers on active duty in 1921; and although the Air Service Act of 1920 authorized as many as 2,500 cadets per year, between June 1920 and June 1921 there were only 190 airplane and 15 airship pilots trained.

By the summer of 1922, Patrick felt the Air Service had been practically demobilized and could no longer meet peacetime demands, much less any national emergency. He said as much in his annual report for 1922, adding that inadequate strength and organization of the Air Service, which he had repeatedly reported to the War Department, could only be corrected by congressional action. The report caused immediate repercussions.[74] Secretary Weeks directed Patrick to submit recommendations, and in February 1928 Patrick proposed (1) legislation to increase authorized strength; (2) division of the Army air arm into air service units consisting of balloon and observation units which assist ground troops and air force units composed of pursuit, attack, and bombardment units functioning independently of ground troops; (3) concentration of air force units under command of the General Headquarters rather than dispersing them to corps and field army commanders; and (4) clarification between the coastal defense missions of the Army Air Service and air units of the Navy.[75]

Weeks appointed a board of seven General Staff officers to consider the proposals that General Patrick had submitted. Headed by General Lassiter, the board was composed mostly of ground officers. Except for the board's reporter, Major Dargue, there was only one other air officer, Lt Col Frank P. Lahm. After studying Patrick's proposals, the Lassiter Board gave full endorsement. It declared that unless something was done about the "alarming condition in the Air Service," it would be of negligible benefit to national defense. More than 80 percent of the Air Service inventory of 1,970 airplanes was judged obsolescent or otherwise "unsuitable for combat use." If there were no changes in procurement, the board predicted that attrition would reduce the Air Service to less than 300 airplanes by the summer of 1926. Further, the aircraft industry was "entirely inadequate to meet peace and wartime requirements" and was on the verge of disappearing. The board proposed a 10-year program to build the Air Service to a minimum peacetime strength of 4,000 officers; 25,000 enlisted men; 2,500 cadets; 2,534 airplanes; 20 airships; and 38 balloons, with capability for emergency expansion to 22,628 officers; 172,994 enlisted men; 8,756 airplanes; 31 airships; and 134 balloons. The board estimated this would require approximately $25 million a year.[76]

The most important aspect of the Lassiter Board report was its acceptance of General Patrick's plan to divide the air arm according to tasks. The observation air arm would be an "integral part of divisions, corps, and armies, with a reserve under general headquarters." An attack and pursuit air force would be "an integral part of each field army, with a reserve under general headquarters," and for "special and strategic missions, either in connection with ground troops or independent of them," there would be an "air force of bombardment, pursuit, and airships." This was a compromise giving airpower advocates a greater independence while maintaining the unity of command that so concerned the General Staff.[77]

The Lassiter Board program was a goal accepted by the War Department and the General Staff and by Secretary Weeks, and this was its importance, as history was to show. Even Mitchell eventually would admit that it was the closest thing yet to an "aeronautical policy" for the Air Service. To carry it out, however, proved impossible. It was a goal Army leaders would not pursue at the expense of the rest of the Army. The program called for the Army and Navy to join in requesting appropriations for aviation, and the Navy disagreed with Weeks's suggested division of the aviation budget—60 percent for the Army, 40 percent for the Navy. The program was shelved. In any event it depended on an increase in the military budget, and with economy the first duty of peace, that was not likely.

And so, the first uneasy months and years had passed after the end of the First World War, and the Army Air Service had changed to a peacetime footing of an unsettled sort. Its leadership had been in flux, from Menoher to Patrick. The new chief gave evidence of having control of his organization, but with the ebullient Mitchell as second in command, he could hardly be certain. All the while, the equipment of the Air Service was deteriorating. The technology of the airplane had changed rapidly during these years, just as it had changed with an almost miraculous (or diabolic, depending upon the point of view) rapidity during the war. In 1913, the last full year of peace before the holocaust, the airplane had been little more than a toy; by 1918 it was a fighting machine of proved quality and usefulness. It continued to develop rapidly during the postwar era. But the Air Service seemed only capable of getting its organizational arrangements in order, and even these seemed unendingly fragile. The future was uncertain, except to visionaries such as Mitchell and his more ardent followers.

Notes

1. The cable is quoted in Frederick Palmer, *Newton D. Baker: America at War*, vol. 1 (New York: Dodd, 1931), 383.

2. Ibid., 383–84.

3. The actual cost of America's World War aeronautical effort is subject to debate. See John B. Rae, "Financial Problems of the American Aircraft Industry, 1906–1940," *Business History Review* 39, no. 1 (Spring 1965): 102; and Edgar S. Gorrell, *The Measure of America's World War Aeronautical Effort* (Northfield, Vt.: Norwich University, 1940), 7–10. According to Rae, the cost was $365,708,488.70. Gorrell set the net cost at $608,865,307.50.

4. See Alfred F. Hurley, *Billy Mitchell: Crusader for Air Power* (New York: F. Watts, 1964), 37. Hurley notes that Mitchell believed the full development of aviation was "only a question of time and further effort." See also Walter Millis, *Arms and Men: A Study of American Military History* (New York: G. P. Putnam's Sons, 1956), 225. Millis notes the deepest penetration as 160 miles and the bomb tonnage as 138. The same figures are found in Harry H. Ransom, "The Air Corps Act of 1926: A Study of the Legislative Process" (PhD diss., Princeton University, 1953), 68. Both Ransom and Millis apparently got their figures from Gorrell, 52. Alfred Goldberg, ed., *A History of the United States Air Force, 1907–1957* (Princeton, N.J.: D. Van Nostrand, 1957), 29, gives a general description of the frustration of American airmen at the end of the war.

5. Wesley Frank Craven and James Lea Cate, eds., *The Army Air Forces in World War II*, vol. 1, *Plans and Early Operations, January 1939 to August 1942* (1949; new imprint, Washington, D.C.: Office of Air Force History, 1983), 37. Craven and Cate note the relatively conservative nature of Mitchell's "independent" operations plans. See also Laurence S. Kuter, "Air Power—The American Concept," unpublished article, Laurence S. Kuter manuscripts (MSS), Special Collections, US Air Force Academy Library, Colorado. Kuter describes the "202 Squadron Program," which was written in 1917 by Lt Col Edgar S. Gorrell and approved in early 1918 by Gen John J. Pershing. According to Kuter, it was the "earliest, clearest, and least known statement of the American conception of the employment of air power." Kuter's analysis was quoted but not footnoted in Goldberg, 30–31.

6. Henry H. Arnold, *Global Mission* (New York: Harper, 1949), 86. See also Diary of William Mitchell, October 1918, Mitchell MSS, Library of Congress (LOC), Washington, D.C.

7. Arnold, 96–100, 121, 157–158. Arnold saw in Mitchell certain characteristics that are commonly attributed to prophets or visionaries. For instance, Arnold observed that Mitchell "seemed to brush aside the possibility that a lot of people still might not understand his theories, and he could not be convinced that air power was not being blocked by deliberate and well-organized enemies," a conspiracy of "entrenched Admirals" and "Old-fashioned Generals" (96). He considered "small gains . . . as a contemptible compromise" (121).

8. See William Mitchell, *Winged Defense: The Development and Possibilities of Modern Airpower—Economic and Military* (New York: G. P. Putnam's Sons, 1925), viii, for quote about "ancient prerogatives." In Benjamin D. Foulois and Carroll V. Glines, *From the Wright Brothers to the Astronauts: The Memoirs of Benjamin D. Foulois* (New York: McGraw-Hill, 1968), Foulois, whose opinion must be considered against evidence that he and Mitchell disliked each other intensely, wrote that Mitchell in his heyday "had become a fanatic much in the way that the Moros were in the Philippines. He had become a juramentado and was ready to run amok!" (197). See also Eugene Beebe, "The Reminiscences of Eugene Beebe (1959–1960)," Oral History Collection, Columbia University (hereinafter Beebe, OHC); Ira C. Eaker, "The Reminiscences of Ira C. Eaker (1959–1960)" (hereinafter Eaker, OHC); Leroy T. Lutes, "The Reminiscences of Leroy T. Lutes (1959–1960)," (hereinafter Lutes, OHC). Eaker, Lutes, and Beebe refer to the indoctrination of airmen in the Air Corps. Said Lutes, "To favor a separate Air Force—that was a religion at that time, no question about it. Anyone who didn't accept that wouldn't go far in the Air Corps." Eaker said, "If you didn't accept it, you didn't belong. I guess there were a dozen or so, and generally those officers were the non-flying non-conformists who didn't support the radical ideas of these people who wanted to have a separate flying service." Said Beebe, "Did

anybody in the Air Force oppose the idea of a separate air arm? No, not to my knowledge. I can't remember a soul who ever did."

9. Palmer, 7, 9.

10. William G. McAdoo, *Crowded Years: The Reminiscences of William G. McAdoo* (Boston: Houghton Mifflin, 1931), 342; and Daniel R. Beaver, *Newton D. Baker and the American War Effort, 1917–1919* (Lincoln, Nebr.: University of Nebraska Press, 1966), 8.

11. Palmer, 8.

12. Ibid., 10.

13. A little book which offers considerable insight into Baker's thinking is Willis Thornton's *Newton D. Baker and His Books* (Cleveland: World Publishing Co., 1954). Baker was an avid reader with the habit of writing comments in the margins of the books he read. Using Baker's private library, Thornton edited Baker's comments into a small but interesting book of 85 pages. For a highly critical assessment of Baker's performance as secretary of war, see Ernest W. Young, *The Wilson Administration and the Great War* (Boston: Houghton Mifflin, 1922), chap. 7.

14. Arthur Sweetser, *The American Air Service: A Record of Its Problems, Its Difficulties, Its Failures, and Its Final Achievements* (New York: D. Appleton and Co., 1919), introduction.

15. This quotation comes from Baker's testimony before the House Committee on Military Affairs, which was looking into the disappointing performance of the 1st Aero Squadron during Pershing's punitive expedition against the Villistas in Mexico. It is quoted in Palmer, 284, and in Foulois and Glines, 136–37. It should be noted that the Pershing expedition took place before Billy Mitchell became an airman.

16. Hearings before the House Committee on Military Affairs on a United Air Service, 66th Cong., 2d sess. (1919), 395 (hereinafter Hearings, United Air Service).

17. Other evidence of this feeling of being different can be found in the Mitchell diary, November 1918, 301; Mitchell MSS; Thomas De W. Milling, "The Reminiscences of Thomas De W. Milling (1959–60)" (hereinafter Milling, OHC); Beebe, OHC; Carl A. Spaatz, "The Reminiscences of Carl Spaatz (1959–60)" (hereinafter Spaatz, OHC); and Frank P. Lahm, "The Reminiscences of Frank Lahm (1959–60)" (hereinafter Lahm, OHC). Milling, who was one of the very first Army officers to learn to fly—he and Henry H. Arnold were taught to fly by the Wrights—said plainly, "We flying men were like a fraternity" (Milling, OHC, 57–58). Spaatz noted some of the hostility between flying and ground officers during the interwar period was caused by the extra pay the flyers received. He added an interesting comment that he did not believe the friction was as great among bachelors as among married men. Said he, "It's the female element in the thing that is responsible for a lot of the friction," Spaatz, OHC, 32–33. Beebe, who entered the service in the middle of the interwar period, said about flying pay: "I never considered my pay was for hazard. I knew the hazard was there, but I thought it was because I was a little better educated and had a little bit more to offer maybe," Beebe, OHC, 79–80. Goldberg explains that there had to be "a constant influx of young pilots because fliers were not considered fit for combat after the age of thirty-five" (34).

18. Arnold, 85.

19. *Annual Report of the Secretary of War, 1919* (Washington, D.C.: Government Printing Office [GPO], 1919), 68–75 (hereinafter Secretary of War, 1919). Baker had opposed strategic bombing during the World War. He told Chief of Staff Peyton March to inform the Air Service that America would not take part in a bombing operation that "has as its objective promiscuous bombing of industry, commerce or population, in enemy countries disassociated from obvious military needs to be served by such action." See Hurley, 37; and Beaver, 169. For further reference to the moral issue of strategic bombing, see Goldberg, 31; Craven and Cate, 38–44; and Lutes, OHC, 1–2. Mitchell's argument is well presented in Craven and Cate. His argument, which became the standard argument of strategic bombing advocates, was essentially that

strategic bombing would bring war to an end more rapidly and was therefore more humane than other means of conducting warfare.

20. The emphasis on prudence by military planners in the interwar years is partially explained by their uncertainty as to America's foreign policy and the requirements it placed on the military. For an analysis of this, see Fred Greene, "The Military View of American National Policy, 1904–1940," *American Historical Review* 69 (January 1964): 354–77. See also Craven and Cate, 21.

21. Arnold, 86–89. See also Hurley, 37–38.

22. *Hearings before Subcommittee No. 1 (Aviation) of the Select Committee on Expenditures in the War Department*, 66th Cong., 1st sess., 2 vols. (Washington, D.C.: GPO, 1919), 274 (hereinafter cited as Frear Committee). For a short biographical sketch of Charles T. Menoher, see *Army and Navy Journal*, 13 March 1926.

23. Douglas MacArthur, *Reminiscences* (New York: McGraw-Hill, 1964), 60. See also D. Clayton James, *The Years of MacArthur*, vol. 1, *1880–1941* (Boston: Houghton Mifflin, 1970), 166–67, in which he states that "Menoher was at all times in unquestioned command, while at the same time he maintained an amazingly harmonious relationship with his ambitious, high-strung chief of staff (MacArthur)."

24. Francis P. Duffy, *Father Duffy's Story* (New York: George H. Doran, c. 1919), 102–3.

25. 42d Division Operations Report, 25 July–3 August 1918, quoted in James, 192–93.

26. Arnold, 100.

27. The description of Gen Joseph T. Dickman comes from Thornton, 35, and from the foreword by General Pershing in Joseph T. Dickman, *The Great Crusade, A Narrative of the World War* (New York: D. Appleton and Co., c. 1927).

28. A list of the members of the Dickman Board and its conclusions on air matters can be found in records of the Adjutant General (AG) 580 (8-4-34), Record Group (RG) 407, National Archives (NA); see also Craven and Cate, 43; Ransom, 141–42; and R. Earl McClendon, *The Question of Autonomy for the United States Air Arm, 1907–1945* (Maxwell AFB, Ala.: Air University, 1950), 74–75.

29. Report of the Chief of the Air Service (25 August 1920) in *Secretary of War, 1919*, 1451. In Hearings, United Air Service, 17; and Frear Committee, 274. General Menoher testified before the Frear Committee that 220 regular officers remained in the Air Service as of 6 August 1919. Robert Frank Futrell in *Ideas, Concepts, Doctrine: A History of Basic Thinking in the United States Air Force, 1907–1964* (Maxwell AFB, Ala.: Air University Press, 1974), 32, uses the figure 200 as the number of regular officers in mid-1919. Arnold explained the Air Corps' unusual position during the demobilization fever by pointing out that the Air Corps was entirely a wartime creation. "It couldn't very well go back to the 16 planes and 26 pilots that had started on the Mexican Border in 1916. . . . If the Air Service was reduced now in proportion to the rest of the Army, it would disappear entirely," Arnold, 88–89.

30. House Report 637, Frear Subcommittee Report on Aviation, 66th Cong., 2d sess., vol. 1, 70; and Ransom, 140–41.

31. House Report 637, 66th Cong., 2d sess., vol. 2, 70.

32. Frear Committee, 475.

33. Ibid., 476.

34. Foulois and Glines, 185–86.

35. The full text of the Crowell Commission Report, along with Secretary Baker's letter of transmittal, is printed in the *Hearings before the Senate Committee on Military Affairs on S.2693: Reorganization of the Army*, 66th Cong., 1st sess., 1919, 196–209. Reference to the Crowell Commission can be found in McClendon, 75–80; Hurley, 48–49; Ransom, 144–45; and Arnold, 97.

36. McClendon, 79–80.

37. Report of a Board of Officers Convened to Report Upon the New (S.2693) and Curry (H.R. 7925) bills, Which Propose the Creation of an Executive Department of Aeronautics (hereinafter Menoher Board Report). The full text of the report can be

found in *Hearings before the House Committee on Military Affairs on Department of Defense and Unification of Air Service,* 19 January to 9 March 1926, 60th Cong., 1st sess., 908–17 (hereinafter *Hearings, Department of Defense*). For a synopsis of the Menoher Board conclusions plus excerpts from the answers to the board's telegraphic inquiry of senior officers, see AG 580 (8-4-34), RG 407, NA. For analysis of the board's report and its impact, see McClendon, 85–89.

38. *Hearings, United Air Service,* 411.
39. Menoher Board Report.
40. Ibid.
41. Ibid.
42. *Hearings before the Senate Committee on Military Affairs on Reorganization of the Army,* S.2691, S.2093, S.2715; 66th Cong., 1st sess., 1268–69; McClendon, 88–89ff.
43. Summary of Mitchell's testimony dated 14 August 1919, Mitchell MSS. Portions of Mitchell's analysis of the board are quoted in Ransom, 200–201.
44. Secretary Baker approved the Menoher Board Report (with minor exceptions) and sent a copy of it to Sen. J. W. Wadsworth (R-N.Y.), chairman of the Senate Committee on Military Affairs, Baker to Wadsworth, 31 October 1919, *Hearings, United Air Service,* 39–41. General Menoher in his testimony before the House committee explained that the secretary's reservations concerned one of the board's suggestions to create a director of aeronautics as the head of a bureau to coordinate procurement of aircraft and nonmilitary aviation matters. The director was to report directly to the president, and Secretary Baker thought that the president already had more than enough to do without another agency reporting to him.
45. Menoher Board Report.
46. For a taste of the airpower arguments as it was presented at the time, see *Hearings, United Air Service.* Most of the airpower advocates testified at these hearings including Mitchell, Arnold, Milling, Rickenbacker, and Assistant Secretary of War Crowell. See also McClendon, 90–92.
47. Gen Charles T. Menoher to Gen John J. Pershing, letter, 16 December 1919, Pershing MSS. Menoher included clippings from the *New York Times* and the *Literary Digest.*
48. Pershing to Menoher, 12 January 1920, letter, Pershing MSS, LOC.
49. Hearings, United Air Service, 389. For General Menoher's opinion of these comments by Secretary Baker, see 407.
50. For a discussion of the congressional actions on the New and Curry bills, see McClendon, 85–89.
51. *Congressional Record,* 66th Cong., 1st sess., 2151.
52. Ibid., 2185.
53. Ibid., 2249.
54. Ibid., 2301–2. See Ransom, 206–10 for an analysis of the Senate debate.
55. For the sections of the 1920 act applying to the Air Service, see *US Statutes at Large, 1920,* vol. 40, sec. 13a, 768, *Armed Forces Reorganization Act of 1920.* See also Goldberg, 29–30; Arnold, 98; McClendon, 25; and I. B. Holley Jr., *Buying Aircraft: Materiel Procurement for the Army Air Forces* (Washington, D.C.: Office of the Chief of Military History, Department of the Army, 1964), 40–44. Holley notes that the act made the planning factor for the size of the Air Service men rather than airplanes and that this served as a detriment to planners later who thought of the Air Service's strength in terms of aircraft rather than men. For analysis of the broader meaning of the act to the Army as a whole, see General MacArthur's comments in "Annual Report of the Chief of Staff," 41–74, in *Secretary of War, 1935.* See also John W. Killigrew, "The Impact of the Great Depression on the Army, 1929–1936" (PhD diss., Indiana University, 1960), iv. Good discussions of the general impact of the act can also be found in Russell F. Weigley, *History of the United States Army* (New York: Macmillan, 1967), 403–4; and Mark S. Watson, *Chief of Staff, Prewar Plans and Preparations* (Washington, D.C.: Historical Division, Department of the Army, 1950),

63. Watson notes that the limitation of the power of the General Staff was "evidence of Congress's continuing suspicion of militarism." This suspicion of militarism was ever-present in all discussions of military matters in the twenties—including the airpower controversy.

56. Historical Office of the Army Air Forces, *The Official Pictorial History of the AAF* (New York: Duell, Sloan and Pearce, 1947), 58–59; Carroll V. Glines, *The Compact History of the United States Air Force* (New York: Hawthorn Books, 1963), 99; Robert Frank Futrell, *Development of AAF Base Facilities in the United States 1939–1945*, USAF Historical Study (Maxwell AFB, Ala.: USAF Historical Division, Air University, 1947), 1–12; and Air Training Command Pamphlet 190-1, *History of the United States Air Force*, 1961, 3-2, 3-5.

57. There are many sources for Mitchell's attack on the Navy in 1920. The best is Hurley, especially 59–68. See also Chase C. Mooney and Martha E. Layman, *Organization of Military Aeronautics, 1907–1935* (Congressional and War Department Action), Army Air Forces Historical Study 25 (Washington, D.C.: Army Air Forces Historical Division, 1944), 54–59.

58. Arnold, 96.

59. Hurley, 66; Mooney and Layman, 54.

60. For the best description of the *Indiana* incident, see Mooney and Layman, 54–55. See also House Document No. 17, 67th Cong., 1st sess., 19 April 1920, 1; in the midst of the battleship controversy, the administration changed in Washington and there was some evidence that the new president, Warren G. Harding, had an interest in aviation. Within a month after taking office, he initiated an investigation by the National Advisory Committee for Aeronautics to study regulation of air navigation and "cooperation among the various departments of the Government concerned with aviation." The subcommittee, less than two weeks later, reported against maintaining a large air force and was in favor of the Air Service remaining within the War Department. Harding endorsed the report and transmitted it to Congress. Even though the result was not what they hoped it would be, airmen were apparently favorably impressed by the fact that Harding had been interested enough in aviation to initiate an investigation, even if the result was not what they hoped it would be.

61. An interesting account of the bombing tests by a participant can be found in Milling, OHC, 62–72, 95–99.

62. Ibid., 97–99.

63. *New York Times* article quoted in the *Congressional Record*, 67th Cong., 1st sess., 4709.

64. *Congressional Record*, 67th Cong., 1st sess., 500.

65. The full text of the Joint Board report is available in the *Congressional Record*, 67th Cong., 1st sess., 8625–26. For the composition of the Joint Board, see Watson, 79. For further reference to the Joint Board's reaction to the bombing tests, see Hurley, 78; Mooney and Layman, 57; and Goldberg, 31.

66. See Mitchell's report described in US Naval Institute *Proceedings* 47 (November 1921): 1828–29.

67. For the various opinions as to why Menoher was replaced as chief of the Air Service, see Hurley, 69; Futrell, *Ideas, Concepts, Doctrine*, 37; Arnold, 104–5; and "Colonel Patrick Chief of Air Service," *Army and Navy Journal*, 24 September 1920.

68. Arnold, 106.

69. Futrell, *Ideas, Concepts, Doctrine*, 37; Eaker, OHC, 19–20.

70. "How Gen. Patrick Learned to Fly," *Army and Navy Journal*, 8 September 1923; Futrell, *Ideas, Concepts, Doctrine*, 39; and Mason M. Patrick, *The United States in the Air* (Garden City, N.Y.: Doubleday, Doran, and Co., 1928), 86–89.

71. Maj Gen Mason M. Patrick to Maj Gen H. E. Ely, commandant, Army War College, letter, 21 February 1925, quoted in Futrell, *Ideas, Concepts, Doctrine*, 43.

72. Arnold, 105–6; Foulois and Glines, 195; Patrick, 86–89; and Eaker, OHC, 19–20.

73. Hurley, 79, 86.

74. Mooney and Layman, 58–59; McClendon, 109; Futrell, *Ideas, Concepts, Doctrine*, 41; and "Report, Chief of Air Service," *Army and Navy Journal*, 31 December 1920.

75. McClendon, 109–110; Mooney and Layman, 59–61; Futrell, *Ideas, Concepts, Doctrine*, 41–43; and Weigley, 412–13.

76. See memo from Col B. H. Wells, assistant chief of staff, War Plans Division (WPD), to deputy chief of staff, subject: "Annual Report, Chief of Air Service, Fiscal Year, 1922," 20 September 1922, WPD 888, RG 165, NA; acting adjutant general to Brig Gen Briant H. Wells, 17 March 1923, WPD 888-1, RG 165, NA; and "Report of a Committee of Officers Appointed by the Secretary of War," WPD 888-3, RG 165, NA. See also the conclusions of the Lassiter Board and a list of its members in AG 580 (8-4-34), RG 407, NA; "Needs of Air Service Reported by Committee," *Army and Navy Journal*, 20 August 1923; and House Report 1653, 68th Cong., 2d sess. (14 December 1925), 33–34.

77. Holley, 44–46; McClendon, 110–112; and Hurley, 83–85.

Chapter 2

Creation of the Army Air Corps

For aviators, the decade of the 1920s marked a golden age, an era of great improvement in equipment and flying skills, of constant competition to fly higher, farther, faster, longer. Despite limited funds, Army flyers competed fiercely and with considerable success in the race for new world records. Army pilots broke world altitude records three times from 1919 through 1921 in an experimental LePere biplane. On 4 October 1919, Maj R. W. Shroeder and Lt G. E. Elfry set a two-man record when they flew to 31,821 feet. On 27 February 1920, Shroeder flew alone to an altitude of 33,113 feet. That record stood until 28 September 1921, when Lt J. A. Macready climbed to 34,508 feet in a LePere that had a turbo-supercharger to increase performance of the plane's Liberty engine. Macready's only oxygen supply was a pressure cylinder to which he had attached a tube with a pipestem mouthpiece. In his open cockpit, he was protected from the minus 60 degrees Fahrenheit temperature by a leather and sheepskin flying suit.[1]

Endurance and long-distance flights brought public attention to Army aviators. This pleased Air Service leaders anxious to draw attention to the Air Service and its capabilities. On 2 May 1923, Macready and Lt O. G. Kelly took off from Roosevelt Field, New York, in a giant Liberty-powered Fokker T-2 monoplane to attempt a nonstop coast-to-coast flight. Averaging 94 miles per hour they made the 2,520 mile flight in 26 hours and 50 minutes. On 23 June of the following year, Lt Russell L. Maughan made his "dawn-to-dusk" cross-country flight. Taking off from Mitchel Field before dawn—at 2:59 A.M.—Maughan, after five stops for fuel, arrived over Crissy Field, San Francisco, one minute before dusk. In his Curtiss PW-8 pursuit, he had averaged 156 miles per hour for 2,850 miles. While this flight was spectacular, an even more spectacular flight was in progress. In specially built Douglas biplanes, Army aviators were attempting a round-the-world flight. Four of the rugged Douglas planes led by Maj Frederick L. Martin took off from Seattle on 6 April 1920. On the second leg of the flight, the lead plane, the *Seattle*, became lost and crashed in the Alaskan mountains. Major Martin and his mechanic, SSgt Alva L. Harvey, trekked out of the wilderness to Port Moller and returned to the United States. Lt Lowell H. Smith took Martin's place as flight commander, and the remaining three planes continued on to Japan and then along the China coast to India. Just beyond Shanghai they passed the

Frenchman, Capt Peltier D'Oisy, who had started earlier from Paris and was also attempting to fly around the world. In addition to the Americans and the French, airmen from Britain, Italy, Portugal, and Argentina were racing for world-flight honors. It took Smith and his men 16 days to make the trip from India to England. From Scotland to Iceland they encountered fog and delay, and Lt L. Wade and Sgt H. Ogden crashed in the *Boston* between the Faroe and Orkney Islands. Fortunately, a replacement airplane was available, and Wade and Ogden continued in *Boston II*. Finally on 28 September 1924, 175 days after they began, the American round-the-world flyers landed the *Chicago*, the *New Orleans*, and *Boston II* in Seattle, completing a circumnavigation of the globe. Having won the competition, they received a rousing welcome, medals from President Calvin Coolidge, and glowing praise from their proud chief, General Patrick.[2]

Americans found aviation fascinating, but still were not much concerned about its orderly development in the Army Air Service. To many Americans, the 1920s were synonymous with good times—prosperity seemed everywhere. The flapper's image was on the magazine covers; the businessman was the man of the hour. American interests were at home, on Wall Street and in the bustling cities and enlarging industries. Military and naval appropriations were cut repeatedly. Reflecting on the situation the Army had faced during his term, Pershing in 1924 issued his final report to the secretary of war. He recalled that the last few years had been a period of economy and sounded an almost plaintive warning against further cuts: "We are down to rock bottom."[3]

Business Methods in the War Department

Money lay at the center of the Army's troubles during the 1920s, but it also (unfortunately for the Army) lay at the center of the calculations of the Republican administrations of that era. This was particularly so of the Coolidge administration.[4] Calvin Coolidge, who had a reputation as a silent, strong, stern Puritan,[5] was committed to frugal administration of government in accord with no-nonsense business principles. He warned that wastefulness by governments, as well as by individuals, was synonymous with immorality, that the stability and growth which set the United States apart from the rest of the world rested upon production and, most important, upon conservation. If Americans squandered their resources, the result would be economic dissipation followed inevitably by moral decay. Economy, he once said, was the highest form of morality.[6]

In the minds of Americans, nothing was more wasteful in time of peace than large expenditure on military preparedness. This was the conviction of the increasing numbers of pacifists who formed organizations promoting disarmament and the outlawry of war.[7] There were also people who were not pacifists but who believed that the traditional American policy of intense commitment and extravagant expenditure when emergencies arose was a better policy than inflicting upon the American people the constant burden of a large standing army. In Senate debates on War Department appropriations, Sen. John S. Williams (D-Miss.) argued forcefully that preparedness was a policy of fear unbecoming for the land of the free and the home of the brave. The World War, he said, had proven that "a great, strong, rich people like ourselves . . . can meet the most efficient and well-prepared military force that the world has ever dreamed of . . . and whip it to its knees, but if in the meantime you had kept your people burdened all those 50 years, they could not have done it, they would have neither the spirit nor the financial ability nor the morale to do it."[8]

Coolidge offered not only to relieve the burden of maintaining a large standing army, but through introduction of business methods in the War Department to reduce the cost of maintaining such a military establishment as was absolutely necessary. Administration of the War Department, said the *Republican Campaign Textbook of 1924*, was the most notorious case of muddling inefficiency in the previous Democratic administration. In the last year under the Democrats, War Department expenditure had soared to over a billion dollars. After four years of Republican rule, the annual cost of the War Department had been cut by more than $750 million. This, the Republicans announced, was "one of the most striking examples of what was done by introducing business in government."[9]

Few, if any, Army leaders shared the administration's enthusiasm for drastic cuts in the War Department budget. Cuts meant fewer personnel and little money for replacement and modernization of equipment. Force reductions were a threat to the life of the Army.[10] Lack of funds for modern equipment threatened efficiency. From 1921 through 1923, the enlisted strength of the Army fell from 213,341 to 132,106 to 118,348. The number of commissioned officers fell from 13,299 to 11,820. Equipment was almost entirely war surplus that was not only wearing out but becoming obsolescent.[11] Army leaders argued that appropriations should increase if the Army was to meet its responsibilities. Defense plans of the 1920s were not aggressive in any sense. Aside from maintaining garrisons in America's overseas possessions—notably the Philippines, Hawaii, and the Panama Canal Zone—the Army's responsibility was limited to continental defense.[12] For this task,

Army leaders desired a force just large enough to administer, organize and train a civilian reserve, meet minor emergencies, and absorb the first shock of any aggression.[13] The size of this force was the source of much debate. Most Army leaders contended that the 280,000 men authorized by the National Defense Act of 1920 was a minimum. But maintenance of an army of even those modest proportions was unattainable within the limit set by President Coolidge's economic policy. As a rock-bottom position, Pershing, backed by Secretary Weeks, argued vigorously for increased appropriations to support an army of 150,000 men.[14]

Pershing's arguments, which were carried on by his successor, Maj Gen John L. Hines and Hines's successor, failed to sway Coolidge and were not incorporated in annual budgets submitted to Congress. This was a major frustration for Army leaders, because once the president approved the budget they were prohibited by the Budget and the Accounting Act of 1921 from taking their case to Congress.[15] Congressmen often seemed to forget this restriction. "Now, why should you not come up here and frankly tell us the amount is not sufficient?" Brig Gen Dennis E. Nolan was asked during an appropriations hearing. Nolan replied that Congress had passed a budget law prohibiting any official of the government arguing for more money than is permitted under the budget sent up by the president. He added laconically, "That is a matter of law."[16]

The Army's protagonists in budget matters were the president and his agent, the director of the Bureau of the Budget. Once the argument was lost with them, it was lost. And with President Coolidge, the Army lost more than it won.[17] He did not see Army needs as critical. "Who's gonna fight us?" he once asked.[18] It was a good question. The great oceans were still barriers to invasion from Europe or Asia. War with Canada was unimaginable. Though relations with Mexico were near a nadir, the Mexicans were divided and exhausted by years of civil war. He unctuously advised worried War Department officials to find ways to reduce costs "without weakening our defense but rather perfecting it." According to Army estimates, the budget cuts the president had in mind would mean reduction in the Air Service from 760 planes to 628. For the Army it would mean elimination of 15,000 men, 2,500 officers, all the Philippine scouts, and abandonment of mobilization plans.[19]

Army leaders continued to argue for appropriations, but recognized reality and established financial policies to meet as best they could the "needs of the whole army."[20] They avoided expensive programs that might absorb the entire budget. To give any one of the Army's programs priority in the budget would mean disaster for the rest. This was particularly true of War Department Major Project Number 4, the Lassiter plan for expansion of the Air Service. The Air

Service was the most expensive branch of the Army, and the Lassiter program would make it considerably more expensive. Discounting overhead such as pay and housing for Air Service personnel, the Lassiter program would have cost an estimated $90 million a year, more than a third of the Army budget. "The truth is simple," said Brig Gen Fox Conner, who directed a study of financial aspects of expanding the air arm. "In view of its other vital needs and the economic policy of the Government, the War Department has as yet been in no position to submit estimates for carrying into effect any part of the Lassiter Board Programme. . . . There would be little left for the rest of the Regular Army."[21]

Secretary Weeks had tried to get funds by convincing Secretary of the Navy Edwin Denby to agree to a joint Army and Navy aviation program. The Navy had a five-year program to expand its aviation component. If in a joint program Weeks could induce the Navy to extend its plan to 10 years, it would reduce the annual cost. Extra appropriations for the Lassiter program would be more acceptable to the president and Congress. But neither Denby nor his successor, Curtis D. Wilbur, would have anything to do with the idea. They were willing to help the Army upgrade its aviation arm, but not at the expense of the Navy. The Lassiter program was shelved, a casualty of the War Department's efforts to remain within Coolidge's budget.[22]

The fact that the War Department had accepted the Lassiter program and had at least tried to carry it out was encouraging to the chief of the Air Service. Patrick understood the budget restrictions on the War Department, that Army leaders were fighting parsimony in the Budget Bureau and pacifism in Congress.[23] He understood the objection to extravagant claims by aviation enthusiasts. A proponent of airpower, he had spent most of his career in the Army. He understood the principles of war, the guide for his classmate Pershing and his many old friends on the General Staff and in command throughout the Army. He respected their opinions and agreed that some of his young airmen lacked broad understanding.[24] He advocated airpower with moderation, reason rather than emotion.[25] In 1923 and 1924, there was evidence that Patrick was making converts. In his words, Army leaders were "being educated" in the importance of airpower, becoming sympathetic to needs of the Air Service.[26] They did not give up their conviction that aviation was an auxiliary arm—indispensable, but an auxiliary. Nor did they abandon their concern over the plane's limits: its vulnerability to antiaircraft artillery, its limited range and carrying ability, and its inability to defend itself on the ground.[27] Still, they did show interest in military aviation, a new open-mindedness with regard to its potential.[28] They accepted the idea that the Air Service could in some circumstances function as an air force operating independently of ground troops.[29] They agreed that the bombing experiments of 1920, along with another series of tests on the battleships *Virginia* and *New Jersey* in the fall of 1923, had shown that aircraft could sink any naval vessel in existence. They agreed with Patrick's contention that the first phase of a war would likely be an air phase, and for that reason a portion of the Air Service should be considered an M-day force. This meant constant readiness. The Air Service should be capable of rapid expansion. Finally, Army leaders agreed that "flyers at the beginning of an emergency must be men trained in time of peace" and that to maintain a reserve of commercial aviators, as well as manufacturing capability for rapid production of military aircraft, the government should encourage and support commercial aviation.[30]

Patrick was heartened by progress in aviation technology. He could boast that the United States was abreast and perhaps a bit ahead of the world in aviation technology, largely as a result of Air Service research and development in experimental planes and engines at McCook Field, Dayton, Ohio. "We can build motors and aircraft as good or better than those built by anyone else," he told George F. Fry of the *New York Journal*. He was proud of the Army's pursuit aircraft which, if few in number, were as modern as those of any other air service.[31] Most pursuit squadrons were equipped with Thomas-Morse MB-3As. When the Army ordered 200 from Boeing Aircraft Company in 1920, they were, according to Mitchell, as good if not better than any other pursuit type in the world. In September 1923, the Army ordered production of the PW-8, first of the Curtiss Hawk series, which would be the dominant Army pursuit type for nearly a decade. Its chief rival would be a new Boeing design, the PW-9. Both aircraft were fast for their time, with top speeds in excess of 165 miles per hour, and they were maneuverable.[32]

Progress in attack and bomber aircraft was not so encouraging. Experimental aircraft were tested but none proved satisfactory. The first attempt to design an aircraft to attack ground troops was by the Engineering Division at McCook in 1920. The result was the GAX (Ground Attack Experimental), a twin-engined, triplane armed with a 37-mm cannon and eight .30-caliber machine guns. Later designated the GA-1, it proved in service tests in Texas to be slow, difficult to maneuver, and generally unacceptable. Another failure was the JL-12. Boasting 400 pounds of armor plate, it had 28 machine guns mounted in the floor, 12 aimed slightly forward, six aimed straight down, and 10 slightly to the rear. It could literally produce a rain of bullets, but it suffered the same performance limits as the GA-1. In 1922, Boeing built three single-engined attack planes designated GA-2s, but these too were failures, as was the

Aeromarine PG-1 (Pursuit, Ground) built in 1923. In 1924, attack squadrons along with observation squadrons were still equipped with war surplus DH-4s.[33] First-line bombers in 1924 were still MB-3s. Experimental bombing planes, including the three-engined LWF Owl and the giant Barling Bomber (XNBL-1), proved disappointments; they offered no advance over the Martins.

Nevertheless, it appeared to General Patrick in 1924 that the major problem of the Air Service was neither conservatism of Army leaders nor technological backwardness. It was a problem of numbers. In his judgment, the service did not have enough pilots or aircraft to fulfill its role in national defense.[34] Like most of the Army's problems, this difficulty was directly related to President Coolidge's economy program. Expansion of the Air Service was generally accepted as one of the Army's most critical needs even by allegedly conservative leaders in the War Department. In his final report as chief of staff, Pershing said categorically that expansion was the Army's most vital need, more important than bringing overseas garrisons up to strength. When one considers the strategic importance Army planners placed on garrisons in the Panama Canal Zone, Hawaii, and the Philippines, this was a considerable remark. But without money, nothing could be done for the Air Service, overseas garrisons, or any other Army need.[35] Patrick could ask for increased appropriations, but he could not expect to receive them.[36]

Patrick also knew that to some extent his problems were self-inflicted. The personnel shortage in the Air Service could have been alleviated by transfer of officers from other branches, but except in the case of second lieutenants he opposed this course because it would reduce command opportunities for Air Service officers. The personnel problem was a difficult issue complicated by the promotion complaints of young flying officers who found themselves at the bottom of the Army's single promotion list. Patrick and most flying officers wanted a separate promotion list. They argued that only flyers should command flyers, that a separate promotion list would improve morale in the service; and combined with a retirement program to meet the special needs of their dangerous profession, it would make the Air Service attractive to recruits. Their argument was not without its faults. A separate list would have resulted in a rash of promotions, but then promotion would have been slower than before. Field-grade positions would be filled with young men, postponing indefinitely the promotion of individuals below them.[37]

The airplane shortage and the fact that many aircraft were obsolete also was, in part, a result of Patrick's decision to emphasize research and development (R&D) of new aircraft rather than standardization and procurement of designs that would have been obsolete before they could have been put into service. Funds for aircraft procurement fell from $6 million in 1921 to $2.5 million in 1925. Monies spent on R&D fell, but not so drastically. Considering the hard times, the Army during 1920–26 spent a surprisingly large sum on R&D in aviation. After 1926, the amount spent on R&D remained constant, but as a percentage of the total budget it fell rather significantly.[38]

Under the circumstances, Patrick was satisfied that the Air Service was developing normally.[39] The Air Service had been rather a mess, he said, when he took charge in 1921. Though seriously undermanned and equipped largely with aircraft of World War vintage, except for pursuit aircraft, it was making progress. He believed the best way to solve its problems was through calm deliberation and steady effort.[40]

"Almost Treasonable Administration of the National Defense"

Unfortunately, the political atmosphere in Washington would not allow calm deliberation. Congress was in an ugly mood, Patrick wrote a friend on 5 March 1924.[41] A few days earlier, he had informed another friend:

> In the midst of these political matters like the Tea Pot Dome affair and the assault upon the Attorney General, an attack has been made upon the Air Service and it, too, is to be "investigated." According to the best of my information, this assault is engineered and directed by three men, one a disgruntled inventor affected with a persecutory mania, I think mentally unbalanced, another a discredited employee who was dismissed from the Department of Justice, and the third an ex-convict and a perjurer.[42]

The disgruntled inventor to whom he referred was James Vernon Martin. Formerly a lieutenant in the Navy Reserve, Martin had billed himself as "Captain James V. Martin, US Master Mariner and Pioneer Designer, Builder and Flyer of Aeroplanes, Holder of the World's Record of Over-All Aeroplane Efficiency."[43] Shortly after the war, he had designed a bomber which he claimed was capable of transoceanic flight.[44] The Air Service acquired a prototype of the bomber for testing at McCook Field, but during engine tests the airplane's transmission fell apart, so it was never flown. For reasons never explained, the airplane later was destroyed by firing incendiary machine gun bullets into it. Martin was incensed. He claimed his airplane was destroyed because he was not one of the manufacturers favored by Air Service officers, that they feared his airplane would outperform the Barling Bomber in which Air Service officers had a vested interest.[45] The Air Service denied Martin's charges, but the fact that the Barling Bomber failed miserably in performance tests put the Air Service in a most embarrassing position. A giant triplane of more than 43,000 pounds, the Barling Bomber was so underpowered it could not climb high enough to clear the Appalachian Mountains between Dayton, Ohio, and Washington.46

Rep. John M. Nelson (R-Wisc.) took up Martin's case in Congress. Relying upon evidence compiled by Martin's lawyer, Nelson charged that the deplorable state of the Air Service was a result of monopolistic practices by the Manufacturers' Aircraft Association, aided and abetted by Air Service officers who were conducting a propaganda campaign to force Congress to subsidize the aircraft industry.47 His charges led to the formation of a "Select Committee of Inquiry into the Operations of the U.S. Air Services" chaired by Rep. Florian Lampert (R-Wisc.)48

The Air Service began to prepare to defend its research and development program and procurement procedures, but it became apparent that the investigation would include much more than these activities. Three months before the hearings, a representative of the Lampert Committee told Maj Raycroft Walsh, Air Service liaison to the committee, that the first subject would likely be the "Present Organization of the Service." Walsh was requested to provide 12 copies of the Lassiter Board report (because the report was a classified document, the committee had to settle for 12 copies of the War Department press release on the report).49 The issue of an independent Air Service was to be raised again.

Hearings of the Lampert Committee, which began in October 1924 and lasted five months, tended to revolve around the testimony of Billy Mitchell. Brushing aside the War Department's gesture of good faith in the Lassiter program and the progress of naval aviation under Moffett, Mitchell restated his charges cked by both the Navy and the War de at in personnel and equipment the Un n fifth among air powers of the world. d repeated warnings from the chief of n's air defenses were deteriorating. nse, he said, was claimed by both th ulted in "absolute duplication and a te services could not progress as long as es having a "vested interest against and Post Office were directed by men tion nor training in aviation matters. aviation in the hands of aviators—a s service. Besides providing improved vice would be more efficient and econ

The m before the committee was General P ny Air Corps. Patrick first made the proposal in a letter to the Adjutant General on 19 December 1924: he was "convinced that the ultimate solution of the air defense problem of this country is a united air force," but the time was not yet ripe for such a "radical reorganization." He suggested that "certain preliminary steps may well be taken, all with the ultimate end in view." Creation of a semi-independent Air Corps, like the Marine Corps, was one of the steps he had in mind. Others included the Lassiter program, assignment of all aerial defense of coasts conducted from shore bases to the Army Air Service, a separate promotion list, a separate budget, and a new uniform suitable for flyers. This last point may appear picayune but among flyers it was a hot issue. The high-standing collar on the Army service uniform, they argued, was "wholly inappropriate for use by flying personnel."[54]

Mitchell claimed the War Department took no action on Patrick's letter.[55] Exactly what sort of action he had in mind is not clear, but the War Department did take some action. The letter was referred to the War Plans Division of the General Staff, which did a point-by-point analysis recommending on 7 January 1925 that the Air Corps plan be disapproved. General Patrick had said that "in any future emergency involving our military forces, particularly in the early phases thereof, the air force must be considered one of the vital factors." The War Plans Division considered it "so vital a factor that neither Army nor Navy can dispense with it as an integral part of its functioning organism." The unity of command of ground and air forces could not be compromised. Endorsing the Air Corps idea would do just that, particularly since such action by the War Department would be tantamount to acquiescence in "ultimate creation of a unified air force." Officers of the War Plans Division warned that while an air force could attack, it could not occupy or hold ground. A unified air force would need a separate supply service and other support functions. It would logically encompass "antiaircraft artillery, Signal Corps, Chemical Warfare Service and Coast Defenses." It should require additional ground troops and perhaps even naval forces. It would duplicate or supplant functions of the Army and Navy. The War Plans Division agreed with Patrick's contention that aerial defense from shore bases should be under the Army Air Service, but that such an arrangement in no way necessitated a separate Air Corps. They agreed that under present circumstances the need for appropriations for the Air Service was more pressing than those of some other branches, but such a problem did not justify a separate budget for the Air Service.

Officers of the War Plans Division admitted that priorities might change, favoring another branch. "The broad problem of national defense requires that the needs of each defense element be considered separately and in relation to the needs of every other branch and to the needs of the combined elements. . . . To remove the Air Service from this coordinating influence would be a step fraught with grave, if not indeed, disastrous consequences." Airpower propaganda had a "strong appeal" among those seeking simple, complete solutions to the problem of national defense. A separate budget would make it easy for the uninformed or politically inspired to favor the Air Service at the expense of a balanced defense program. To Patrick's plea for a separate promotion list, the reply from the War Plans Division was that Air Service officers by virtue of extra pay for flying were already a favored class and further discrimination in their favor would not be to the interest of the Army. The uniform issue was seen as a symptom of the separation already evident. They pointed out that aviators were authorized to wear overalls when flying. For economy, if for no other reason, they could continue to wear the same uniform as the rest of the Army when not flying. Finally, War Plans noted that enactment of the Lassiter Board recommendations was awaiting agreement between the Secretaries of War and the Navy.[56]

General Drum, who reviewed the findings of the War Plans Division, felt it was not enough simply to disapprove the proposal of the chief of the Air Service. The points in that proposal were a challenge to established policy of the secretary of war against a separate Air Service. The statements of General Patrick should not be allowed to stand without more thorough explanation. Drum said that Patrick "should be called upon to show grounds in every case. If his contentions are correct, remedies should be applied; if they are not correct, they should be withdrawn."[57] Drum's suggestion was overruled. Patrick was not asked to withdraw his proposal and it was, as Drum apparently feared, destined to reappear, to the embarrassment of the War Department.

While War Plans was analyzing Patrick's Air Corps plan, the entire War Department, indeed virtually everyone with an interest in national defense, was following the testimony of Mitchell in the Lampert Hearings. Former secretary of war Baker wrote to ex-chief of staff March that General Mitchell " is cutting up high jinks again. . . . His lack of discipline is undoubtedly distressing, but after all it may be that this dramatic insubordination will make Congress more disposed to provide for real strength in the air, and I fancy this must be the direction of even defensive preparedness in the future."[58] As a spectator, Baker could afford to be philosophical; the incumbent secretary of war could not. And on the morning of 19 January 1925, when headlines in the *Washington Herald* proclaimed, "Aviation Chief Scores Army and Navy Autocrats—Hot Criticisms by Mitchell," Weeks's patience ended.[59] He decided to call Mitchell's hand, to challenge him to prove his charges. Weeks had sent Patrick excerpts from Mitchell's testimony with the offensive passages underlined. Patrick was directed to "call on General Mitchell to submit without delay a statement of facts that substantiated each assertion contained in the underscored portions of each extract of his testimony."[60] Mitchell's answer to the secretary was a detailed defense of his testimony prefaced with a review of his qualifications as an expert on military aviation and the unrepentant statement that "the evidence I gave before the Committee of Congress was in the form of my opinion expressed rather mildly."[61]

There followed General Mitchell's famous (infamous, said his supporters) exile to Texas. His term as assistant chief of the Air Service had expired in the midst of the above turmoil, and, as many observers in Washington expected, he was not reappointed. Weeks explained to the president that Mitchell's "whole course of action has been so lawless, so contrary to the building up of an efficient organization, so lacking in reasonable team work, so indicative of a personal desire for publicity at the expense of everyone with whom he is associated that his actions render him unfit for the high administrative position."[62] Returned to his permanent rank of colonel, he was ordered to Fort Sam Houston as air officer.[63] James E. Fechet succeeded him as assistant chief of Air Service.[64]

Meanwhile, Weeks was responding to Mitchell's latest criticisms. In a letter to Rep. Randolph Perkins (R-N.J.), one of the Republican members of the Lampert Committee, the secretary explained that operating the Air Service was a complicated and expensive business, not unlike that of operating a "great railroad system." Development and purchase of new equipment required large expenditure over and above the already high cost of simply maintaining service. Secretary Weeks was again pointing out that the principal problem with the Air Service was money. He assured Perkins that the War Department was making every effort to economize in order to make available the maximum possible sum for new equipment. War Department leaders were not opposed to new airplanes for the Air Service; they were facing realities of the budget. To Mitchell's charge that Army leaders were conservative, Weeks replied, "If the statement . . . is meant to indicate an attitude the opposite of radicalism, the charge of conservatism might be sustained; but that does not mean that they are not progressive."[65]

After the uproar over Mitchell's testimony and exile, there was calm for several months. On duty in Texas, Mitchell was busy learning his new job, fishing, and revising his testimony, articles, and essays for a book he entitled *Winged Defense*.[66] The Lampert Committee ended hearings on 2 March but delayed issuing its report to give committee members time to study the thousands of pages of testimony, a task they were not overly anxious to begin. As Congressman Perkins put it, "Most of us are pretty tired and want to forget the 'Inquiry' for a few weeks."[67]

Winged Defense was published on 29 August 1925, and perhaps its appearance would have been enough to shatter the calm. By chance, however, it came out shortly before a series of tragic events that seemed to play into Mitchell's hands. On the first of September, news broke that Commodore John Rodgers and the crew of a Navy PN-9 seaplane had disappeared on the first attempt to fly the Pacific from the West Coast to Hawaii. That tragedy was still in the headlines when before dawn on 3 September the Navy airship *Shenandoah* ran into a squall-line over Ohio. During the desperate battle to get the dirigible turned around, it broke into three parts. The control compartment containing Comdr Zachary Lansdowne and 13 crewmen fell to earth, killing all 14 men. Miraculously, the remaining 28 crewmen of the *Shenandoah* managed to maneuver another section of the dirigible as a free balloon, bringing it down safely.[68]

Mitchell rose to the occasion. Secretary of the Navy Wilbur had issued a statement that included the unfortunate comment that "in view of the experience of the navy planes in the Arctic expedition, the failure of the Hawaiian flight and the *Shenandoah* disaster, we have come to the conclusion that the Atlantic and Pacific are still our best defenses."[69] To Mitchell and his followers, this attempt to deprecate airpower by reference to these naval disasters was infuriating.[70] Responding to requests from newspapers, Mitchell worked feverishly on a statement that he delivered at a press conference early on the morning of 5 September, two days after the *Shenandoah* crash.[71] He remarked that "these accidents are the direct result of incompetency, criminal negligence and almost treasonable administration of the national defense by the war and navy departments." Then he repeated all his old charges, with less restraint than ever. He passed out mimeographed copies of his statement, which was almost 6,000 words long. The press had a field day with the story.[72] It was evident that the radical airman was challenging the War Department to court-martial him.

A "Bolshevik Bug in the Air"

Mitchell's principal antagonist was not the War Department, but President Coolidge, and the president was no easy antagonist. The quiet gentleman from Northampton, Massachusetts, had made his political reputation belatedly, opposing unruly public servants in the Boston police strike of 1919. He was a strict disciplinarian, but a patient man, willing to let problems come to a crisis before wasting energy addressing them.[73] During the tumult over Mitchell's exile, Coolidge apparently recognized that the Air Service issue was beginning to be serious, and perhaps also that he might have to deal with the ungovernable Colonel Mitchell. Four days after concurring in the decision not to reappoint Mitchell as assistant chief of the Air Service, Coolidge wrote his classmate from Amherst, Massachusetts, and his friend for nearly 30 years, Dwight W. Morrow.[74] "I have in mind," he said, "that I may like to have you look into the subject of airplanes for me."[75] He asked Morrow to "think this over and think who you might wish to join you in case I call you."[76] Six months later, while the War Department was concluding a preliminary investigation prior to announcing the court-martial of Mitchell, Coolidge judged the time was right to address the problem of aviation. On 12 September 1925, he announced that he had directed Morrow and eight other distinguished men to look into the aircraft situation.[77] The Morrow Board investigations would divert attention from Mitchell's court-martial. It may also have been Coolidge's hope that recommendations would offer an alternative more favorable than that expected from the Lampert Committee, which still had not made its report.[78] Several days after Coolidge's announcement, the War Department made public its intention to court-martial Mitchell. Not made public at the time was the fact that Coolidge himself had preferred the charges.[79]

Mitchell's increasingly reckless campaign to influence public opinion had given the president a strong moral issue on which to base his move: militarism. In a speech to a convention of the American Legion, Coolidge reminded the legionnaires that "our forefathers had seen so much militarism and suffered so much from it that they desired to banish it forever." Then, obviously referring to Mitchell and his activities, he said, "It is for this reason that any organization of men in the military service bent on inflaming the public mind for the purpose of forcing Government action through the pressure of public opinion is an exceedingly dangerous undertaking and precedent." He declared that "it is for the civil authority to determine what appropriations shall be granted, what appointments shall be made, and what rules shall be adopted for the conduct of its armed forces."[80]

The Morrow Board was widely acclaimed as a fair and sensible approach to the air controversy. The respected men he had chosen inspired confidence that hearings would be conducted properly. The Hearst newspapers called Morrow "the kind of man to dissolve clouds of technicalities and override prejudice."[81] On 17 September the board began four weeks of public hearings, before retiring to write its report in the Wardman Park Hotel, where Morrow reserved a suite.[82] On the board were Maj Gen James G. Harbord, retired;

Rear Adm Frank F. Fletcher, retired; Howard E. Coffin, a consulting engineer and aeronautics expert; Sen. Hiram Bingham (R-Conn.), member of the Committee on Military Affairs; Rep. Carl Vinson (D-Ga.), member of the Committee on Naval Affairs; Rep. James S. Parker (R-N.Y.), chairman of the Committee on Interstate and Foreign Commerce; Judge Arthur C. Denison, of the Sixth Circuit Court of Appeals; and William F. Durand of Stanford University, president of the American Society of Mechanical Engineers and a member of the National Committee for Aeronautics. Of members of the board, Senator Bingham was expected to be most friendly toward the Air Service. He was a former Air Service officer, had written a book on the Service during the First World War, and had recently been instrumental in winning approval for the new "turn-down collar" uniform for the Air Service.[83] Aiding the board in unofficial status were Edward Warner of the Massachusetts Institute of Technology, Maj Leslie MacDill of the Army Air Service, and commanders Jerome Hunsaker and H. C. Richardson of the Naval Air Service.[84]

For air enthusiasts, Mitchell's testimony before the Morrow Board was a great disappointment. The "brilliant defiance" they expected was dulled when Morrow cleverly allowed the fiery colonel to burn himself out in uninterrupted testimony. Mitchell apparently had intended to read his book, *Winged Defense,* until it sparked controversy from the board. When no questions came, he found himself reading for four hours straight. Reflecting on the scene in his memoirs, General Arnold recalled how "we of the Air Service practically squirmed, wanting to yell: 'Come on, Billy, put down that damned book! Answer their questions and step down, that'll show them!'" Mitchell did not put the book down until he was exhausted. Morrow adjourned the board for the day. Next day Mitchell had his opportunity to answer questions, but opportunity to gain control of the situation was lost.[85]

After hearing the testimony of 99 witnesses, many of them flying men, the Morrow Board submitted its report on 30 November 1925. Approved by Coolidge and backed by the prestige of the members of the board, the report was to become perhaps the principal influence on the passage of legislation in 1926 forming a basic air policy for the nation. Addressing the allegations of Mitchell, the report assured the nation that there was no danger of attack from the air and denied that in wars "against high-spirited peoples" strategic bombing could break their will: "Man cannot make a machine stronger than the spirit of man." It denied that a large air force would constitute a move toward peace: "Those who believe in the preponderating effect of air power . . . are not talking of disarmament when they suggest the sacrifice of battleships. They are talking of discarding the weapon they think is becoming useless and substituting therefore what they believe to be a more deadly one." It declared that civil and military aviation functions of the government should remain separate; private agencies, as well as the federal government, should contribute to development of aviation; there should be no Department of National Defense and no separate Department of Air; and in any air policy, the budget must be a consideration.[86]

Morrow and colleagues had come to essentially conservative conclusions; they favored no radical change in aviation policy. "We aimed," Morrow said later, "to put the problem in the process of settlement, in process of a more careful and sustained study."[87] This tactful procedure pleased the War Department, leaders of which had made a methodical presentation. For the most part, the board had accepted their arguments.[88] Their antagonists, the airmen, were, of course, far from pleased. Even the moderate Patrick was greatly disappointed that the board had not accepted what he considered constructive recommendations.[89] The board had rebuffed his independent Air Corps plan which he had outlined on the first day of the hearings.[90]

Meanwhile, the court-martial of Mitchell had begun on 28 October 1925. It was a big event in Washington.[91] After a while, it became dull and repetitious, but it began with excitement. Shortly before ten o'clock on the day of the trial, Colonel Mitchell and a small party including his wife Betty, his sister Harriet, and his attorneys Rep. Frank Reid (R-Ill.), a member of the Lampert Committee—the "Bolshevik member"[92] according to Patrick—and Col Herbert A. White made their way through the crowd that had gathered in front of the ramshackle, old warehouse that the Army had chosen as the site for Mitchell's trial. They entered the building and ascended to the second floor where, as a reporter for the *Army and Navy Journal* put it, a "dinky little room" had been arranged to accommodate the court.[93] Inside was a small group of about 60 spectators who talked in low voices and shifted about on the hard iron folding chairs the Army had provided. Sprinkled through the audience were several young officers and a few congressmen. There were approximately 40 gentlemen of the press. Most of the spectators were fashionably dressed young women who perhaps sensed romance in this trial of a handsome Air Service officer before a court of stodgy old Army generals.

Explosions of light from photographers' flashes and the scramble of newsreel cameramen for positions announced entry of the Mitchell party. For a moment there was an air of romance in that dinky little room. Clad in the new uniform of the service with its stylish fold-down collar and lapel, Colonel Mitchell was, indeed, the picture of a dashing air officer. Rows of medals and service ribbons added a riot of color above his left pocket and testified to gallantry and accomplishment. He moved to the table and chairs reserved for the defendant's party and sat down. Close behind him and slightly to one side was his wife. Comely and dignified, she seemed the essence of a woman offering total support to her man. Throughout the trial she would sit close by him, often putting her arm around him or giving him reassuring pats on the shoulder.

After a moment, the young captain who commanded the detail in charge of the courtroom gave a command in a low voice to his old sergeant whose service stripes extended well past his left elbow. The sergeant bellowed, "Stand up as the court enters!" The audience rose in unison as the 12 generals of the court quietly filed in. Their high-collared, olive-drab tunics appeared stiff and formal in contrast to Mitchell's suavity. They were professional soldiers; and like Colonel Mitchell, their tunics were decorated with symbols of accomplishment. Every one of them wore the Distinguished Service Medal, and four of them the Distinguished Service Cross, in combat decorations second only to the Medal of Honor. The president of the court, Maj Gen Charles P. Summerall, was the ranking major general of the Army. In the First World War, his V Corps had formed the center of the attack that broke the German lines in the Argonne in November 1918. Another member of the court, Douglas MacArthur, now the youngest major general in the Army, had fought under Summerall in the Argonne.[94] The other generals had similar combat credentials. To assist the court in legal matters, a 13th officer had been assigned to the court. He was Col Blanton Winship.

Formalities completed, Congressman Reid rose to challenge three members of the court. A big man with an aggressive, rapid manner of speaking and a propensity to use sweeping gestures to emphasize points, he hurled his arguments. Brig Gen Albert J. Bowley should be removed, he charged, on grounds of "prejudice and bias." In a speech before the American Legion in Greenville, South Carolina, in October 1924, Bowley had said among other things that "the public is prone to be carried away by exaggerated statements as to the importance of one branch of the service. Pictures are painted showing flocks of airplanes dropping bombs on New York City, with the skyscrappers toppling right and left. Stories of how the metropolis of the country can easily be destroyed appeal to the imagination of the public and they are prone to lose their balance." Bowley admitted the speech but denied prejudice or bias in the matter for which Colonel Mitchell was on trial. The court retired to consider the argument. General Bowley was excused. Also challenged and excused without contest was Maj Gen Fred W. Sladen.

Then Reid leveled an attack at the president of the court, Summerall. Reid submitted Mitchell's report of an inspection trip in 1923 when still assistant chief of the Air Service. Mitchell had severely criticized Hawaiian air defenses for which Summerall was then responsible. The congressman argued that Summerall had taken Mitchell's points personally and was thereby "biased and prejudiced." An emotional scene followed. "I learn here for the first time," General Summerall said, "of Colonel Mitchell's personal bitter hostility toward me. I cannot consent to sit longer as a member of this court, and I ask[ed] that I be excused." The court was declared closed. Within a few minutes, the remaining members of the court announced that Summerall was excused. He left the courtroom. One correspondent reported that men who knew Summerall well "had said they had never seen him so ruffled." To reporters outside the courtroom, the general exclaimed, "Now it's all over. We're enemies, Mitchell and I."

In the more mundane days which followed that first day of excitement, Mitchell was able to turn much of the testimony into a debate over airpower, but the trial did not achieve the results he expected. Coolidge had succeeded. In the mind of the public, the trial was the martyring of Colonel Mitchell, but on the issue of airpower and aviation policy they accepted the opinion of the Morrow Board, which made its report 17 days before the verdict in Mitchell's trial, as the judgment of a higher court.

Despite efforts of Mitchell and a parade of friends and supporters, mostly from the Air Service, to prove his charge of "incompetency, criminal negligence and almost treasonable administration of the national defense by the War and Navy Departments," on 17 December 1925 he was found guilty of violating the 96th Article of War. In the opinion of all the court except one member (alleged to have been General MacArthur), he had acted in a manner prejudicial to "good order and military discipline," bringing discredit upon the Army. His sentence was a five-year suspension from rank, command, and duty, with forfeiture of pay and allowances. Mitchell chose to resign, and Coolidge accepted his resignation.

Billy Mitchell's crusade and trial would be debated by airmen for years to come. Some of them contended during the turmoil, and later, that Mitchell's final insubordination was detrimental to the Air Service. Edgar Stanley Gorrell was a respected member of that inner circle of airmen who could claim to be aviation pioneers. He was the author of America's first strategic bombing plan during the First World War and in civilian life was vice-president of the Stutz Motor Car Company. He felt it was time for Mitchell to be shut up, that the stormy petrel of the Air Service was not trying to help the nation but trying to feather his own nest, to further his own prestige.[95] Thomas Milling and Benjamin Foulois, two of the first three certified military aviators in the American Army, held similar opinions. They could not condone lack of discipline nor agree that good had come from it.[96] General Patrick felt all along that Mitchell's methods were wrong and would only "befog the entire situation," dimming the prospect for the Air Service.[97] Hap Arnold, another aviation pioneer and Mitchell supporter, reflected on the trial years later and concluded that a different verdict would probably have had no effect on the development of aviation, that the dream he and Mitchell had for the Air Service would not be possible until the late 1930s, when a "combination of technical advances and the state of international relations" would induce a mushroom growth of airpower.[98] Mitchell supporters Carl Spaatz and Ira C. Eaker concluded, however, that the Mitchell episode had been essential to bring to public attention the neglect of military aviation.[99]

A few days before the end of the trial, two weeks after the Morrow Report, the Lampert Committee issued its report. It gave a much darker picture of the condition of aviation in America than did the Morrow group. It made 23 recommendations, the most important being establishment of a Department of National Defense, a five-year development program for aviation, representation for the Army and Navy air services on the Army General Staff and the Navy General Board, and separate, all-inclusive budgets for the air services. A longer and detailed concurring report was filed by Congressman Reid, counsel for Mitchell. The most important aspect of his report was repetition of Mitchell's ideas on airpower.[100]

With the Morrow and Lampert studies complete, the Mitchell court-martial finished, the next move was up to Congress. The House Committee on Military Affairs considered bills patterned after the Morrow Board recommendations, the Lampert Committee recommendations, and General Patrick's Air Corps plan. Hearings rehashed all the arguments of the past years.[101]

The first proposal considered by the House Military Affairs Committee was a bill submitted by Representative Curry in December 1925, patterned after recommendations of the Lampert Committee. It proposed a Department of National Defense. To counter this proposition, Rep. John M. Morin (R-Pa.) introduced a bill incorporating the recommendations of the Morrow Board. The Morin Bill had approval of the War Department. Debate in the hearings became a tug-of-war between the two proposals. Patrick repeated his suggestion that an acceptable compromise would be a semi-independent Air Corps along the lines of the Marine Corps within the Navy, and J. M. Wainwright submitted a bill incorporating these suggestions.[102] Commonly known as the Patrick Bill, the

Wainwright measure met immediate opposition from the War Department. Fox Conner of the General Staff saw the measure as an attempt by airmen to "escape control by the Chief of Staff, the Adjutant General or the Inspector General." He dubbed the measure a "promotion scheme." Expressing an opinion commonly held in the General Staff, he said that the Air Service as then organized was well balanced with relation to the rest of the Army. The Patrick Bill would destroy that balance. It would make the Air Corps a favored branch.[103] Concurring with the General Staff in opposing the Patrick Bill, Secretary of War Dwight F. Davis (Weeks had retired because of ill health) sent a long letter to the committee chairman, Representative Morin, attacking the bill point by point. Davis gave emphasis to Patrick's proposal that the Air Corps have a separate budget. He argued that the only possible reason for such a budget would be to get more money. Under President Coolidge's economy program, an increase in funds for the Air Service would have to be paid by reduction elsewhere in the War Department budget. The War Department in the past had taken funds from other branches to meet needs of the Air Service and might do so again, but such decisions had to be made with needs of the entire Army in mind. "The Air Service requires fiscal control," he added.[104]

Meanwhile, Mitchell and friends caused something of a "rhubarb" by their continued effort to mobilize public opinion to influence the Congress. Major Arnold and others "continued going out to Billy's home in Middleburg, Virginia, and also over to Capitol Hill, and writing letters to keep up the fight."[105] One of their activities gave Secretary Davis opportunity to take action against them. Allegedly using a mimeograph machine in the Air Service headquarters in Washington, they printed circulars which they apparently planned to distribute.[106] Davis directed the Inspector General to investigate these activities which he said were designed to raise support for the Patrick–Wainwright measure. The implication was that Patrick had something to do with it. In reply, the ever-quotable Mitchell charged that "the War Department was trying to bludgeon General Patrick into silence. . . . He has taken my place and now they are going after him."[107] The headline in the *Army and Navy Journal* read "Air Measures Menaced by Ugly Dispute."[108]

Patrick issued a statement denying he was being bludgeoned into silence.[109] Quietly he conducted his own investigation, announcing on 17 February 1926 that "only two officers in this office were concerned in an attempt to influence legislation in what I regard as an objectionable manner. Both of them were reprimanded, and one of them, no longer wanted in my office, will be sent to another station."[110] The officer reprimanded was Major Dargue. Major Arnold was the officer no longer wanted and was exiled to Fort Riley, a cavalry post where he took command of an observation squadron. In a letter to a friend in New York, Patrick explained that one or two somewhat misguided officers had let their zeal lead them astray. He remarked wistfully, "Things were really in fairly good shape until this teapot tempest trouble."[111]

Patrick understood that it was either going to be a compromise or no legislation, and tried to calm things in a speech in Chicago. He asked extremists on both sides to "kindly take a seat" while Congress worked things out. The decision, he said, "rests with Congress, which will probably take its stand somewhere between the extremes of the enthusiasts and those who call themselves conservative."[112]

The compromise would likely be in favor of the War Department. The president had made clear that he favored legislation to carry out recommendations of the Morrow Board, but no further. In his own inimitable style, Coolidge told reporters in a press conference, "Now, I want to have a good Air Service here, the same as I want to have a good Army and Navy, but I don't want to run to extremes about it."[113]

The compromise arrived at, after a stormy executive session of the Military Affairs Committee on 3 March 1926, rejected both the Morin Bill (the War Department measure) and the Patrick Bill by a vote of 11 to 10. The bill advocating a department of air was defeated 16 to 5. The slate clean, a compromise exchanged a commitment from the War Department to pursue a five-year aircraft development program "to the extent that financial considerations permit" for an agreement by General Patrick to go along with a bill advancing the Morrow recommendations.[114] After a few revisions, the committee bill passed on 2 July 1926.[115] The resultant Air Corps Act of 1926 changed the name of the Air Service to Air Corps, established the five-year program, and provided an assistant secretary of war for air. Other provisions addressed the issues of pay, promotion, and General Staff representation, largely along lines recommended by the Morrow Board. Not at all what the air enthusiasts wanted, it probably was the most they could have secured under the circumstances.

Army leaders were pleased that the air arm remained under War Department control and that the first steps had been taken to restore discipline. To them the whole affair had been, to a great degree, a disciplinary problem. In these times of tight budgets the whole Army had to work together if it was to survive. So they emphasized the team spirit. They were willing to sacrifice for the benefit of the air arm if it was for the good of the Army team as a whole. What they could not countenance was rebellion, men like Mitchell going outside the Army circle to preach airpower and bring outside pressure on the Army to favor the air arm unduly. In December 1925, as the Mitchell trial ended, General Pershing wrote to Gen William M. Wright: "There seems to be a Bolshevik bug in the air . . . and all these men who have grouches seem to think they must run to the press and have them aired."[116] Most Army leaders felt it was high time the Army fumigate and innoculate against the Bolshevik bug.

It had taken a long time, seven years after the Armistice, to shake down the organization of the air arm of the United States Army, and any observer from abroad must have thought that the only thing the airmen could do well was to squabble with their superiors in the War Department. All the while the types of planes becoming available to air forces around the world, and the requirements upon pilots flying those planes, were multiplying in a remarkable manner, as technology was changing and the aircraft industry was coming of age. To people like Mitchell, the future still seemed a wild, dreamy affair in which wars would be fought in the air while noncombatants watched helplessly below. In this great aerial Armageddon the traditional armies and navies would be useless. The entire argument had risen to an intense level in the court-martial of Mitchell. The opponents of Mitchell seemed so marked out for posterity as they had filed into the room, those generals in their old First World War high collars, facing the nattily attired man of the air. And yet, like so many of the confrontations of life, this one was more appearance than reality. Mitchell, of course, would have his influence in the coming war in the person of young Major Arnold and through the work of his other supporters. But the zealots saw only their own problems and possibilities. They were like (to use a metaphor from the horse age) animals with blinders. The major generals of the court-martial scene were themselves fighters of a sort that the world would need again, in another world war. The war of the future, so dimly perceived in that middle year of the 1920s, the year 1926, was to have a place for both visionaries and realists. Both of them would be right, and in some respects both would be wrong.

Notes

1. Historical Office of the Army Air Forces, *The Official Pictorial History of the AAF* (New York: Duell, Sloan and Pearce, 1947), 59; Martin Caidin, *Air Force: A Pictorial History of American Airpower* (New York: Rinehart, 1957), 30; and Wilbert H. Ruenbeck and Philip M. Flammer, *A History of the Air Force* (Chicago: University of Chicago Press, 1967), 15.

2. *The Official Pictorial History of the AAF*, 65–69; Caidin, 34–35; and Mason M. Patrick, *The United States in the Air* (Garden City, N.Y.: Doubleday, Doran, and Co., 1928), 116–17.

3. This quotation comes from Gen John J. Pershing, final report, 12 September 1924, War Plans Division (WPD) 2189, Record Group (RG) 165, National Archives

(NA). Additional evidence of Pershing's frustration can be found in Mark S.Watson, *Chief of Staff, Prewar Plans and Preparations* (Washington, D.C.: Historical Division, Department of the Army, 1950), 18. See also Gen George C. Marshall, speech, in H. A. DeWeerd, ed., *Selected Speeches and Statements of General of the Army George C. Marshall, Chief of Staff, United States Army* (Washington, D.C.: The Infantry Journal, 1945), 58. Marshall notes that Pershing found the situation "very discouraging."

4. Repeated references to the Republican Party's commitment to economy in government can be found in *Republican Party National Committee Campaign Textbook* (Washington, D.C.: Republican National Committee) for 1924, 1932, and 1940–1944. Hereinafter cited as Republican Campaign Textbook.

5. Newton D. Baker to Peyton C. March, letter, 26 July 1924, March manuscripts (MSS), Library of Congress (LOC), Washington, D.C.

6. See President Coolidge's inaugural address, 4 March 1925. Also Arthur M. Schlesinger Jr., *Crisis of the Old Order, 1919–1933* (Boston: Houghton Mifflin, 1957), 58–59. Coolidge was so committed to the doctrine of economy that he demanded his inauguration be held amid the "severest simplicity." For a short but interesting editorial on Coolidge's inexpensive inauguration, see the *Washington Evening Star* (11 February 1925).

7. This period from the midtwenties through the early thirties, was the heyday of pacifism. Numerous pacifist societies were organized with the purpose of breaking the "war habit." Many of the most popular novelists of the day—Ernest Hemingway, William Faulkner, and John Dos Passos to name a few—reflected antiwar sentiment in their novels. War was abhorred not only for its inhumanity but for its immoral wastefulness. As William Allen White put it: "War is waste. And the greatest wasters win. . . ." William Allen White, *Forty Years on Mainstreet* (New York: Farrar and Rinehart, 1937), 180.

8. Sen. John S. Williams added that "the last lunatic who thought us not worthy of counting in case of war is not in Holland, and he ought not to be punished, because he was a lunatic." See *Congressional Record*, 66th Cong., 3d sess., 1921, 1349–50.

9. *Republican Campaign Textbook, 1924*, 363–66. The sentiment against defense spending was bipartisan in the twenties. The 1924 Democratic Party platform stated, "We demand a strict and sweeping reduction of armament by land and sea, so that there shall be no competitive military program or naval building."

10. See Watson, 25–26, for a quotation from George C. Marshall describing the Army's "fight for its very life" in the 1920s and 1930s.

11. Ibid., 15–16.

12. See Fred Greene, "The Military View of American National Policy, 1904–1940," *American Historical Review* 69 (January 1964): 354–77. See also Alfred Goldberg, ed., *A History of the United States Air Force, 1907–1957* (Princeton, N.J.: D. Van Nostrand, 1957), 42; and Wesley Frank Craven and James Lea Cate, eds., *The Army Air Forces in World War II*, vol. 1, *Plans and Early Operations, January 1939 to August 1942* (1949; new imprint, Washington, D.C.: Office of Air Force History, 1983), 35.

13. "Statement of Major General John L. Hines," in Pershing MSS, LOC.

14. John J. Pershing to Secretary of War John W. Weeks, letter, 21 November 1923, Pershing MSS. See also the *Annual Report of the Secretary of War, 1923* (Washington, D.C.: GPO, 1923) (hereinafter cited as Secretary of War, 1923).

15. John W. Killigrew, "The Impact of the Great Depression on the Army, 1929–1936" (PhD diss., Indiana University, 1960), 8–9; Russell F. Weigley, *History of the United States Army* (New York: Macmillan, 1967), 401.

16. Watson, 22.

17. It is interesting that General Pershing admired Calvin Coolidge for his firmness in rejecting the bonus demands of World War veterans. "I am glad we have a

man in there who does not pussyfoot," he wrote to Gen John L. Hines, 2 January 1924, Hines MSS, LOC.

18. Harry H. Ransom, "The Air Corps Act of 1926: A Study in the Legislative Process" (PhD diss., Princeton University, 1953), 124. A credible threat to the national security did not begin to appear obvious until the early 1930s. Arnold recognized this in his memoirs when he noted that the "combination of technical advances and the state of international relations" were not conducive to the rapid growth of airpower in the twenties. See Henry H. Arnold, *Global Mission* (New York: Harper, 1949), 158. Gen Charles P. Summerall, as late as October 1929, conceded that military men had to accept the judgment of the president and the State Department that there was "reasonable assurance of a long-continued peace." See "Notes used in Report," in box 22, "Final Report of Chief of Staff, November 30, 1930," Summerall MSS, LOC.

19. Calvin Coolidge to secretary of war, letters, 22 May 1925, quoted in memorandum to chief of staff from Brig Gen Fox Conner, 29 May 1925, WPD 2189, RG 165, NA. See also Alfred F. Hurley, *Billy Mitchell: Crusader for Air Power* (Bloomington: Indiana University Press, 1975), 100. For a popular account of the effect of President Coolidge's economy program on the Air Service, see *Literary Digest*, 10 October 1925, 10–11.

20. Maj Gen Dennis E. Nolan, memorandum to chief of staff, 28 January 1925, Office of Chief of Staff (OCS) 15294-7, RG 165, NA. See also the testimony of Brig Gen Hugh A. Drum in the Morrow Board hearings.

21. "Statement on the Financial Side of the War Department's Policies with Reference to Aviation," Brig Gen Fox Conner, 16 October 1925, Pershing MSS. This statement was presented before the Morrow Board hearings. Gen Nolan summarized Conner's statement in a letter to Pershing, noting that it was apparent from the facts presented by Conner that the War Department treated the Air Service as a favored son rather than as a stepchild. Dennis E. Nolan to John J. Pershing, 10 November 1925, letter, Pershing MSS.

22. Edwin Denby to John Weeks, letter, 18 February 1924, and "Document of Curtis Wilbur, Secretary of the Navy presented to the Morrow Board," 25 September 1925. Both of these are in the Morrow Board records, LOC. See also "Memo from General John J. Pershing for Mr. Dwight W. Morrow," 17 October 1925, Pershing MSS.

23. Mason M. Patrick to Maj F. P. Reynolds, letter, 29 October 1923; Mason M. Patrick to S. S. Bradley, letter, 18 October 1921; and Mason M. Patrick to P. R. G. Groves, letter, 3 April 1924. All of these letters are in Patrick MSS, RG 18, NA. See also Robert Frank Futrell, *Ideas, Concepts, Doctrine: A History of Basic Thinking in the United States Air Force, 1907–1964* (Maxwell AFB, Ala.: Air University, 1974), 52. Futrell notes Patrick's understanding of the relationship between relaxation of world tensions and the willingness of Americans to pay for national defense. Ira C. Eaker, who worked in Patrick's office during this period, said that "our principal problem, against the accomplishment of our objectives, was budgetary." Ira C. Eaker, "The Reminiscences of Ira C. Eaker," Oral History Collection (OHC) of Columbia University, 27–28 (hereinafter cited as Eaker, OHC).

24. Mason M. Patrick to R. C. Kirtland, letter, 4 December 1923; Patrick M. Mason to Training and Plans, memorandum, 4 December 1923; Oscar Westover to Mason M. Patrick, letter, 16 May 1925; and "Address, 17 January 1927, to Mid-Day Club, Cleveland, Ohio." All of these are in Patrick MSS, RG 18, NA. See also Futrell, 39; Eaker, OHC, 21; and Benjamin D. Foulois and Carroll V. Glines, *From the Wright Brothers to the Astronauts: The Memoirs of Benjamin D. Foulois* (New York: McGraw-Hill, 1968), 207–8.

25. "Expansion of Air Power Needed for Army and Navy," *Army and Navy Journal*, 27 October 1923.

26. Gen Mason M. Patrick, testimony before the Morrow Board, quoted in *Army and Navy Journal*, 26 September 1925.

27. John J. Pershing to Dwight W. Morrow, 17 October 1925. See also Brig Gen Hugh A. Drum, testimony before the Morrow Board, quoted in *Army and Navy Journal*, 26 September 1925; and J. H. Pirie to Mason M. Patrick, letter, 10 October 1925, Patrick MSS, RG 18, NA. The war plans for this period considered the limitations of aircraft and concluded that the aircraft of that day offered neither special problems nor opportunities. For a discussion of this see Greene, 369. The controversy over antiaircraft artillery versus aircraft was a particularly difficult problem for General Patrick because of the report of the so-called McNair Board in 1923, which asserted the superiority of antiaircraft artillery. The Air Service went to considerable lengths to disprove the conclusions of that board. See Central Decimal Files 334.7, "The McNair Board" in RG 18, NA.

28. W. D. Sherman to Mason M. Patrick, letter, 20 February 1923; R. C. Kirtland to Mason M. Patrick, letter, 12 March 1923; H. A. Smith to Mason M. Patrick, letter, 7 January 1925; H. A. Smith to Mason M. Patrick, letter, 13 March 1925; H. A. Smith to Mason M. Patrick, letter, 27 March 1925; and H. E. Ely to Mason M. Patrick, letter, 2 October 1925. All of these are in the Patrick MSS, RG 18, NA.

29. Mason M. Patrick to John J. Pershing, letter, 27 December 1922; and G. C. Marshall to Mason M. Patrick, letter, 8 January 1923, both filed under "Howard E. Coffin," in Pershing MSS. The degree to which General Pershing and his staff accepted General Patrick's arguments and their exceptions and qualifications to Patrick's major points are demonstrated in this correspondence concerning the draft of an article Patrick had prepared for General Pershing's signature. The article was to be published in the *Aeronautical Digest* for which Howard E. Coffin was editor. Marshall and other members of Pershing's staff edited Patrick's article, agreeing that "an Army of the future must possess an up-to-date, adequate, efficient, highly trained Air Force," adding significantly that "*within the limits of appropriations* the War Department is doing everything in its power to insure that end" [emphasis added]. See also Mason M. Patrick to Roy C. Kirtland, letter, 17 November 1923; Mason M. Patrick to H. A. Toulmin, letter, 19 February 1924; and Mason M. Patrick to Roy C. Kirtland, letter, 13 March 1924. All are in Patrick MSS, RG 18, NA.

30. G. C. Marshall to Mason M. Patrick, in Patrick MSS, RG 18, NA. See also "Course at the Army War College 1925–1926 Command: Fundamental Principles for Employment of the Air Service," Morrow Board Records, LOC.

31. Mason M. Patrick to G. B. Fry, letter, 14 March 1924; Mason M. Patrick, memorandum to R. W. Ireland, 5 January 1925; and Mason M. Patrick, memorandum to R. W. Ireland, 6 January 1925. All are filed in Patrick MSS, RG 18, NA. See also Mason M. Patrick testimony before the Morrow Board quoted in *Army and Navy Journal*, 26 September 1925. See Goldberg, 33. The emphasis on pursuit was significant because according to the Air Service Training Regulation 444-15, "Fundamental Conceptions of the Air Service," prepared by Maj W. C. Sherman under direction of General Patrick, pursuit aviation was the "backbone of the air forces." See also Futrell, 40; and Thomas H. Greer, *The Development of Air Doctrine in the Army Air Arm, 1917–1941*, USAF Historical Study 89 (Maxwell AFB, Ala.: USAF Historical Division, Air University, 1953), 16.

32. Ray Wagner, *American Combat Planes* (Garden City, N.Y.: Hanover House, 1960), 72–75; and K. S. Brown et al., *United States Army and Air Force Fighters, 1916–1961* (Letchworth, Herts, England: Harleyford Publications, Ltd., 1961), 28–29.

33. Wagner, 53–54; and Ronald R. Fogleman, "The Development of Ground Attack Aviation in the United States Army Air Arm: Evolution of a Doctrine, 1908–1926" (master's thesis, Duke University, 1971), 81–82.

34. Patrick to Fry, 14 March 1924.

35. A copy of Pershing's final report is available in records of the War Plans Division, WPD 2038, RG 165, NA. Pershing's opinion remained the same a year later. See John J. Pershing to Dwight W. Morrow, 17 October 1925, Pershing MSS.

36. For Patrick's review of the sums he had and the appropriations the Air Service received in the years 1923–1925, see his testimony before the Morrow Board quoted

in *Army and Navy Journal*, 26 September 1925. See also Dennis E. Nolan to John J. Pershing, 10 November 1925, Pershing MSS.

37. See "General Statement of Maj Gen Mason M. Patrick to Board of Officers Appointed to Study Personnel Legislation for the Air Service," undated, Patrick MSS, RG 18, NA. See also Craven and Cate, 9; Goldberg, 33–34; and Nolan to Pershing, 10 November 1925, Pershing MSS. Pershing had no objection to a separate promotion list for the Air Service. See Pershing to Morrow, 17 October 1925, Pershing MSS.

38. Director of the Bureau of the Budget, memorandum to the president, 20 October 1925, in Morrow Board records, LOC. See also Goldberg, 32–33; *Army and Navy Journal*, 12 January 1924; and House Report 1653, 68th Cong., 2d sess., 1924, 21–23. See Martin P. Claussen, *Materiel Research and Development in the Army Air Arm, 1914–1945*, USAF Historical Study 50 (Maxwell AFB, Ala.: USAF Historical Division, Air University, 1946), 22–23, 48–50. On page 50 of Claussen there is a chart showing the annual expenditures for R&D from 1920 through 1940; see also Craven and Cate, 54; and I. B. Holley Jr., *Buying Aircraft: Materiel Procurement for the Army Air Forces* (Washington, D.C.: Office of the Chief of Military History, Department of the Army, 1964), 44–46.

39. Gen Mason M. Patrick, memorandum to secretary of war, 31 December 1924, Central Decimal Files 333.5, RG 18, NA.

40. Mason M. Patrick to F. P. Reynolds, letter, 3 March 1924. See also Mason M. Patrick to J. H. Williamson, letter, 27 February 1925. Both are in Patrick MSS, RG 18, NA.

41. Mason M. Patrick to William R. Wood, letter, 5 March 1924, Patrick MSS, RG 18, NA.

42. Patrick to Reynolds, 3 March 1924, Patrick MSS, RG 18, NA. See also Mason M. Patrick to Dexter M. Ferry, 7 April 1924, Patrick MSS, RG 18, NA.

43. See Lt James Vernon Maxwell, "How US Funds are Squandered" and the record of his discharge, both in the Hazel Lewis Scaife MSS, LOC. The Scaife papers amount to only one box in the Manuscript Division in the Library of Congress, but they relate exclusively to the 1919–1924 aircraft scandal and tell an interesting, sometimes lurid, story.

44. "Trans-Oceanic Airplane . . ." *Scientific American*, 6 November 1920.

45. Chief of Engineering Division, McCook Field (McIntosh) to Executive in Office of Chief of Air Service (Frank), letter, 7 February 1924, Central Decimal Files 333.5, RG 18, NA.

46. Goldberg, 33.

47. Scaife had written an exposé of the aircraft manufacturing situation in the spring of 1921 that Nelson read into the *Congressional Record*. See H. L. Scaife, "What Was the Matter with the Air Service?" *Current History* (of the *New York Times*) 14 (April 1921): 3–18; and *Congressional Record*, 67th Cong., 1st sess., 1922, 1353–56. Scaife even suggested that the Japanese were involved in the conspiracy against the US Air Service. See *Washington Times*, 10 May 1922, clipping in Scaife MSS.

48. *Congressional Record*, 68th Cong., 1st sess., 1922, 1625–30, 1665, 3444, 3126, 3293, 4815–17. See also "Congress Must Face Air Service Problem," *Army and Navy Journal*, 12 January 1924; "Nelson asks Probe of the Air Service," *Army and Navy Journal*, 2 February 1924; and Chase C. Mooney and Martin E. Layman, *Organization of Military Aeronautics, 1907–1935*, Army Air Forces Historical Study 25 (Washington, D.C.: Army Air Forces Historical Division, 1944), 63.

49. Memo from Maj Raycroft Walsh to Lampert Board Committee, 28 July 1924, Central Decimal Files, RG 18, NA. The committee made a point in the first page of its report of the broad scope authorized for its inquiry by H.R. 192. The resolution authorized the committee to investigate almost anything "in any way connected with any or all transactions of the said United States Army Air Service, the United States Naval Bureau of Aeronautics, the United States air mail service, or any agency, branch, or subsidiary of either." See House Report 1653, 68th Cong., 2d sess., 14 December 1925, 1 (hereinafter cited as Lampert Report).

50. Hurley, 95; Mooney and Layman, 64; Foulois and Glines, 199–200; and R. Earl McClendon, *The Question of Autonomy for the United States Air Arm, 1907–1945* (Maxwell AFB, Ala.: Documentary Research Division, Air University, 1950), 113–14. The hearings of the Lampert Committee were published in six volumes and are available on microfilm. *Hearings Before the Select Committee of Inquiry into the Operation of the United States Air Service*, 68th Cong., 1st sess., 1924, 6 vols. (Washington, D.C.: GPO, 1926) (hereinafter cited as Lampert Hearings).

51. Lampert Hearings, 1682.

52. Quoted in Mooney and Layman, 64, and in McClendon, 114.

53. Lampert Hearings, 1687, 1896, 1928; Mooney and Layman, 64–66; and the documents in WPD 888-30, RG 165, NA.

54. Mason M. Patrick to the adjutant general, letter, 19 December 1924, WPD 888-22, RG 165, NA. Portions of Patrick's letter were introduced by Mitchell into the Lampert Committee. See Lampert Hearings, 1895–96. Mitchell also used the letter in his testimony before the Morrow Board. For other references to Patrick's original air corps proposal, see McClendon, 127–28; Futrell, 43–44; Mooney and Layman, 66; Foulois and Glines, 201; and Hurley, 98–99. Further evidence that Patrick felt a unified air service was the ultimate answer is in his *The United States in the Air*, 190. Patrick took his air corps suggestion directly to the secretary of war in late December 1924. See chief of Air Service, memorandum to secretary of war, 31 December 1924, Central Decimal Files 333.5, RG 18, NA.

55. William Mitchell testimony before the Lampert Committee. See Lampert Hearings, 1895–96.

56. See "Notes on Reorganization of Air Forces for National Defence," 24 December 1924; and assistant chief of staff, WPD (Brig Gen Leroy Eltinger), memorandum to chief of staff, 6 January 1925. Both are in WPD 888-22, RG 165, NA.

57. Brig Gen H. A. Drum, assistant chief of staff, G-3, memorandum to the assistant chief of staff, WPD, 7 January 1925, WPD 888-22, RG 165, NA.

58. Newton D. Baker to Peyton C. March, letter, 14 February 1925, March MSS.

59. A. E. Danton, adjutant general to chief of Air Corps, letter, 29 January 1925, Central Decimal Files 333.5, RG 18, NA.

60. Ibid.

61. William Mitchell to chief of Air Service, letter, 5 February 1925, Central Decimal Files 333.5, RG 18, NA.

62. John W. Weeks to Calvin Coolidge, letter, 4 March 1925. A copy of this letter is in Mitchell MSS, LOC. Portions of it are quoted in Ransom, 240; and Foulois and Glines, 200.

63. Patrick noted that the position Mitchell had at Fort Sam Houston was "a position of responsibility, particularly as there was more Air Service activity in this than in any other corps area." See Patrick, *The United States in the Air*, 180–81. The fact that Fort Sam Houston was not a coast assignment was probably a consideration in Mitchell's assignment. See George B. Duncan to Mason M. Patrick, letter, 11 March 1925, Patrick MSS, RG 18, NA. See also Arnold, 116.

64. James E. Fechet, who happened to be a close friend of Mitchell, was apparently Patrick's personal choice. See James E. Fechet to Mason M. Patrick, letter, 18 March 1925; Mason M. Patrick to James E. Fechet, letter, 31 March; and James E. Fechet to Mason M. Patrick, letter, 3 April. All are in Patrick MSS, RG 18, NA. Fechet had been the commanding officer at Kelly Field, San Antonio, Texas.

65. Randolph Perkins to John W. Weeks, letter, 26 February 1925; and John W. Weeks to Randolph Perkins, 28 February 1925. Both are in the Central Decimal Files 333.5, RG 18, NA.

66. William Mitchell to James E. Fechet, letter, 6 July 1925, Fechet MSS, RG 18, NA.

67. Randolph Perkins to Mason M. Patrick, letter, 10 March 1925, Central Decimal Files 333.5, RG 18, NA.

68. See Lt Comdr C. E. Rosendal, USN, "Last Cruise of Shenandoah Vividly Described by Survivor," *Army and Navy Journal*, 30 September 1925. See also Arnold, 118; and Foulois and Glines, 201.

69. *New York Times*, 4 September 1925.

70. Isaac D. Levine, *Mitchell: Pioneer of Air Power* (New York: Duell, Sloan and Pearce, 1943), 325.

71. Ransom, 245; and Levine, 327.

72. *New York Times*, 6 September 1925.

73. Coolidge once told an impatient senator, "Don't you know that four-fifths of all our troubles in this life should disappear if we would only sit down and keep still." See Schlesinger, 57–58. To a friend some years later, Coolidge said, "Public administrators would get along better if they would restrain the impulse to butt in or to be dragged into trouble. They should remain silent until an issue is reduced to its lowest terms, until it boils down into something like a moral issue." Mitchell gave him his moral issue. See Hurley, 91, 99–101. Carl Spaatz said of Coolidge's reaction to Mitchell, "No politician in the White House likes a mess on his hands. I think probably in his own mind he resented Mitchell for stirring up the whole thing and putting him in a position where he had to do something." See Spaatz, OHC, 29.

74. Hurley, 99; and Harold Nicolson, *Dwight Morrow* (New York: Harcourt Brace and Co., 1935), 267–68. See also Foulois and Glines, 201.

75. Nicolson, 281.

76. Hurley, 99.

77. Dwight Morrow learned of Coolidge's decision from the newspapers. Coolidge made the announcement on Saturday, 12 September, posting a letter notifying Morrow on the same day. Morrow read about the appointment of the board in his Sunday paper but did not receive the president's letter until Monday morning. See Nicolson, 280–82. See also Mooney and Layman, 71; and *Report of the President's Aircraft Board*, 69th Cong., 1st sess., 1924, S. Doc. 18, 1 (hereinafter cited as Morrow Report).

78. Arnold, 119.

79. Hurley, 101.

80. For text of speech, see *New York Times*, 7 October 1925.

81. *Army and Navy Journal*, 30 October 1925.

82. Nicolson, 282–85.

83. See Hiram Bingham, *An Explorer in the Air Service* (New Haven: Yale University Press, 1920). Also Mason M. Patrick to Hiram Bingham, letter, 6 June 1925; and Mason M. Patrick to Hiram Bingham, 14 September 1925. Both in Patrick MSS, RG 18, NA. The uniform approved for the Air Service was a compromise. It had the turn-down collar the airmen had requested but it was not blue. That "would differentiate Air Service officers too much from those of other branches." General Patrick wore the first of the new uniforms to be seen in Washington. When asked, "How long did it take you to get that, general?" Patrick replied, "Three years." See the *Philadelphia Public Ledger*, 10 October 1925, clipping in Patrick MSS, RG 18, NA.

84. Hurley, 101–2.

85. See Arnold, 119–20. See also Hurley, 103; Foulois and Glines, 202; and Nicolson, 282–84. Nicolson notes that Mitchell "arrived on the witness stand carrying an enormous globe. This exhibit, as the long hours of his evidence dragged onwards, became an object of extreme physical embarrassment." The contrast between the "sensational" Mitchell and more dignified and tactful witnesses such as Orville Wright and Commander Rodgers of the Navy was a detriment to the airman's cause. See *Army and Navy Journal*, 10 October 1925; and the Morrow Report, 7–8.

86. A summary of the findings of the Morrow Board is in the files of the Adjutant General (AG) 580 (8-4-34), RG 407, NA. See also Hurley, 105–6; *Secretary of War 1926*, 34–35; Mooney and Layman, 71-72; and Holley, 46. As already noted, the board's report is available in Senate Document 18, 69th Cong., 1st sess. The recommendations of the Morrow Board for changes in the Air Service were as follows:

CREATION OF THE ARMY AIR CORPS

1. To avoid confusion . . . between the name of the Air Service and certain phases of its duties, its name should be changed to Air Corps. The distinction between service rendered by air troops in their auxiliary role and that of an air force acting alone on a separate mission is important.

2. In order that the Air Corps (Air Service) should receive constant sympathetic supervision and counsel, we recommend that Congress be asked to create an additional Assistant Secretary of War who shall perform such duties . . . as may be assigned him by the Secretary of War.

3. It seems desirable to give aviation some special representation on the General Staff . . . we therefore recommend that the Secretary of War create, administratively, in each of the five divisions of the War Department General Staff, an air section.

4. We recommend that Congress be asked to provide two more places for brigadier generals in the Air Corps (Air Service) . . . one such officer to be placed in charge of procurement . . . another preferably to head the group of air-training schools near San Antonio, Texas.

5. To provide rank commensurate with command during present shortage of field officers in the Air Corps (Air Service) . . . temporary rank should be given to active flying officers who will serve to fill . . . vacancies in field ranks . . . in the Air Corps (Air Service). . . . All must concede the justice and propriety of putting only experienced flying men on immediate command of flying activities.

6. Considering the extra hazardous nature of flying . . . the principle of extra pay for flying should be recognized as permanent in time of peace.

7. We recommend that suitable appropriations be requested in order to provide training of reserve officers and in order to provide necessary training planes and subsidiary flying fields for the use of the reserve.

8. We recommend a very considerable increase in the number of institutions where ground instruction is given to the Reserve Officers Training Corps units . . . and adequate provision be made . . . for annual summer flying training, so that members of the Air Corps Reserve Officers' Training Corps may qualify as military aviators and be able to receive their commissions in the same manner and at the same time as other members of the Reserve Officers' Training Corps.

9. We recommend that a careful study be made of the desirability of increasing the use of enlisted men as pilots in the Air Corps. Rather than the Lassiter Board's plan for a ten year development program for the Air Corps the Board recommended a five year program.

87. Quoted in Nicolson, 285.

88. Pershing was particularly impressed with the Morrow Board's work. See John J. Pershing to Martin Egan, letter, 22 December 1925, Pershing MSS. See also Nicolson, 286.

89. Mason M. Patrick to C. B. Amorous, letter, 24 February 1926, Patrick MSS, RG 18, NA. See also Arnold, 120; and McClendon, 122.

90. See Patrick testimony before the Morrow Board, quoted in *Army and Navy Journal*, 26 September 1925. It is interesting to note that shortly after Patrick testified, the War Department did what General Drum had suggested to do nine months earlier. General Patrick was required "to submit in five days a complete plan for the implementation of the Corps idea." See Hurley, 102; and McClendon, 128–29. See WPD 888-31, RG 165, NA, for the War Plans Division file on Patrick's proposal and General Staff reactions to it. For General Patrick's official opinions of the various recommendations of the Morrow Board, see Patrick's reply to memo from G-4, 7 December 1925, in Central Decimal Files 334.7, RG 18, NA.

91. There are numerous descriptions of the famous Billy Mitchell court-martial. For the flavor of the times, a review of the newspaper accounts can be enlightening. See especially the accounts in the *New York Times* from October through December of

1925, and for the military slant, see the *Army and Navy Journal* of the same period. Particularly interesting is the *Army and Navy Journal*'s coverage of the first day of the trial. See *Army and Navy Journal*, 31 October 1925. There are materials relating to the trial in Mitchell MSS. In Air Service records, see Central Decimal Files 250.4, "Mitchell Court Martial 1923–26, RG 18, NA. See also the papers of Maj Gen John C. Hines on his service as chief of staff during the Mitchell trial. These papers are located at the US Army Military History Research Collection, Carlisle Barracks, Pennsylvania. The Hines MSS in the Library of Congress has very little relating to Mitchell.

92. Mason M. Patrick to J. V. McClintic, 8 January 1925, Patrick MSS, RG 18, NA.

93. Hilton Butler, "A Military Court in Action—Word Picture of the Famous Trial," *Army and Navy Journal*, 31 October 1925.

94. For an interesting account of Douglas MacArthur's participation in the trial, see D. Clayton James, *The Years of MacArthur, 1880–1941* (Boston: Houghton Mifflin, 1970), 307–11.

95. Edgar S. Gorrell to Mason M. Patrick, letter, 9 September 1925, Patrick MSS, RG 18, NA.

96. Foulois and Glines, 202; and Milling, OHC, 99.

97. Boschke to Mason M. Patrick, letter, 22 September 1925; Mason M. Patrick to Boschke, 27 September 1925; Mason M. Patrick to Edgar S. Gorrell, letter, 11 September 1925; C. B. Amorous to Mason M. Patrick, letter, 8 February 1925; and Mason M. Patrick to C. B. Amorous, letter, 2 February 1925. All are in Patrick MSS, RG 18, NA. See also Patrick, *The United States in the Air*, 181.

98. Arnold, 158.

99. Spaatz, OHC, 29; and Eaker, OHC, 16.

100. For the report of the Lampert Committee, see H.R. Report 1653, 68th Cong., 2d sess., 14 December 1925. A summary of the Lampert Committee conclusions and recommendations is available in AG 580 (8-4-34), RG 407, NA. See also McClendon, 117–18; and Mooney and Layman, 68–73. General Patrick's official opinion on some of the recommendations of the Lampert Committee is in memo for assistant chief of staff, WPD, from General Patrick, 23 December 1925, WPD 388-37, RG 165, NA.

101. For the best detailed analysis of the legislative actions on the air issue in 1925–1926 see Ransom's dissertation. See also McClendon, 124–32; and Mooney and Layman, 69–77. For a brief summary of the Morrow, Lampert, and Reid options facing the Congress, see *Army and Navy Journal*, 19 December 1925. See also chart entitled "Legislative History of Some Major Sections in the Air Corps Act of 1926 . . ." in an appendix of Ransom.

102. See Mooney and Layman, 75–76; and McClendon, 129–31.

103. For the General Staff analysis of the Patrick Bill, see AG 580 (30 January 1926) (1), subject: HR 8533 re: Creation of US Air Corps as recommended by Chief, Air Service, Maj Gen Patrick, RG 407, NA. Fox Conner's comments are in memo for the chief of staff, 1 February 1926, in AG 580 (30 January 1926) (1), RG 407, NA.

104. Dwight F. Davis to John M. Morin, letter, 10 February 1926, in AG 580 (30 January 1926), RG 407, NA. The text of the letter is also available in the *Army and Navy Journal*, 13 February 1926. General Patrick's defense of the bill within the War Department is laid out in his endorsement to the adjutant general, 5 February 1926, in AG 580 (15 February 1926), RG 407, NA. Davis was a tough adversary for General Patrick. When he was appointed as secretary of war in October 1925, the conservative editor of the *Army and Navy Journal* described him as follows: "He is no saber rattler, no visionary with huge and expensive armaments to seek or plan, but a hard-headed American citizen, who wants merely a force of Regulars sufficient to protect our interests and uphold our government." *Army and Navy Journal*, 17 October 1925.

105. Arnold, 122.

106. The following is an excerpt from the circular:

> We have tried to put across the idea of reorganization in which the Air Service can be developed and operated so that it will be able to give its maximum of efficiency and effectiveness.

There are two Senators from your State and a Representative from your district. Also you must know people of prominence in your State who can communicate with the Senators and Representatives, people whose communication will be given more than casual consideration. It is to your interest that you get in touch with these people, as your future in the service will depend largely upon legislation in this session of Congress. Get them to back the reorganization of the Air Service along the lines as outlined herewith, so that their Senators and Representatives in Washington will know what the folks back home want. This is your party as much as it is ours. We all must get busy and do it now. Next month will be too late. We are relying on you to do your share of this work. Do not throw us down.

See *New York Times*, 9 February 1926.

107. Ibid.

108. John Callen O'Laughlin, "Air Measures Menaced by Ugly Dispute," *Army and Navy Journal*, 13 February 1926.

109. Press release dated February 1926, Patrick MSS, RG 18, NA. See also *New York Times*, 18 February 1926; and *New York Times*, 19 February 1926.

110. *New York Times*, 18 February 1926.

111. Mason M. Patrick to Frank E. Smith, letter, 15 February 1926, Patrick MSS, RG 18, NA. In a press conference on 23 February 1926, President Coolidge was apparently referring to these latest activities of Mitchell followers when he said, "We have had to bring it rather sharply to the attention of men in the service that they ought to obey that injunction in service rules which requires that they shouldn't volunteer to influence legislation." See Howard H. Quint and Robert H. Ferrell, eds., *The Talkative President: The Off-the-Record Press Conferences of Calvin Coolidge* (Amherst, Mass.: University of Massachusetts Press, 1964), 163.

112. Quoted in *New York Times*, 20 February 1926.

113. Quint and Ferrell, 162.

114. *New York Times*, 4 March 1926.

115. Ransom, 318–19.

116. John J. Pershing to W. M. Wright, letter, 22 December 1925, Pershing MSS. See also Nolan to Pershing, 10 November 1925, Pershing MSS; and E. B. Johns's editorial in *Army and Navy Journal*, 12 September 1925. The sort of Mitchell propaganda that so upset Army leaders can be seen in an article entitled "When the Air Raiders Come," which was published in *Collier's* magazine shortly after Mitchell resigned from the Army. Mitchell painted a horrifying picture of New York City under a surprise air attack by some unnamed enemy. Describing the panicking New Yorkers, he wrote,

> Elevators drop them down in loads; stairways are jammed. From the subway kiosks there begin to emerge frightened, panic stricken men and women. The streets are tightly filled before a third of the office workers have poured out. Tardy ones claw and clutch and scramble, clambering on top of those who have fallen. Before long there is a yelling, bloody, fighting mass of humanity. . . . The fortunate ones are they who die under the heels of their fellows. They will never know that the awful thing, threatened so long, has come to pass. They will never know that a hostile air fleet has at last attacked New York and found it easy prey because the United States has no adequate air defense force.

At the top of the article there is a photograph of biplane bombers looking to the modern reader about as menacing as the Keystone Cops. At the bottom of the article is a "doctored" photograph of the New York skyline, with bombs bursting and skyscrapers falling this way and that. The article gives one a good feel for Mitchell's style as a propagandist. See William Mitchell, "When the Air Raiders Come," *Collier's* 77 (1 May 1926): 8–9, 35.

Chapter 3

At War with the Navy

After less than a decade of heated publicity, celebrated aerial demonstrations, congressional debates, and even a court-martial, daring young men had established a new branch of the Army. They wore their own uniform and had the bonus of flight pay and a promotion rate comparable to other branches; a new assistant secretary of war for air, F. Trubee Davison, who had been a supporter of aviation for years; and, best of all, the promise of an increase in aircraft and flight facilities through the five-year plan approved by President Coolidge in 1926. In the air they were continuing to set records, demonstrating their prowess. Against both the Navy and foreign competitors, Army flyers in 1925 won the Pulitzer Trophy and the international Schneider Cup. Lt Cy Bettis on 12 October won the Pulitzer race in a specially built Curtiss R3C2 racer. Two weeks later, in the same plane fitted with pontoons instead of wheels, Lt James A. "Jimmy" Doolittle won the Schneider seaplane race. In the winter of 1926–27, General Patrick's flying instructor, Major Dargue, led a flight of five Loening amphibians on a goodwill tour of 25 Pan-American countries, covering some 22,065 miles. And in the summer of 1927, Lt Lester J. Maitland and Lt Albert F. Hegenberger succeeded where the Navy had failed. With Maitland at the controls and Hegenberger navigating, they flew their Fokker Tri-Motor from the continental United States to Hawaii.

The aerial achievements of the Air Corps were impressive, but on the ground, its battle for independence and for control over its own budget had just begun. The War Department still controlled the purse strings, and the five-year plan was jeopardized by Coolidge's failure to authorize extra funds to carry out the plan and by competition with the Navy for available funds.

The problem of budgeting the five-year-program would dominate Trubee Davison's term as assistant secretary.[1] His task was to persuade others in the War Department that it was in their best interest to support Air Corps expansion. He would pledge that the Air Corps would "study ways of making the best possible contribution to the success of the Army as a whole," but he was, above all, the defending champion of the Air Corps's right to expand as technology advanced. Aviation, he said when he began his term in 1926, "has certainly not yet reached the end of its phenomenal development."[2]

Davison had been chosen by Coolidge probably upon recommendation of Dwight Morrow, who had been a friend and business associate of Davison's father. While unknown in most Army circles, Davison was readily accepted by flying officers. Trubee, as he liked to be called, had been interested in aviation since before the World War. As a freshman at Yale in 1915, he was a supporter of the Allies. His enthusiasm led him in the summer of 1915 to volunteer to drive ambulances in France and in the summer of 1916 to organize the Yale Aviation Unit, which was equipped with flying boats paid for by Davison's father and one of his father's friends. The young men of the Yale unit were to receive much praise for their initiative. After the war, Adm William S. Sims, referring to the contribution of American naval aviation to the war, said that "the great aircraft force which was ultimately assembled in Europe had its beginnings in a small group of undergraduates at Yale." Fate denied Davison a chance to share in the group's combat experiences. On a training flight over New York harbor in the summer of 1917, he crashed his airplane; and when the crew of a nearby yacht freed him from the tangled wires of the wreckage, his back was broken.[3] His piloting career had ended, but not his interest in aviation nor his energetic and enthusiastic manner. After the war and graduation from Yale, he sought a career in public service. Davison was aided by influential friends and a large inheritance from his father. The elder Davison, who had been a partner in the J. P. Morgan banking house, specified in his will that the fortune was to permit Trubee "to devote himself to the public welfare."[4] He was elected to the New York state legislature, and later, during the year prior to appointment as assistant secretary of war, gained prominence as chairman of an unofficial National Crime Commission that included such worthies as former Secretary of State Charles Evans Hughes and former Secretary of War Newton D. Baker.

As assistant secretary of war for air at age 30, he was charged with a problem in which there was considerable national interest. His authority, however, was not all that it appeared. The law creating his position had not outlined his duties; his power was restricted to that given him by the secretary of war. He received no authority over the Air Corps budget. He could argue the Air Corps case within the War Department and attempt to influence budget decisions, but he could not determine them.[5]

The ever-present problem of the budget set the Air Corps at odds with other branches of the Army. In an era of severely limited budgets, the Air Corps, with its highly expensive machines to buy and maintain, never thought it was getting enough. The other branches, of course, always thought it was getting too much. As a General Staff study put it, "The amount of money appropriated for aerial defense is limited each year," and any expansion was "very likely to be at the expense" of other services.[6] Maj Gen John L. Hines, the chief of staff, a tough commander who emphasized team spirit—individual discipline, self-sacrifice, no favoritism—described the situation as he saw it. The War Department, he said, was in "the position of a penurious parent who is attempting to satisfy the appetites and desires of a large, robust and energetic family. Few members of our family fail to make known their wants, but they do not always fully appreciate the equally important needs of their military relatives." He warned that Army planners should not forget that peacetime organization of the military was a "compromise between military expediency and cost," with cost generally dictating. "Every officer," he declared, "should understand the principle of the military supremacy of the dollar in time of peace."[7]

Fears of Army leaders about where the money for the Air Corps five-year plan was coming from were well founded. Funding of the plan was to be done by normal procedures subject to control of President Coolidge and his budget director. Coolidge had made his position on the plan clear. "Now," he said, "if it is desirable to have more in the Air Service and more officers, why I think some provision ought to be made to meet that expenditure by a reduction of expenditures in some other direction, especially so on account of the present condition of the treasury."[8] The Army would have to pay for the expansion of the Air Corps, but not immediately, because the five-year plan was delayed a year. The Air Corps Act came too late to be included in the budget for the fiscal year (FY) 1927 (July 1926–June 1927). Expansion began with FY 1928. Thereafter, every year for five years, the Air Corps was built with funds and men pared from other branches of the Army.[9]

The idea that a limited budget produces controversy applied especially to the relationship of the Army's Air Corps with the Navy, heretofore the favored branch of the military. The Navy had plans for air development and was proceeding with its five-year plan for expansion of shore-based as well as carrier-based aircraft. It was this latter point that caused concern in the War Department. Army leaders acquiesced in expansion of the Air Corps partly because they had little choice, partly because they could see a need to stay abreast in aviation with modern armies in the world, but perhaps because they realized that they had to make an attempt to meet requirements of coastal defense or run the risk of losing that task to either proponents of a separate air force or to the Navy.[10]

Warning from the Air Corps: The Navy Is Coming Ashore!

Back in September 1925, in the midst of the uproar over Billy Mitchell's charges against the War and Navy departments, General

Patrick had suggested that the answer to the air dilemma was for the War Department to lead the way in revising national defense doctrine and establishing responsibilities of the land, sea, and air arms in national defense plans. Even the most casual observer, he argued, could see that the way to economize in the air arm was to eliminate the duplication between the Army's air arm and the Navy's shore-based air units. This could be accomplished by basing defense doctrine on what he described as three tactical defense requirements against any major attack on the United States or its territories. The requirements were determined by three possible phases of any attack: the sea-action phase, the air-action phase, and the land-action phase. The dominant role was held respectively by sea power, airpower, and land power. He contended that responsibility for action and therefore command authority should be held by the arm playing the dominant role. The logic was obvious. In the sea phase, which would take place "beyond the effective range of shore-based aircraft," the Navy would dominate the action supported by the Army and its air arm. If the Navy could not hold the attacking force and it penetrated within range of land-based bombers, the air-action phase would begin and command would shift to the Army's air arm with the Navy's and Army's land forces in support roles. If the enemy were not stopped in the air-action phase and should threaten the shore, command would shift to the Army land commander. By dividing the functions and responsibilities of the air, sea, and land forces and by organizing and equipping the forces accordingly, Patrick contended that duplication could be eliminated not only between the Army and Navy air arms but between the Army's air arm and its coastal artillery. The General Staff was involved in preparing testimony for the Morrow hearing when Patrick submitted these suggestions in a report entitled "Study in Economy of Administration," and there was no immediate reaction.[11]

General Patrick's suspicions about the Navy coming ashore seemed to be confirmed six months later when the Navy revealed that its five-year plan included a large increase in shore-based aircraft—from 334 planes for 1927 to 583 at the end of five years (this compared to a planned 534 planes afloat).[12] Patrick was sure that the Navy was engaged in a clever plan to take over all coastal defense. Traditionally, coastal defense had been the responsibility of the Army. Freed from the duty of patrolling the coastline, the Navy could concentrate the fleet to pursue offensive operations at sea. This was in accord with the principles of America's renowned naval strategist, Capt Alfred T. Mahan. The range of the Army's coastal artillery was to be the dividing line between Army and Navy responsibilities. But now that the airplane had increased the range of both the fleet and coastal defense, it appeared to Patrick that the Navy was intent upon taking over both functions. There would be no direct assault upon the Army's position; naval officers were too clever for that. They would deny that they coveted the Army's coastal defense. At the same time, they would oppose any decision on the line between Army and Navy responsibilities. Patrick reasoned that they would quietly build up their shore establishments (Hawaii, Panama, and San Diego). Then they would argue that to avoid duplication the aerial functions in "coast defense should be turned over to the Navy Department, which is already provided with the equipment and facilities for that purpose." If they accomplished that, the next step would be to claim that in interest of unity of command the Navy should control all coastal defense. The implications of the Navy's assault upon the Army's functions would not stop. If the Navy controlled coastal defense, it would have the only need for bombers and pursuit aircraft in peacetime. This really meant, Patrick said, that "when the seacoast fortifications and air defense of our coasts are turned over to the Navy, there will be a great reduction in the land armed forces. So far as the air component of the Army is concerned, this may logically be reduced to nothing more than the observation aircraft accompany this much reduced Army." To avoid these dire consequences, he urged the War Department to take immediate measures to obtain a proper air program of its own.[13]

Patrick had his private source of information about the Navy's "footholds on the beach." Had he been called upon to provide evidence he could have presented many letters from friends of the Army who were watching and reporting on the Navy's activities in Hawaii, Panama, and San Diego. Typical of Patrick informers was retired Maj Gen J. E. Kuhn of Coronado, California. "I am not trying to 'start' anything," wrote Kuhn as he told Patrick of Navy attempts to supplant the Army at Rockwell Field on North Island near San Diego, but merely wanted to make sure Patrick was informed.[14] Patrick replied that he had been fighting Navy encroachments for four years and intended to battle to the end. "It's a tough fight, but if we are beaten, we will go down with our flag flying. I do not propose to surrender."[15] This was just nine days before he detailed his suspicions to the War Department.

Hines and staff were not to be stampeded by Patrick's warnings. They did not believe the threat of encroachment to be serious. It appeared that Patrick's purpose was to take advantage of controversy between the Army and Navy and to secure for his own branch the predominant role in coastal zones. The War Plans Division assured Hines and the General Staff that while aviation had complicated the situation, the problem remained a line between Army and Navy responsibility for defense, between sea power and land power, but that there was no need for a three-way division.[16]

Still, there was an urgent problem, and aviation lay at its center. Since the World War, technology had increased the range and striking power of the airplane, causing constant reevaluation of Army and Navy air forces. This generated controversy between the two services. Congress had taken up the problem in 1919 and 1920 and, after much debate, the House included in the appropriations bill for 1920 a proviso that "hereafter the Army Air Service shall control all aerial operations from land bases, the Naval Aviation shall have control of all aerial operations attached to a fleet." The Navy convinced the Senate to change the provision by adding that the Navy also could have "shore stations whose maintenance is necessary for operation connected with the fleet, for construction and experimentation, and for training of personnel."[17] The change satisfied the Navy but not the Army, particularly Army aviators. In the years that followed, and as the Navy built up its shore installations, controversy arose over the meaning of "shore stations whose maintenance is necessary for operation connected with the fleet."

When it appeared that some of the Navy's shore-based aviation duplicated functions of the Army air arm and was only tangentially related to the operation of a fleet, Army leaders pressed for a definition that would limit the Navy's activities ashore. That was part of what Secretary Weeks was trying to do in early 1924 when he proposed to coordinate the Lassiter plan for Air Service expansion with the Navy's aviation expansion program. "My idea is that we should agree on our relative missions," he told Secretary of the Navy Denby.[18] This would provide the basis for a joint request for appropriations. Denby rejected the suggestion. He told the secretary of war that he could see no relation between appropriations for Army and Navy aviation. Ignoring the Navy's land-based aircraft, he implied that all the Navy's aviation was, by definition, fleet aviation. "There seems to me," he said, "to be no more reason for pooling the appropriations for fleet-shore aviation than there is for pooling the appropriations for battleships and forts."[19]

In 1924, Denby's successor, Curtis D. Wilbur, reiterated these views,[20] while Rear Adm William A. Moffett, head of the Bureau of Aeronautics and senior Navy member of the Joint Aeronautical Board, said that neither the Army nor Navy should try to tell the other what types and how many planes it should have.[21] Resistance by the Navy to a redefinition of the functions of Army and Navy aviation persisted throughout the Mitchell uproar in 1925 and the congressional activity of early 1926 that resulted in the Army Air Corps Act.

Now that both the Army and Navy had approved the five-year air plans competing for appropriations, it occurred to Army leaders that the Navy might be more responsive to a decision on the issue. There was criticism in Congress over costs of the two plans, and if the War and Navy Departments did not try to eliminate the possibility of duplication, Congress might do it in a way that would benefit neither the Army nor Navy.[22] After a comprehensive review of studies by the General Staff and the Air Corps, along with the opinion of the judge advocate general, the War Plans Division drafted a proposal for revision of the aviation policies of the Army and Navy. While it declared that there had been comparatively little duplication of equipment and installations thus far, considerable duplication could result if the present policies were not changed. The changes suggested did not require legislative action; in fact, the War Plans Division advised against bringing Congress into the question if it could be avoided. If the War and Navy departments could not reach an agreement, the issue should be referred to the president for a decision, not to the Congress. Having thus laid the ground rules for changing the policy, the War Plans Division suggested that the Army's authority over coastal defense extend to the operating range of land-based aircraft and that the Navy retain control over sea-lanes within the coastal zone. Its air activities in support of that function were to be limited to reconnaissance and patrol of the coastal sea zone, convoy operations, and "attacks on isolated vessels and detachments," all of these activities to be done with "scouting and patrol types of naval aircraft." Land-based bombardment and pursuit aviation was to be in the domain of the Army Air Corps. Relating these proposed policies to the touchy question of who might buy what kinds of airplanes, the War Plans Division contended that joint aircraft policy should limit procurement of aircraft and establishment of bases by the War and Navy departments to that necessary to perform their respective primary functions. Functions of Army, Navy, and Marine Corps aircraft should be clearly shown as derivations of the general functions of the Army, Navy, and Marine Corps.[23]

These proposals, particularly the last, were hardly what General Patrick had envisioned, but he concurred in the suggestion to send them to the Joint Board for consideration. "I still think," he said, "that it leaves open the door to some duplication of land stations . . . which in my opinion is undesirable, but which as the law now stands, I cannot see any way to avoid."[24] After the Joint Board considered the proposals and the studies made to define the primary and secondary functions of Army and Navy aircraft, it finally made a ruling that became policy after approval of the secretary of war and the secretary of the Navy in early December of 1926.

The critical provision in the policy was one sentence: "To avoid duplication in peace-time procurement, the Navy's land-based aircraft procured for the conduct of the secondary functions of naval air component will be limited to those primarily designed and ordinarily used for scouting and patrolling over the sea."[25] To the Army, this meant that the Navy was prohibited from procuring or maintaining bombardment, pursuit, or attack airplanes on land bases. However, as later developments proved, the Navy still had its own interpretation of "primary functions."

Not a Matter of Law

The Army's satisfaction with the Joint Board's decision evaporated when it became clear that the Navy still intended to supply torpedo planes to Pearl Harbor and to Coco Solo in Panama. In a meeting of the Joint Aeronautical Board in early May 1927, Patrick and Admiral Moffett clashed. Patrick argued that the Air Corps already had bombing planes at Hawaii and Panama and that Navy torpedo planes would duplicate their mission. He admitted it was difficult to separate Army and Navy aerial functions since there was no coastline in the air, but as long as a separate air force was unacceptable, the only way for the Army and Navy to avoid duplication was to agree upon a division of functions and live by it. Moffett agreed that Army bombers and Navy torpedo planes were similar types, but said their wartime assignments were different; there was no duplication. Planes the Navy had planned for Pearl Harbor and Coco Solo were three-purpose aircraft—for reconnaissance as well as for torpedoing and bombing. Since the Army seemed bent on interpreting Joint Board policy in such a way as to prevent the Navy from procuring shore-based bomber aircraft, which Moffett argued were essential to the Navy's wartime mission, he proposed a change in wording of the policy. To the controversial sentence that limited the Navy to aircraft "primarily designed and ordinarily used for scouting and patrolling over the sea," he would add "and for attacking enemy vessels over the sea by torpedoing and bombing."[26]

Patrick, Moffett, and other members of the Aeronautical Board again referred the problem to the Joint Board, which wrangled over it for more than a year. War and Navy Department planning staffs spent hours preparing studies to support their positions. Among War Department planners, there was growing support of Patrick's theory that the Navy intended to take over all bombardment aviation. Majors J. D. Reardon and J. N. Greely, assigned by the head of War Plans to write a review of the military role of aircraft, reported that expanding Navy air might force the Army Air Corps inland from the coasts; this was "not an imaginary danger."[27]

"The Navy is violating the law," said Brig Gen James E. Fechet, assistant chief of the Air Corps. The chief of staff ordered the judge advocate general to investigate that possibility. No law could be found prohibiting the Navy from building land-based torpedo planes; if the Navy was violating anything, it was an agreement with the Army.[28] To officers of the General Staff, the latter was problem enough. It raised again the worry that if the Army and Navy could not agree under the existing law, Congress would change the law and the old question of an independent air corps might surface once more. Col Stanley D. Embick, acting chief of War Plans, warned Gen Charles P. Summerall, then chief of staff, that "it could afford a cogent argument for those who advocate a consolidated Air Corps or a Department of National Defense."[29]

Summerall was not one to provide arguments for an independent air corps or a department of national defense. Described by some observers as the Cromwell of the American Army, he was a man of conviction, which is a polite way of saying he was stubborn. In combat, he had been fearless in imposing his will upon the enemy. In peacetime, he channeled his energies into the battle for command. He was efficient, fiercely loyal to the Army, ruthless toward competitors, coldly intolerant of inefficiency or opposition from subordinates. Respected throughout the Army, he was anything but well liked. This was especially true among air officers who considered Summerall the archetype of Army conservatives who knew nothing of the potential of aviation nor cared to learn. They were correct in part. Summerall had a vast ignorance of the technical aspects of aviation. To him that was the domain of the airmen. His interest in the Air Corps was on a different level.[30] Since the Air Corps was a necessary branch of the Army, he was interested in keeping it under Army control. Since it was an unusually expensive branch, he was interested in keeping its cost down. And since the coastal defense was essential to the Army, for budget reasons if no other, he was interested in defending the Air Corps against Navy encroachment.[31] These concerns put him in agreement with the General Staff in the controversy with the Navy. To avoid the risk of losing control of the Air Corps, he felt that every effort should be taken to keep the issue out of Congress. To keep costs down, competition between the Army's and Navy's five-year plans had to be avoided. To protect the Army's coastal defense mission, he believed Navy encroachment had to be stopped. All this emphasized the necessity of a binding agreement with the Navy as soon as possible.

Brig Gen George S. Simonds, chief of War Plans, believed that the only way to solve the problem was to "shove it right up to the C-in-C, the President of the United States." It was the kind of issue that should be solved by command, "not by litigation and quarrelling among the subordinates on each side."[32] Known to his friends as Sue, Simonds was respected in Army circles for judgment and ability to see things in the broadest perspective. On this issue some officers on the General Staff agreed with him. Submitting the problem to the president had been a recognized alternative. Shortly after the Aeronautical Board put the problem back on the Joint Board, Colonel Embick had suggested that the president should be asked to decide in case the Joint Board was unable to agree. After struggling with the problem throughout the rest of 1927 and the early part of 1928, Army members of the Joint Board did propose putting the issue before the president, but Navy members would not agree.[33]

In the summer of 1928, prompted by a congressional resolution to "make a full investigation of the problem of the control of seacoast defense," the Joint Board began to move toward agreement. Senator Bingham had introduced the resolution on 23 February, and it passed the Senate in May and was referred to the Rules Committee.[34] Upon request of General Summerall, Rep. W. Frank James (R-Mich.), acting chairman of the House Committee on Military Affairs, put off the investigation until the next session of Congress by getting the resolution referred to his committee.[35] This was to give the Joint Board time to come to an agreement, which it finally did on 16 August. Perhaps because machinations in Congress caused more anxiety among Army leaders than among Navy leaders, the agreement was more a compromise for the Army than the Navy. The board found "no duplication of functions or missions and therefore no duplication of types of planes" in the two services' five-year programs. The Army agreed that neither service should interfere with the other's development and procurement of planes necessary to accomplish its mission. At Pearl Harbor and Coco Solo, the Navy would not include any special combat planes in its program, that is, bombers or pursuit, but would limit its aircraft either to scouting or patrol types or the so-called three-purpose plane that would normally be for scouting and patrolling and only incidentally for bombing.[36]

Unfortunately, for the War Department this agreement by the Joint Board failed to accomplish its purpose, just as had previous agreements. For a while the controversy did subside. Everyone in Washington was preoccupied with the presidential campaign between Herbert C. Hoover, Coolidge's secretary of commerce, and the governor of New York, Alfred E. Smith. The campaign provided newspapers with copy and the Washington bureaucracy with diversion while they waited for the nation's officials to return from the hustings. There was a lull in bureaucratic infighting and General Simonds could report to Maj Gen Malin Craig, then Army commander in the Canal Zone: "No news or gossip in the War Department."[37] With Hoover the winner, Congress was back in session early in 1929, and the lull had ended. With return to "business as usual" in Washington, the coastal defense controversy and threats of congressional investigation revived, despite the Joint Board agreement.

Army fears about congressional intervention seemed justified when Senator Bingham on 12 January 1929 acknowledged the Joint Board agreement but declared that there was evidence of "incomplete reconciliation" of Army and Navy views on coastal defense. It was not likely, he claimed, that the issue would be resolved until either the president or Congress took a hand. Implying that the president's inaction left the matter up to Congress, he indicated his intention to try to revise his resolution to create a joint committee to investigate; and as Army planners tensed in anticipation, Senator King expressed hope that in connection with these investigations Congress would take up the question of a department of national defense. "With these quarrels and contentions," he said, "these overlappings, and this uncertainty as to jurisdiction in these departments, it is obvious that there should be one department of national defense."[38]

During the next weeks, the War Department tried to block Bingham's maneuvering. While admitting that the Joint Board agreement had not put the issue to rest and that controversy between the Army and Navy on coastal defense would likely reappear, the Army argued that a legislative solution would make matters worse. In a letter to Sen. David A. Reed (R-Pa.), chairman of the Military Affairs Committee, Secretary Davison laid out the Army's views. Extremely rapid development of aviation, he said, required constant "redetermination of the roles of all arms in both the Army and the Navy." The recent Joint Board decision was not a permanent solution nor was it so intended. As development continued, problems would change, requiring new solutions. He contended that the Joint Board gave the Army and Navy flexibility. Legislation establishing the role of aviation in coastal defense could destroy flexibility.[39]

The maneuvering ended on 4 March 1929, with Bingham the victor, for his resolution passed the House of Representatives. The Joint Committee on Aerial Coastal Defense made up of five senators and congressmen was formed with Bingham as chairman.[40]

The Bingham Committee began its investigation in late April with questionnaires to the War and Navy departments and letters soliciting opinions of noted military and naval authorities, including Admiral Sims and General Pershing. The War and Navy departments collaborated on the questionnaire, agreeing on every item except one concerning joint occupancy of North Island. Knowing its facilities gave it the stronger claim, the Navy said the Army should leave. The Army would not agree, especially since there was no arrangement on where facilities for the vacating service would be established or how they would be financed. The question caused the new Hoover administration's Secretary of War James W. Good and Secretary of the Navy Charles F. Adams to exchange several letters. But during the committee hearings, which were held in early May, Bingham made clear that his target was the fundamental issue of whether the Army or Navy should have primary responsibility for defending the coasts against an attacking fleet of aircraft carriers.[41]

In a heated cross-examination of General Summerall and Assistant Secretary Davison, it became clear that Bingham favored the Navy. Quoting long passages from Admiral Sims's letter to the committee, he challenged the chief of staff and assistant secretary to tell him why defending against such an attack, obviously the responsibility of the Navy on the high seas, should suddenly become the Army's responsibility when the attackers came in range of land-based aircraft. Summerall tried to explain that the shift of responsibility would not occur instantaneously, that the defense would be a joint operation—the Navy commanding when its interests were dominant, the Army when an actual threat to the coast gave it the dominant interest. This, Bingham argued, would require Army and Navy flyers to work together, and he doubted that they could. Quoting Sims, he maintained that even if the Army pilots were all Lindberghs, they still could not operate efficiently with the fleet because of their shore-based training. To operate with the fleet, pilots had to have "the kind and amount of training that can be gotten only by living and training with the fleet." Summerall retorted that "that is not what we are talking about at all," and he and Bingham argued until the hearing adjourned. Summerall's last words were, "It is an Army job to attack everything within the coastal zone which the Army protects. And it is a Navy job to go with the fleet and to patrol the coast."[42]

Bingham's next move seemed an effort to force an arbitrary solution of the problem. Three days after his exchange with Summerall, the senator wrote Secretary of War Good, asking that he refer the following question to the attorney general:

> Is there anything in existing statutes which would prevent the Navy from establishing a shore base and equipping it with adequate aircraft intended to operate as an air force capable of delivering an independent blow directed against an enemy aircraft carrier or carriers three hundred miles out at sea? This question is based upon the assumption that the aircraft in question are to be used in connection with the Fleet when the Fleet is in the waters near to the station, and that the aircraft is suitable for such use and that the shore base is near or adjoining an important harbor or naval base.[43]

Good replied that he did not have authority to refer such a question to the attorney general.44 Secretary of the Navy Adams apparently did not feel so restricted, for he sent two questions to Atty Gen William D. Mitchell in response to a similar request from Bingham. He asked "whether the Army appropriations act of 5 June 1920, 41 Stat. 954, or any other statute, is properly to be construed as restricting naval control of aerial operations over the sea from shore stations established and maintained by the Navy." If so, he asked whether such law should not be judged "invalid as constituting an unauthorized restriction upon the constitutional power of the President as Commander in Chief of the Army and Navy." The Navy's judge advocate general prepared a long brief.45 Secretary Good, informed by Adams of the Navy's action, had the Army's judge advocate prepare a brief. It rephrased the Navy's first question to require a decision not only as to the Navy's right to control aerial operations from shore bases, but as to the character of such shore stations that the Navy might be authorized.46 Again, all the debating came to nothing. Attorney General Mitchell on 17 January 1930 informed both departments that the matter was "beyond the proper limits of my authority."47

This much-discussed, much-probed law was vague on the coastal defense issue, else there would not have been so much disagreement. Perhaps that was the reason the attorney general shied away from it. More likely the issue was, as General Simonds put it, a matter of command rather than of law. Too much was at stake for both the Army and Navy to agree calmly between themselves. The agreement that would ultimately come, the MacArthur–Pratt Agreement, would be based more on the ingenuity of one man than on any reconciliation between the War and Navy departments.

The MacArthur–Pratt Agreement

While the attorney general was deliberating on his decision not to decide, the Army obtained a new secretary of war, and the Navy covered itself with glory—at least in the Navy's opinion—in maneuvers against the Panama Canal, which was defended by the Army.

The 1929 summer maneuvers in the Canal Zone were to demonstrate the superiority of a carrier attack force over land-based defenses, and they were a great success. Although the defenders of the canal knew the day of the planned mock attack and had as many airplanes as the attacking fleet, the "enemy" was able to come within 150 miles of the Pacific side of the Panama Canal before launching bombers in the predawn darkness from the carrier *Saratoga*. "The enemy air fleet was over the Panama Canal by the time that the defenders knew it was coming," boasted Assistant

Secretary of the Navy Ernest L. Jahncke. Dropping their bombs on the Pedro Miguel and Miraflores locks before returning to the carriers, the attackers left the Panama Canal, theoretically at least, "an impassable wreck." In a speech in his hometown of New Orleans, Jahncke warned that the next war would be decided in the air by the Navy. "When you can get your aircraft even 250 miles off your enemy's coast," he said, "the majority of your airplanes will reach their objectives and drop their bombs with deadly effect. The only answer to an attack like that is an equal or superior force of your aircraft carriers, protected by both their own armament and an escort of fast cruisers and destroyers, able to put out to sea at top speed and attack the enemy before his air fleet can be launched. A Navy limited to the surface of the sea might as well be scrapped."[48]

"Such propaganda makes me very hostile," wrote General Craig in a letter to Simonds, his friend in the War Department. Beginning with the usual "My dear Sue," Craig complained that during the maneuvers the Navy "completely ignored" the Army. While he admitted that the fleet's aircraft work was excellent, it was also "pure propaganda." He claimed that the Army knew every move of the *Saratoga* and that Army aircraft, though few in number, did their job. The Navy had ignored the Army. It was not, he concluded, a joint maneuver in any sense of the word.[49] In the view of Army leaders, the Navy's conduct in the Panama maneuvers and the propaganda that followed was further evidence of an intention to belittle the Army and take the mission of defending the coasts. But aside from private complaints of the Army commander in the Canal Zone to his friend Sue, there was little evidence to refute Jahncke's claims. The battle against the Navy was becoming more and more an uphill fight.

Fortunately for the Army, Patrick J. Hurley, who had made a career out of uphill fights, became secretary of war on 9 December 1929. Some three weeks earlier, Secretary Good had died from an attack of appendicitis. A westerner from Oklahoma, Hurley was a self-made man. When 11 years old, he had done a man's work for the Atoka Coal and Mining Company driving a cantankerous old mule named "Kicking Pete." When the mule one day kicked him, he picked up a two-by-four and brained Kicking Pete. Now he was a millionaire and at 46 the youngest member of the president's cabinet. In his rise from mule driver to cowboy, to lawyer, to rancher, to oilman, to millionaire, to secretary of war, Hurley had picked up some of the trappings of culture. He possessed money, education, fine houses, and a charming wife. When "all spiffed up" for a state dinner at the White House or to review the troops, he looked as royal as any duke. But he never quite lost the rough edges of an Oklahoma boy made good. Enthusiastic, energetic, a bit overconfident, he favored the direct approach to problems, and the shortcut if he saw one. That was the way he would approach the coastal defense controversy. He would meet it head on, and, unlike his easy-going predecessor who had given General Summerall a free hand, Hurley would insist on being in the action.[50]

In early January of 1930, even before Attorney General Mitchell put the problem back in the laps of the secretaries of war and the Navy, the General Staff had begun a review of the controversy. The annual battle of the budget was underway in Congress, and the Navy had made no sign that it intended to withdraw its request for torpedo planes for Pearl Harbor in Hawaii and Coco Solo in Panama and for facilities for their maintenance and operation. In the War Plans Division, General Simonds pondered the Army's alternatives. The matter could again be put before the Joint Board. But that agency had already made "an honest attempt to make an obscure law workable" and failed. Now that both the Army and Navy judge advocates had prepared long briefs, they would undoubtedly be involved in the board's proceedings. Lawyers could only muddle the situation. He considered the possible results of a new Joint Board agreement. If the Joint Board agreed with the Army, there was no assurance that the Navy would abide by the agreement. In his opinion, they had not done so in the past. If the Joint Board disagreed with the Army, the Army would lose "its present favorable position of having both the law and the approved Joint Board decisions behind it." If the Joint Board was out, then what of taking the issue to Congress? The Army did have its champions on Capitol Hill. Just recently, Rep. Henry E. Barbour (R-Calif.), chairman of the Subcommittee on Army Appropriations, had noted Navy encroachments into "certain activities that have to do with land defense" and suggested "a study be made with a view to placing the entire land defense with the Army." That sounded good, but Simonds knew that congressional action on this issue still contained dangers. The naval lobby and proponents of a consolidated department of national defense were much alive. Considering all the possibilities, it appeared to Simonds, now more than ever, that only the president could end the controversy.[51]

Whereas Secretary Good had shied away from the idea of going to the president, Hurley did not. On 18 February 1930, he posted a letter to Hoover. "In the interest of economy," he wrote, "and in the interest of a sound organization of the National Defense, I feel that the question as to whether or not the Navy may establish land-based tactical airplane units should be given a definite decision by you as the Commander-in-Chief of the Army and Navy." He included a study by the General Staff supporting the Army's position. "Should you agree to the Army view," he said, "may I suggest that the object may be accomplished by instructions issued by you to the War and Navy Departments and to the Director of the Bureau of the Budget as follows," and he quoted a passage prepared by the War Plans Division that would limit Navy land-based airplanes to trainers and experimental models.[52]

Hurley's letter prompted a rebuttal from Jahncke, acting secretary of the Navy in the absence of Secretary Adams, and that letter was in turn rebutted by Hurley. Jahncke's argument was that the Army should not be concerned with types of airplanes the Navy used or where those planes were based but with their functions. He assured the president that the Navy was not infringing on functions to which the Army could lay legitimate claim. The Navy could use sea-based planes to perform these functions, he admitted, but land-based planes were more economical.[53] Hurley's rebuttal emphasized the economic part of the problem. In peacetime, he argued, economy would not permit the services all their wartime functions. They must limit themselves to their primary functions. Referring to the writings of Mahan, he noted that the Navy's function was to be prepared to defeat or contain an enemy fleet on the high seas. While coastal defense was a primary mission for the Army during peace, it was not for the Navy; indeed, he argued, none of the functions of the Navy's land-based aircraft could be considered primary. Implying that the Navy's intent was to push the Army back from the coast, Hurley warned that the "defense of the coast is inseparable from that of the interior. The whole must be left to the Army, or turned over in entirety to the Navy."[54]

Hurley's attempt to press Hoover for a decision failed. The president recognized that there was a problem and that it had economic as well as military implications. The military aspects of the problem he passed back to the two secretaries to work out. "In order that we may have some conclusion" on the economic aspects of the problem, as he put it, he asked the Bureau of Efficiency to investigate the matter.[55] Designed for the task of investigating other agencies for lack of budget restraint, the bureau had been criticized during the 1920s and early 1930s for its mushrooming cost and inefficiency.

By this time, the enmity between Army and Navy officers involved in the controversy had reached such a level that an understanding was almost impossible. The two services reconnoitered each other like feuding clansmen. Surveillance included closely watching each other's activities both on and off duty, observing which officers were assigned where, and even keeping count of buildings being put up. In his letters to "Dear Sue," Craig, in the Canal Zone, described such intrigues as sending two Army officers incognito to find a suitable landing strip in the Caribbean for ferrying Army aircraft from the United States to the Canal Zone. To ensure that the Navy knew nothing of this activity, Craig even arranged for the trip's cost, $175, to be sent from Washington rather than go through the post quartermaster.[56] It was clearly understood by both Army and Navy commanders that one of their jobs was to keep close watch on each other. As Craig observed to Sue, "These high-ranking Navy officers are splendid fellows personally, but they are coached to a fare-you-well on questions in which the Navy is interested and, if they do not put over their jobs, up comes a new one who is fully up to date."[57]

In Washington, informal meetings were occasionally held between representatives from the two departments. One such meeting was held on the morning of 6 August 1930. It began with a snafu, and went downhill from there. Hurley had made the arrangements with Adams; they would meet in Hurley's office. Adams was to bring his assistant secretary for air, David S. Ingalls. Hurley expected to have the "usual delegation"—Davison, Summerall, Fechet, now chief of the Air Corps, and Simonds. But when Adams and Ingalls arrived at Hurley's ornate office in the War Department, only Hurley was there. Davison, Simonds, and Fechet were out of town, and Summerall, who was to have informed them of the meeting, was in the hospital. With a few panic phone calls for help, a team of pinch hitters was found, including General Foulois, then assistant chief of the Air Corps, and Col R. S. Pratt of War Plans.

The meeting resulted in a great deal of argument and little else. Adams and Ingalls insisted that the Navy was living up to the Joint Board agreement. Colonel Pratt contended that by substituting tactical planes for patrol planes, the Navy was not living up to the agreement, and produced a table to show the "great increase" in tactical planes at Pearl Harbor and Coco Solo. The increase, Adams retorted, was part of the Navy's five-year program, which the Joint Board had approved. To which Pratt replied that he understood that while the Navy program gave the number of planes, it did not specify types. He added that the Army's objection was not to the Navy procuring patrol planes, but to substituting bombing planes for patrol planes. "I am not certain that my statement as to the Naval Five-Year Program was correct," Pratt admitted later, "but as I anticipated when I made it, Mr. Adams wasn't certain about it either."[58]

Later in the meeting, Adams said that it was inconceivable that the Navy could not keep a hostile fleet from approaching the coast and therefore coastal defenses were an "unnecessary expense." This statement set "Pat" Hurley off. Now, he said, he could see that his subordinates were right when they had told him the Navy intended to push the Army off the coast. For years the Army had given in to the Navy. It could give no more; it would have to "fight for its very existence." Then, as Pratt later explained, "Adams tried to smooth over what he had said, but unfortunately for him he had spilled the beans." When Foulois chimed in to give examples of Navy encroachments—their "squatting on Bolling Field," their attempts to shoulder the Army off North Island—Hurley snorted that in early days back in Oklahoma men were shot for that sort of thing.[59]

Throughout the meeting the two secretaries did most of the talking, addressing each other very formally as "Mr. Secretary"—except when Adams was trying to smooth things over by using first names. Several times Adams charged that Hurley's taking the matter to the president had been unethical. Hurley's reply was that he had done so only after Adams had taken the matter to the attorney general. That was different, Adams argued, because Senator Bingham had directed it. Hurley replied that Bingham was "entirely pro-Navy" and had once told him that "he intended to see the Navy gets Panama and Oahu." When Adams and Ingalls left Hurley's office they were still convinced that the Navy was well within its rights to build torpedo planes. Hurley and aides remained convinced that the Navy was trying to come ashore.[60]

Both departments reported to President Hoover on their failure to find any common ground. Assistant Secretary of War Frederick H. Payne, who reported for the War Department because Hurley had gone out of town, charged that "in recent years naval forces have been allowed to develop to such an extent that the Navy now has the nucleus of a self-contained Department of National Defense." This, he argued, was a trend that could be harmful to both the Army and the Navy. That it threatened to hurt the Army was obvious, but it threatened to destroy the mobility of the Navy. He suggested to the president that the "present effort of the Navy to build up shore-based aviation is a repetition of the 'gunboat' and 'monitor' policy of defense which existed previous to the Spanish–American War." It would tie the Navy to the shore.[61]

It was perhaps the influence of Payne's letter, but more likely the native cleverness of a new chief of naval operations, which in early October of 1930 brought about an important change in the Navy's aviation policy. Adm William V. Pratt, who took office charge on 17 September 1930, was a progressive admiral of the so-called Sims school. Although he and Admiral Sims had had a falling out after the World War when Pratt was caught in a feud between Sims and Josephus Daniels, the wartime secretary of the Navy, the two men were much alike in their open attitude toward change in the Navy. Sims was a bit more impressed with the potential of naval aviation, but Pratt was by no means a battleship admiral, nor would he weaken naval aviation in any deals with the Army.[62]

Pratt's changes in aviation policy were first announced on 8 October 1930, with a reorganization affecting shore-based aircraft in

Hawaii and Panama. Carrier Division One, which included the aircraft carrier *Langley* and the aircraft tenders *Wright, Sandpiper,* and *Teal,* was to be reassigned to the Scouting Fleet and have attached to it "such naval planes as are operating in the Canal Zone." In Hawaii, the Mine Force (which included the minelayer *Oglala,* four light minelayers, and four minesweepers) was to be the fleet base for the naval aircraft at Pearl Harbor. With this reorganization, the Navy could now call all of its aviation fleet-based aviation. Aircraft at Coco Solo, having been attached to aircraft carriers and aircraft tenders, could conceivably move with the fleet. Aircraft at Pearl Harbor which were reassigned remained where they had been; their move to the fleet was only on paper.[63] On 28 November 1930, Admiral Pratt issued the formal policy change. A memorandum entitled Naval Air Operating Policy was sent to all ships and stations and to Donald P. Evans who was conducting the Bureau of Efficiency's investigation ordered by Hoover: "All aircraft assigned to tactical units will be mobile in order to operate with the fleet. Mobility will be achieved by the use of carriers and tenders." The primary purpose of naval aviation was to develop "the offensive power of the Fleet and of advanced base expeditionary forces." Coastal defense was defined as a secondary purpose, and "Naval aircraft operations in peace do not contemplate the development of the secondary purpose." Further, the memorandum stated, "Airplanes stationed during peace at Coco Solo and Pearl Harbor, as an initial deployment, will be of the long-range patrol type, and will be provided with tenders for assistance in the conduct of distant operations."[64]

With one fell swoop, Pratt had eliminated most of the strategic and technical arguments in the controversy, and he did it without surrendering a dollar of the Navy's aviation budget to the Army. In reality, all he had done was change names and assignments; the only real movement was on paper. "From the standpoint of argument," admitted General Simonds, "the Navy is better off than ever but from the standpoint of efficiency, economy and duplication of Army effort they are just where they were before."[65] The only argument left for the Army was that the long-range patrol planes to be stationed at Coco Solo and Pearl Harbor were still shore based and designed for a secondary purpose. These airplanes, Army officers were quick to point out, were the most expensive military airplanes yet developed. The cost per plane for those on order was estimated from $98,545 to $101,537. For the price of one Navy long-range patrol plane the Army calculated it could buy three pursuit planes, or three attack planes, or one and one-half bombers. With the costs of the Army Air Corps five-year plan cutting deeply into budgets of other branches of the Army, it appeared to Army leaders that the Navy should either find a more important Navy need for the money planned for the long-range patrol planes, a need related to the Navy's primary purpose, or allow funds to be diverted to the Army Air Corps five-year program.[66]

In a final effort to get a decision favorable to the Army, Secretary Hurley again wrote President Hoover. "The recent step taken by the Navy has corrected many of the features objectionable to the War Department," he remarked, "the retention, however, of the smallest land-based force violates a principle which experience has proven must remain in effect, and continues an unsound situation which cannot but develop again into confusion and misunderstanding."[67] To no avail, for on the same day that Hurley sent the letter, the Bureau of Efficiency completed its investigation of the controversy and filed its report which was most favorable to the Navy.[68] For the time being, the Army had lost its case.

On the afternoon of 7 January 1931, Gen Douglas MacArthur, who had been appointed chief of staff less than two months before, and who had been only slightly involved in the controversy, went to Admiral Pratt's office in the Navy Department and the two men discussed the aviation issue. Shortly thereafter, they announced what would become known as the MacArthur–Pratt Agreement. It was contained in a one-page memorandum, the critical passage of which was two sentences: "The Naval Air Force will be based on the fleet and move with it as an important element in solving the primary missions confronting the fleet. The Army Air Forces will be land-based and employed as an essential element to the Army in the performance of its mission to defend the coasts at home and in our overseas possessions, thus assuring the fleet absolute freedom of action without any responsibility for coast defense."[69]

The MacArthur–Pratt Agreement was never more than an agreement between the chief of staff and the chief of naval operations. Pratt had made a personal commitment to spend Navy funds for airplanes which could go to sea.[70] This was in line with his belief that the fleet should have maximum mobility and air striking power. It served the purpose of defusing a controversy with the Army at a point when the Navy was winning. Navy leaders had been clever, and they had been lucky, for the Army thus far had failed to get the president to enter the controversy on its side. This was significant since it was well known in Washington that Secretary of War Hurley was one of Hoover's favorites, whereas the president and Secretary Adams were often not even on speaking terms. It was a wise move for the Navy to get the aviation controversy back down from the presidential level. That's what the MacArthur–Pratt Agreement did. The Navy resisted repeated efforts by the Army to have the agreement incorporated into "Joint Action of the Army and the Navy," the policy statement for Army and Navy coordination. In 1934, after Pratt was no longer chief of naval operations, the Navy repudiated the agreement. Nevertheless, while it was in effect, it was the basis for Army coastal defense, including plans to develop the long-range bomber.

The war with the Navy was not over, but it was not long after that the Army and its Air Corps had to face a far more ominous dilemma than competition with the Navy: the Great Depression. The man waiting in the soup line was indifferent to any military five-year plan.

Notes

1. Almost immediately upon taking office, F. Trubee Davison received a rather detailed memo from Gen Mason M. Patrick emphasizing the necessity of fighting any cuts in the five-year program. As it was, Patrick argued, the plan called for considerably fewer airplanes and men than the minimum the Lassiter report had said was necessary to meet the Air Corps's responsibilities in national defense. Mason M. Patrick, memorandum to assistant secretary of war, subject: Necessity for 1,800 Airplanes Upon Completion of Five-Year Air Corps Expansion Program, 31 July 1926, Record Group (RG) 18, National Archives (NA). For a good outline of the five-year plan, see address by General Patrick at Army War College, 10 February 1927, in "Speeches 1927," Patrick manuscripts (MSS), RG 18, NA.

2. *Army and Navy Journal*, 4 September 1926.

3. *Time*, 12 July 1926, 6.

4. *Army and Navy Journal*, 10 July 1926; *New York Times*, 3 July 1926.

5. Chase C. Mooney and Martin E. Layman, *Organization of Military Aeronautics, 1907–1935*, Army Air Forces Historical Study 25 (Washington, D.C.: Army Air Forces Historical Division, 1944), 79–80. Ira C. Eaker, who was Davison's pilot throughout his service as assistant secretary of war for air, said Davison was ideally suited for his job and that he had great influence considering his youth. See Ira C. Eaker, "The Reminiscences of Ira C. Eaker," Oral History Collection (OHC), Columbia University, 26–30.

6. Memo from the War Plans Division, subject: Controversy between the Army Air Corps Over Use of Aircraft in Coast Defense, December 1928, War Plans Division, WPD 888-58, RG 165, NA.

7. Speeches and Addresses, no. 66, John L. Hines MSS, LOC, Washington, D.C.; and *Army and Navy Journal*, 4 September 1927.

8. Howard H. Quint and Robert H. Ferrell, eds., *The Talkative President: The Off-the-Record Press Conferences of Calvin Coolidge* (Amherst, Mass.: University of Massachusetts Press, 1964), 163; and *New York Times*, 6 March 1926.

9. Memo in "Conference on Decision of the Director of the Budget Regarding Limitation on Army Strength," Central Decimal Files 321.9, RG 18, NA; John Callan O'Laughlin, "Air Increase May Reduce Other Arms," *Army and Navy Journal*, 27 March 1921; Edwin H. Rutkowski, *The Politics of Military Aviation Procurement, 1926–1934: A Study in the Political Assertion of Consensual Values* (Columbus, Ohio: Ohio State University Press, 1966), 24–28; and *New York Times*, 9 December 1926, 18 December 1926, and 11 October 1928.

10. The war plan for air defense of the nation ("Special War Plan Blue") was based upon the worst possible contingency: air war with a combination of Red, Orange, and Crimson (England, Japan, and Canada). See memo for the chief of staff, subject: Plan for Defense Against Air Attack, 19 February 1925, Office of Chief of Staff (OCS) 2055, RG 165, NA.

11. Mason M. Patrick, memorandum to the adjutant general, subject: Preliminary Report-Study of Economy in Administration, 12 September 1925, Central Decimal Files 310, RG 18, NA.

12. Report of Hearings before the Committee on Naval Affairs, H.R. Report 7375, 8 February 1926, extract in WPD 888-53, RG 165, NA.

13. Memo by Mason M. Patrick on "The Navy Five Year Program, Its Possible Effect on the Army," 18 February 1926, Adjutant General (AG) 580 (2-18-26), RG 407, NA. Three weeks later, Patrick suggested that "an exhaustive study" of the proper functions of Army and Navy aircraft should be "immediately undertaken." The General Staff replied that the studies had been made and were ongoing. Mason M. Patrick, memorandum to the adjutant general, subject: Functions of the Army and Navy in Coast Defense, 5 March 1926; and War Plans Division, memorandum to the adjutant general, subject: Functions of the Army and Navy in Coast Defense, 27 March 1926. Both are in AG 580.1 (3-5-26), RG 407, NA.

14. J. E. Kuhn to Mason M. Patrick, letter, 31 January 1926, Patrick MSS, RG 18, NA.

15. Mason M. Patrick to J. E. Kuhn, letter, 9 February 1926, Patrick MSS, RG 18, NA. See also E. N. Jones to Mason M. Patrick, letter, 15 July 1925; E. N. Jones to Mason M. Patrick, letter, 23 July 1925; E. N. Jones to Mason M. Patrick, letter, 25 July 1925; and Mason M. Patrick to E. N. Jones, letter, 3 August 1925. All are in Patrick MSS, RG 18, NA.

16. Memo for the chief of staff, subject: Policy of the Army and Navy Relating to Aircraft, 26 March 1926, WPD 888-27, RG 165, NA.

17. Memo for the chief of staff, subject: Dividing Line between the Functions of Army and Navy Air Forces, 28 February 1925, WPD 888-27, RG 165, NA.

18. John W. Weeks to Edwin Denby, letter, 28 January 1924, WPD 888-58, RG 165, NA.

19. Edwin Denby to John W. Weeks, letter, 18 February 1924, Morrow Board Records, LOC.

20. Curtis D. Wilbur to John W. Weeks, letter, 25 September 1924, WPD 888-17, RG 165, NA.

21. Adm William A. Moffett and Gen Mason M. Patrick, memorandum to secretary of war, subject: Considerations of Estimates for Appropriations for Aeronautics, 2 October 1924, WPD 888-21, RG 165, NA.

22. Memo for the chief of staff, 26 March 1926.

23. Ibid.

24. Memo for the chief of staff, subject: Proposed Revision of the Policy of the Army and Navy Relating to Aircraft, 2 June 1926, WPD 888-27, RG 165, NA.

25. Memo by Lt Col Roy C. Kirtland, subject: Function of Army and Navy Air Components, 17 November 1926, WPD 888-49, RG 165, NA. This memo sparked a bit of controversy in the War Plans Division. See memo by Maj Jarvis J. Bain, Lt Col Charles Keller, and Maj J. D. Reardon, 18 November 1926; also memo by Maj Gen Harvey A. Smith, 19 November 1926. All of these are filed in WPD 888-49 with Colonel Kirtland's memo.

26. Mason M. Patrick and William A. Moffett to the Joint Board, letter, subject: Five-Year Aircraft Programs of the Army and Navy, 28 May 1927, WPD 888-55, RG 165, NA.

27. Memo by Maj J. D. Reardon and Maj J. N. Greely, subject: Military Role of Aircraft, 3 January 1928, WPD 888-46, RG 165, NA.

28. Memo for the chief of staff, subject: Correspondence with Reference to the Existing Law Prohibiting the Navy from Constructing Airplanes Other Than Those Used for Patrolling and Scouting Purposes," 8 July 1927; and "Message from Colonel Hartshom to Colonel Embick, 10:07 A.M., 8 July 1927." Both in OCS 15205-49, RG 165, NA.

29. Memo by Col Stanley D. Embick, subject: Five-Year Aircraft Programs of the Army and Navy, 12 July 1927, WPD 888-54, RG 165, NA.

30. A biographical sketch of Gen Charles P. Summerall is available in the *Army and Navy Journal*, 25 September 1926; former Secretary of War Newton Baker was one of those who dubbed Summerall the "Cromwell of the American Army." Newton

Baker to William R. Wood, letter, 8 September 1924, Summerall MSS, LOC. An example of Summerall's ignorance of the technical aspects of aviation can be found in Claire Chennault, *Way of a Fighter: The Memoirs of Claire Lee Chennault*, ed. Robert Hotz (New York: G. P. Putnam's Sons, 1949), 16–17.

31. "Final Report of Chief of Staff," Summerall MSS, LOC.

32. Simonds to Craig, 25 July 1930, Simonds MSS, LOC.

33. WPD 888-54 and WPD 888-58 in RG 165, NA.

34. Senate Concurrent Resolution 11, 70th Cong., 1st sess., read into the record on 23 February 1928, *Congressional Record*, 70th Cong., 1st sess., 3417.

35. Gen Charles P. Summerall, memorandum to Gen B. H. Wells, subject: Aircraft Seacoast Defenses, 21 May 1928, OCS 15205-59, RG 165, NA.

36. Gen Charles P. Summerall to the Aeronautical Board, letter, 16 August 1928, WPD 888-58, RG 165, NA.

37. Gen George S. Simonds to Gen Malin Craig, letter, 5 October 1928, Simonds MSS.

38. *Congressional Record*, 70th Cong., 2d sess., 1614.

39. Dwight Davis to Sen. David A. Reed, letter, 11 February 1929, AG 580 (1-7-29). See also memo by Maj Delos Emmons, 9 February 1929, AG 580 (2-9-29); Gen Charles P. Summerall to W. Frank James, letter, 11 January 1929, AG 580 (1-7-29); and Dwight Davis to W. Frank James, letter, 23 January 1929. All are in RG 407, NA. In the War Plans Division files, see Dwight Davis to L. E. Snell, 15 January 1929, WPD 888-58, RG 165, NA.

40. *Congressional Record*, 70th Cong., 2d sess., 5233.

41. See Sen. Hiram Bingham to Gen John J. Pershing, letter, 24 April 1929, Pershing MSS, LOC; Proposed letter from secretaries of war and Navy in AG 580 (5-3-20); also Adm C. F. Hughes to Secretary James W. Good, letter, 4 May 1929, AG 580.1 (5-4-29); and James W. Good to Sen. Hiram Bingham, letter, 18 May 1929, AG 580.1 (5-19-29). All are in RG 407, NA. In War Plans Division files, they are cited as Good to Joint Board, 10 May 1929, WPD 888-58, RG 165, NA.

42. Transcript of the hearings are in WPD 888-58, RG 165, NA.

43. Sen. Hiram Bingham to James W. Good, letter, 7 May 1929, WPD 888-58, RG 165, NA.

44. James W. Good to Sen. Hiram Bingham, letter, 18 May 1929, WPD 888-58, RG 165, NA.

45. C. F. Adams to Attorney General William D. Mitchell, letter, 3 June 1929, WPD 888-88, RG 165, NA.

46. James W. Good to William D. Mitchell, letter, 17 June 1929; and James W. Good to W. D. Mitchell, letter, 8 October 1929, WPD 888-58, RG 165, NA.

47. W. D. Mitchell to secretary of the Navy, letter, 18 January 1930. A copy of this letter was sent to Secretary Patrick J. Hurley by the Navy Department. Assistant Secretary of Navy Ernest L. Jahncke to Patrick J. Hurley, letter, 17 January 1930, WPD 888-58, RG 165, NA.

48. Newspaper clipping, "Jahncke on Next War," in Simonds MSS, LOC.

49. Gen Malin Craig to Gen George S. Simonds, letter, 3 July 1929, Simonds MSS.

50. For a good biography of Hurley, see Don Lohbeck, Patrick J. Hurley (Chicago: H. Regnery, Co., 1956). For a colorful sketch of the man, see Robert Sharon Allen and Andrew Russell Pearson, *More Merry-Go-Round* (New York: Liveright, Inc., 1932), 155–86.

51. Gen George S. Simonds, memorandum to the chief of staff, 17 January 1930. See also memo by Simonds dated 25 January and 4 February 1930. All are in WPD 888-58, RG 165, NA.

52. Patrick J. Hurley to President Hoover, letter, 18 February 1930, WPD 888-58, RG 165, NA.

53. Ernest L. Jahncke to President Hoover, letter, 14 April 1930, WPD 888-58, RG 165, NA.

54. Patrick J. Hurley to President Hoover, letter, 29 May 1930, WPD 888-58, RG 165, NA.
55. President Hoover to Patrick J. Hurley, 17 July 1930, WPD 888-58, RG 165, NA.
56. Gen Malin Craig to Gen George S. Simonds, letters, 22 April 1930, 7 May 1930, 27 May 1930, 21 June 1930, and 27 June 1930. See also Gen George S. Simonds to Gen Malin Craig, letters, 12 April 1930 and 21 May 1930. All in Simonds MSS.
57. Gen Malin Craig to Gen George S. Simonds, letter, 11 July 1930, Simonds MSS.
58. Col R. S. Pratt, memorandum to Gen George S. Simonds, 6 August 1930, WPD 888-58, RG 165, NA.
59. Ibid.
60. Ibid.
61. Frederick H. Payne to President Hoover, 10 September 1930, WPD 888-58, RG 165, NA.
62. A rough draft of Adm William V. Pratt's autobiography is in his papers in the Library of Congress. Of his dealings with the Army, he said,

> In time of war, the relations with the Army are that the two services stand shoulder to shoulder. Whatever differences of opinion may arise are subordinated to the major objective of winning the war. In time of peace, many little vexatious differences of opinion spring up and if they are allowed to grow, in short time will assume dimensions entirely out of proportion to their real merit. Fortunately the Army had as its Chief of Staff, Douglas MacArthur. A remarkably brilliant and able soldier, courteous and intelligent, it was a pleasure to work with him. He was always willing to consider the other point of view, and give it such weight as he thought just. Between us we managed to smooth over many obstacles considered insuperable. I am going to say this, even if it hurts navy pride. The Army has always been considered a hard boiled organization; stiff and with ramrods down their backs. The Navy prides itself on being more liberal minded. I daresay that I have been thrown in with more Army men that [sic] the majority of Naval men, for I served a year with it in Panama, was almost a year at the Army War College, and knew several army men at our own War College, before coming to the Office of Operations. When it comes to sitting around a table to discuss and reach a fair minded solution to a tough problem, one which requires a liberal mind to approach, and requires tack and finesse as well as firmness even though he be of a different service, I would rather sit with Douglas MacArthur than some of my own naval confreres [sic]. About the only real difference upon which we could not compromise lay in the field of football.

Manuscript of memoirs, chapter 21, 21–23, Pratt MSS, LOC.
63. Gen George S. Simonds, memorandum, 18 October 1930, WPD 888-48, RG 165, NA.
64. Chief of naval operations, memorandum to all ships and stations, subject: Naval Air Operating Policy, 28 November 1930, WPD 888-38, RG 165, NA.
65. Gen George S. Simonds, memorandum, 18 October 1930, WPD 888-58, RG 165, NA.
66. Donald P. Evans, memorandum to Herbert Daniel Brown, subject: Overlap between the Army and the Navy in the Maintenance of Shore-based Aviation, 15 December 1930, WPD 888-58, RG 165, NA.
67. Patrick J. Hurley to President Hoover, letter, 15 December 1930, WPD 888-58, RG 165, NA.
68. Evans.
69. Maj Gen Van Horn Moseley, memorandum, 10 January 1931, AG 580 (1-10-31) (1), RG 407, NA.
70. Gerald E. Wheeler, *Admiral William Veazie Pratt, U.S. Navy: A Sailor's Life* (Washington, D.C.: Naval History Division, 1974), 356–57.

Chapter 4

The Great Depression

As the United States entered a new decade, the horizons of American aviation were widening, but money was increasingly becoming a problem. The airplane still fascinated the American public. The Air Corps, though almost constantly in contention with budget-conscious Army leaders and the competitive aviators of the Navy, had enthusiastic supporters among the general public and in Congress. But during the Great Depression, the Army had its appropriations reduced almost in half. The 1930s were to be a dreary decade for the Army, a time during which almost all thinking would revolve around the budget. At every turn, Army leaders seemed to face an almost impossible dilemma. The Depression compounded the problem of coping with rapid developments in aviation technology. If it had been possible, the Army's leaders would have put aside until better times the expensive burden of building an air force. Even continuing the moderate Air Corps five-year expansion program meant drastic reduction in other branches to pay the bill.

There seemed little that Army leaders could do to reduce the Air Corps share of the budget. There were pressures to increase it despite warnings that the Army was being unbalanced—that to support the Air Corps, other branches had "gone to the limit in making sacrifices and could sacrifice no more."[1] At first there was the threat from the Navy. If the Army did not continue to build up its air forces, particularly those necessary to perform coastal defense, the Navy might step in and take over that mission, and with it virtually the entire peacetime budget for military aviation. The MacArthur–Pratt Agreement that reserved coastal defense for the Army removed this threat temporarily. Still, Army leaders could not set aside the demands of the Air Corps, if only for this reason. As the Great Depression spread and worldwide tensions increased, the need to defend the nation's coasts became more urgent. The same was true of the Army's need to stay abreast technically, if not in size and strength, with modern armies of other powers.

Army leaders were in the frustrating position of being able neither to fulfill these needs nor ignore them. If they tried to meet them, they risked crippling other elements of the Army. If they tried to postpone them, they risked criticism from airpower enthusiasts. At times when they were advising restraint in Air Corps growth, the chief of staff and officers of the General Staff must have felt that their best allies on aviation issues were their political enemies, the pacifists and supporters of disarmament.

Hoover Orders an Economic Survey of the War Department

Even before the stock market crash of October 1929, President Herbert Hoover had announced that the Army's expenditures were too high. In late July, he called his military advisers to his weekend retreat on the Rapidan in Virginia. They were to make a survey of military activities to see where the budget might be trimmed without undermining national defense. General Summerall, the chief of staff, supervised the General Staff's survey, warning corps area commanders and the chiefs of branches and bureaus that the General Staff would be looking for ways of "extensive reductions in the cost of the Army in all or any of its components or activities." Among his instructions to the General Staff, he ordered evaluation of the cavalry to see if it should not be replaced by motorization or aviation. He directed a study of the relation of aviation to other branches and a close look at the five-year program.[2]

The survey had hardly begun when rumor began that a huge reduction was planned in military aviation. At the national air races in Cleveland, Ohio, during the last week of August 1929, the story was passed around that Hoover was planning to scrap the five-year program. The rumor put aircraft manufacturers attending the races in a near panic. The aviation industry in the next two years would lose contracts totaling $100 million. The White House denied any intention to scrap the program, but moderate reduction of the budget was not ruled out and would likely be considered by the General Staff in its survey.[3]

Brig Gen James E. Fechet, the chief of the Air Corps, along with other service chiefs, was asked for his opinion, which proved not altogether helpful. His answer was that aviation should not be cut back but expanded. As for the five-year plan, he agreed it should be scrapped—and replaced with a larger program.[4]

The final report of the survey was ready for the president on Friday, 1 November 1929. It had been a gloomy week. On Tuesday, 29 October, the efforts of J. P. Morgan and other big bankers had failed to stop the downward slide in the stock market. An avalanche of sell orders triggered a massive liquidation that would last through the first two weeks of November. If President Hoover expected some good news from the survey of military expenditures to offset bad news from Wall Street, he was disappointed. Several days before the report was made, General Summerall had shown his notes on the survey to the president and Secretary of War Good, so there were no surprises in the 175-page report prepared by War Plans. With great logic, the report argued that the military establishment was already at bare minimum and the General Staff had failed to find ways of "making extensive reductions" in the budget without "manifest injury to the national defense."[5] These arguments were convincing; the Army's appropriation for FY 1931 went unscathed. For the Air Corps, the five-year plan would continue, though without the upward revision Fechet wanted.

Reaffirmation of the five-year program was a concession by General Summerall and the General Staff. It violated Summerall's theory of how to get maximum defense out of a limited peacetime budget. He outlined the theory in the notes he showed President Hoover. "In principle," he said, "the peace organization should insure a balanced nucleus for expansion to at least three times its strength, and the components should be a minimum in the most expensive and a maximum in the least expensive categories."[6] The Air Corps was an expensive branch and, according to Summerall's theory, should be at a minimum in peacetime, particularly since the nation's aircraft industry was strong enough to stand on its own and capable of producing enough planes to expand the Air Corps in an emergency. (Air Corps leaders would have debated this point with Summerall, but there was no denying that the aircraft industry had far greater capacity than in 1926, when the five-year program was established.) Summerall did not advise scrapping the program. Politically it would be foolish, since the airplane had captured the popular imagination. He explained that the "Five-Year Program is the product of a civilian board, and received the support of the people and of Congress. It would not be wise for a revision downward to be undertaken except by a similar agency." Summerall suggested that the Air Corps be allowed a separate budget "so that its cost would be made clear to the Congress and the country."[7] He was trying to emphasize that there was far more to the cost of the Air Corps than the mere purchase price of airplanes. Someone had to pay for maintenance and motor pools, hangars and runways, all the overhead associated with maintaining a squadron of airplanes. This cost had often been borne by other branches of the Army and not the Air Corps (fig. 1).

While neither the Army leadership nor air enthusiasts were satisfied with the program, it was founded in law and during the almost continuous budget battles of the first four years of the Great Depression, it provided a convenient fallback position for both sides. Summerall had shied away from asking for downward revisions because it was politically unwise. Air Corps leaders recognized that it was not the time to press for legislative action. In late January of 1930, in response to a request from Secretary of War

THE ARMY AND ITS AIR CORPS

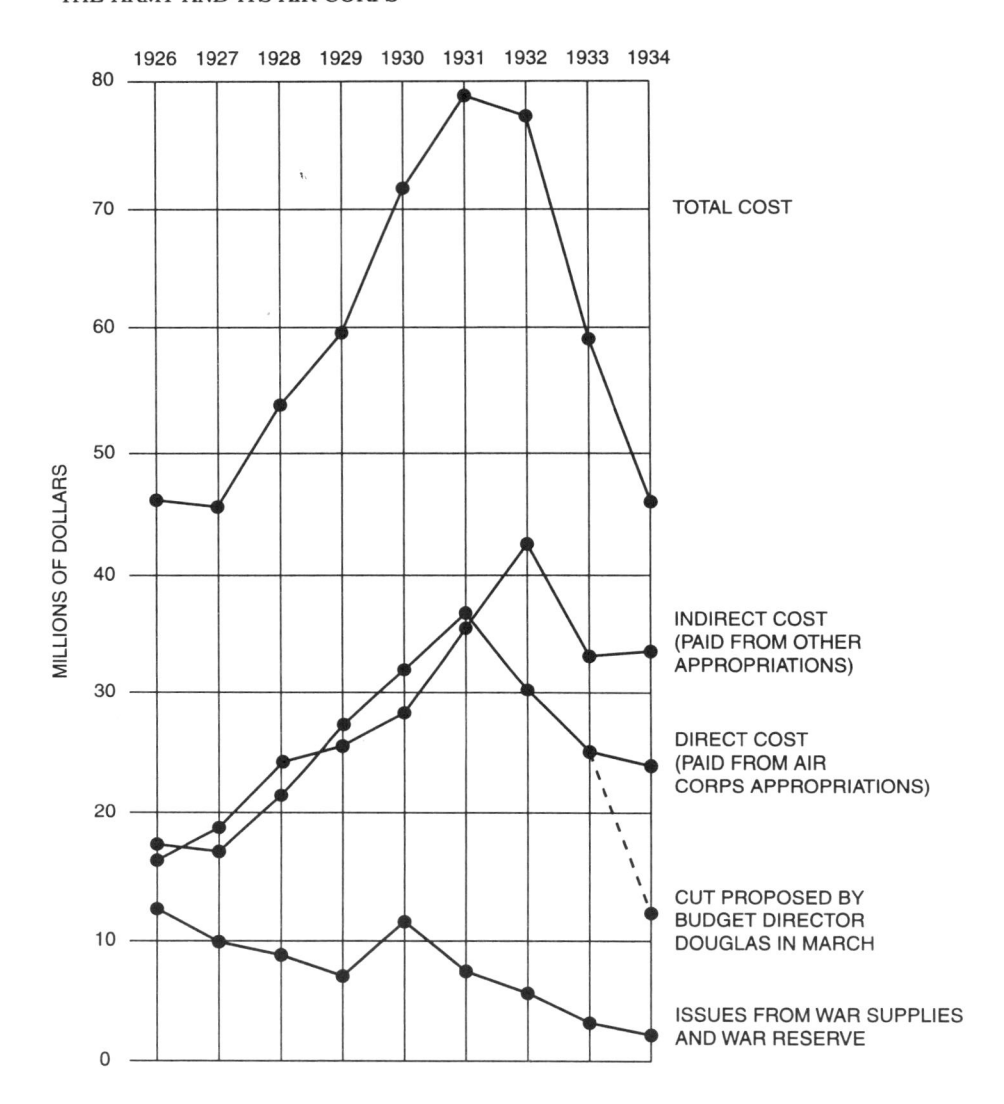

Figure 1. Cost of the Army Air Corps by Fiscal Years

Hurley for recommendations for revision of the five-year program, General Fechet and a board of Air Corps officers declared the program wholly inadequate but were prudently moderate in recommendation for immediate change. They explained that the minimum air force "capable of discouraging hostile attack" on the continental United States, Panama, and Hawaii was 3,100 airplanes, 1,300 more than the five-year goal of 1,800. Still more planes would be needed if the Philippine Islands were also to have air defense.

But a 3,100-plane program, if completed in four years, would cost approximately $62 million annually. Realizing that such an increase was unlikely considering Hoover's views on economy in the War Department, the general and his fellow officers suggested that 2,300 airplanes would be a first step toward a 3,100-plane force. They explained that if the president could be induced to support the 2,300-plane program, it could be initiated with only minor legislative action. All that was needed was congressional acceptance of a liberal interpretation of the existing law so that "obsolete aircraft and aircraft undergoing major repairs at depots may be excluded from the 1,800 serviceable airplanes authorized by the Air Corps Act."[8] The Air Corps eventually got both the War Department and Congress to accept in principle their interpretation of the law. It was agreed that the 1,800 serviceable airplanes authorized in the five-year program would include only aircraft available for duty.[9] As the economic and political situations developed in 1930 and 1931, however, it turned out to be an empty victory.

As the Depression deepened in the summer and autumn of 1930, Hoover came under immense pressure to do something about it before the November elections. With somber determination, he drove himself to meet the pressure. His engineer training and his belief in rugged individualism had conditioned him to believe that with effort, self-sacrifice, and determination, one could overcome almost any obstacle. He would sacrifice and work to the limit of his endurance. All of it was to little avail, and as the months passed his situation became desperate. An "ever-present feeling of gloom . . . pervades everything connected with the Administration," wrote Secretary of State Henry L. Stimson, "I really never knew such unenlivened occasions as our Cabinet meetings. . . . I don't remember that there has ever been a joke cracked in a single meeting of the last year and a half, nothing but steady, serious grind. . . . How I wish I could cheer up the poor old President."[10]

With Hoover, balancing the budget became more and more an imperative. Despite apparent acquiescence in the conclusions of the survey of War Department expenditures of 1929, he told Hurley, in late July 1930 that in this "time of depression," minor administrative savings in the War Department budget were not enough. Spending on major programs would have to be deferred until "such time as government revenues have recovered." Hurley was to do an immediate study to see what cuts could be made in funds already appropriated for FY 1931. The General Staff suggested that $20 million could be held back. The president was not satisfied. The federal budget could not be balanced, he said, without a drastic reduction in current expenditure, and he ordered the War Department to limit expenditures for FY 1931 to $444,200,000, nearly $65 million less than the amount Congress had appropriated.[11]

The Air Corps was affected by the impoundment of funds and its protests were immediate and loud. Assistant Secretary of War for Air Davison wrote Col J. Clawson Roop, director of the Bureau of the Budget, that holding back part of its appropriation would not only undermine ability to perform its mission, but might cause catastrophe in the aviation industry. The Bureau of the Budget had set the Air Corps share of the reduced budget at $33,700,000. The Air Corps argued that without at least $40 million, it could not meet contracts already let. Finally, the Air Corps was allowed $36 million, the extra $2 million from funds of other branches.[12]

All the while, General Summerall was preparing his final report as chief of staff. Not surprisingly, his theme was the budget and the need for a balanced Army. In strong terms, he restated the position of the General Staff on aviation expenditures since the World War:

> No element in our military forces is independent of the others, but each is affected by the state of development of the others. . . . With our increase in aviation there has been no parallel development of the related antiaircraft defense. The state of development of all elements of our forces should be considered simultaneously, and our military policy in respect to the development of our forces, whether in the way of expansion or reduction, should be expressed in general projects extending over a period of years.[13]

Remembering the emotional scene back in 1925 when Mitchell on the first day of his court-martial had been removed from the court on grounds of "prejudice and bias," airmen may have suspected Summerall's rebuke of air enthusiasts. They may have hoped for more sympathy for the Air Corps position from General MacArthur, the new chief of staff, but they would not get it. MacArthur strongly concurred in the conservative views of his predecessor. For the next five years, he would fight for a balanced Army and vigorously oppose congressional proponents of airpower.[14] He was concerned about protecting the personnel of the Army, especially the officer corps. He wrote, "An army can live on short rations; it can be insufficiently clothed and housed; it can even be poorly armed and equipped, but in action it is doomed to destruction without trained and adequate leadership of officers."[15] Unbalanced appropriations would not only favor one component, but it would favor materiel over personnel in the case of the Air Corps.

MacArthur had been chief of staff only a few days when he made his first appearance before the House Subcommittee on Military Appropriations. In the War Department budget for FY 1932, which the subcommittee was reviewing, the Air Corps had suffered a double cut. Hurley had ordered Air Corps estimates reduced from $56,900,000 to approximately $45,500,000. Then the Bureau of the

Budget ordered a further cut of 50 percent in the annual aircraft augmentation program under the five-year plan.[16] MacArthur went along, testifying that considering economic realities, the proposed budget met minimum needs of the Army, adding that it was free from "eccentricities of any individual or group"—a jab at airpower enthusiasts who believed the budget did not meet minimum needs of the Air Corps.[17] MacArthur endorsed the General Staff's solution of keeping up with technology, which was to use available funds for research and development of models rather than attempt to provide forces with the latest equipment. Speaking for the Air Corps, Davison disagreed with that solution. The Air Corps would not be satisfied with advanced test models while its squadrons were equipped with obsolete aircraft. It was Air Corps policy, he said, to use its funds to buy the best airplanes available. He and Fechet argued vigorously for increasing procurement of aircraft, especially bombers. Congress, however, dominated by Republicans (some had lost in the 1930 elections, but their Democratic successors would not be seated until December 1930), approved Hoover's economy measures and was not of a mind to increase appropriation for aircraft.

Even so, the Air Corps fared better than the rest of the Army. With half the final increment of its five-year plan funded, there would be an increase in size of the Air Corps. Though other branches would suffer, such comparisons made little impression on air enthusiasts.

"Just Hog-tied a Mississippi Cracker"

When Congress met in December 1930, the budget was a top priority for every member. Eight months earlier, during one of his "working weekends," President Hoover had met with political advisers to prepare for the budget hearings. As he had done before and since the "economic survey" of the War Department in 1929, Hoover insisted that continuing US Treasury deficits made military retrenchment imperative. He told Hurley, MacArthur, and their aides to study the problem; and while they did, he "went off under a tree to write a speech," for Hoover was not a man to waste time waiting on others.[18]

As reports of the meeting were made public, it became clear that the conferees had decided the Army could stand neither a reduction in personnel nor in funds for training. Still, there were areas that could be cut.[19] It was announced to the press that 20 to 30 unnecessary Army posts would be abandoned, and though not included in the announcement, curtailment of funds for the Chemical Warfare Service and the Air Corps was apparently under consideration.

Newsmen were probably right in suspecting the latter, because three days after the weekend conference, Hoover sent a letter to the secretaries of war and Navy directing them to review the whole matter of air defense for possible savings. He said,

> As you are aware, I have been giving thought to the subject of national defense in directions that might improve efficiency and at the same time bring about imperative economies. . . . Our Army has been reduced greatly and the principles of limitation of naval armaments have been extended to cover all types of naval craft. Yet there seems considerable tendency to further expand the air components of the two services and perhaps to regard them as exempt from application of these principles. If our air strength is out of proportion to our other forces, this . . . is not an efficient way of organizing our defense.[20]

Army leaders were eager to abide by the president's instruction. Not only had he endorsed the idea that other Army needs might be more pressing than those of the Air Corps, but according to Hurley's interpretation of the letter, Hoover had ordered the Army and Navy to make a joint study of aviation needs in order to coordinate their budget requests.[21] Army leaders had favored joint funding of aviation programs since 1924, when Secretary Weeks had tried to get the Navy to coordinate its aviation expansion plan with the Army plan proposed by the Lassiter Board. Joint funding would make it more likely that appropriations for aviation would be distributed to the Army and Navy at a ratio of 18 to 10, the same as the ratio of airplane strengths authorized by the respective five-year programs, rather than 18 to 14 which the Army claimed had been the average ratio of aviation appropriations for the Army and Navy since 1926.[22]

The issue caused a minor dispute between the two services, threatening to revive the Army–Navy controversy which the MacArthur–Pratt Agreement had supposedly put to rest only four months earlier. Having done quite well before appropriations committees on their own, Navy leaders were no more anxious in 1931 than in 1924 to tie their aviation program to the Army's program. Both secretaries referred the matter to the Joint Board as President Hoover had suggested, and the Joint Board directed its Joint Planning Committee to study and report on peacetime requirements of the Army and Navy. Hurley hoped the committee's report would determine the "total air strength needed by the United States for aerial defense and the relative proportions in that total strength allocated to the Army and to the Navy."[23] Upon his direction, MacArthur told the Army members of the Joint Planning Committee to be prepared "to discuss the subject along the broadest lines."[24] Admiral Pratt gave different instructions to the Navy members. They were told to keep the study narrow, to insist upon limiting consideration of Navy aviation to naval officers and Army aviation to Army officers. Pratt's instructions were obeyed to the letter, with the result that the committee's report covered no new ground and was little more than a restatement of the five-year plans.[25]

MacArthur denounced the report as "utterly lacking in responsiveness to the directive from the President." It was clearly the president's intent, he argued, that the "Joint Board would consider the whole matter of air defense from the broad viewpoint of the national defense as a whole." The Navy had blocked the president's instruction, and MacArthur challenged Pratt to explain.[26] Pratt's position was weak, and he knew it, so he prudently retreated. "I am willing to broaden the scope of the inquiry," he told MacArthur.[27] But he was clever and his concession was more apparent than real. As MacArthur complained later, the broadened inquiry was qualified "with such restrictions as to insure a report of no more usefulness than the one which the Army members reject."[28] If there was to be a study of the sort MacArthur and Hurley wanted, it would have to be done by the Army. This had been apparent almost from the day President Hoover ordered the study. Not to be caught short, General Simonds in War Plans had been working on just such a study. Though he had been holding up the study checking and revising figures, the study was available to MacArthur even before he challenged Pratt to "broaden the inquiry."[29] Perhaps MacArthur was giving the Navy one last chance to cooperate. At any rate, the Navy did not cooperate, and MacArthur sent a copy of the study on 14 August to Hurley and also one to Colonel Roop at the Bureau of the Budget.[30]

The Simonds study made clear the General Staff's position on the Air Corps budget. Reviewing the world situation and comparing American air strength with that of leading foreign powers, Simonds and his war planners concluded that the ideal goal for the United States should be a force of 2,950 Army planes and 2,065 Navy planes. "World conditions at the present time are much disturbed and frictions and causes for war are much in evidence," but this was not justification for expanding the air programs. The economic situation, they said, was "additional argument against it, and in so far as concerns the Army, such expansion would result in a further disproportion between the Air Corps and the rest of the Army." They proposed that the Army Air Corps be stabilized at approximately 1,900 planes gross (not 1,800 "serviceable planes" as the Air Corps spokesmen suggested, because that would mean expansion to about 2,000 planes gross and more expense). With regard to the Navy program, they proposed that "Marine Corps and other land-based combat aviation be eliminated from Naval expenditures" and that the Navy "be required . . . to justify the great excess of naval aviation over that of foreign nations (the American naval air service was at the time the largest in the world), their apparently excessive proportion of observation aviation, and the apparently excessive cost of their training system." Naval aviators received 248 hours of flying training as opposed to 165 hours for Army aviators. Finally, Simonds and staff made a suggestion probably designed to irritate the Navy more than anything else: elimination of airplane carriers in the disarmament conference soon to meet in Geneva. Though aircraft carriers had defensive value, they were essentially an offensive weapon, the kind the disarmament conference hopefully would eliminate.[31]

Air Corps leaders had opposed stabilizing Army aviation at 1,800 planes gross, and now with equal vigor supported the attack on the Navy. They held demonstrations in the spring and summer of 1931 to illustrate the ability of the Air Corps to defend the nation's coasts. The first was a mass gathering of 672 airplanes for Air Corps coastal defense exercises held during the last two weeks of May.[32] The 1st Air Division, as this concentration of planes was called, flew about the northeast section of the nation in mass formations that stretched for miles and defended New York, Boston, and other cities from mock air attacks. There were complaints that the maneuvers were warlike and expensive, and columnists Robert Allen and Drew Pearson branded them propaganda, "the greatest air circus held at any time or at any place in the world."[33] Despite criticism, the maneuvers were a great success. The mock attackers were driven off, the Eastern seaboard theoretically saved, and the public duly impressed by the young Army pilots who could fly over 500 thousand air miles without running into each other, or the ground, or killing or injuring anyone.

The second demonstration was the bombing of the old freighter *Mount Shasta*, and it was not a success at all.[34] As combat pilots would say, the mission began to "turn sour" before it began. Prior to 11 August, when the Army mine-planter *General Schofield* cut the *Mount Shasta* adrift off the Virginia coast about 60 miles east of Currituck Light, the Air Corps discovered that there were no 600-pound bombs available; 100- and 300-pound bombs would have to be used. It was doubtful that these light bombs would do the job, and the mission would have been cancelled had there not been so much publicity. Some twoscore reporters and photographers were to cover the event. The Army had arranged for them to be transported to the test site aboard the tug *Reno*, the Coast Guard cutter *Mascoutin*, as well as the *General Schofield*, and several transport planes. A blow-by-blow account of the attack on the drifting freighter was to be broadcast by the National Broadcasting Company, which planned to have a man in an airplane orbiting the test site and another aboard the *Reno*. Three ranking Army generals and three naval observers were to fly in the bombers. According to the press, MacArthur himself would witness the tests from the lead plane piloted by Maj Herbert H. Dargue.

Thus, it was decided that the mission could not be called off—but it should have been, because matters went from bad to worse. Weather moved in, and Dargue's flight of nine bombers that took off from Langley Field in midmorning on the 11th returned several hours later with their bomb racks full. They had been unable to find the *Mount Shasta*. Visibility varied from excellent to fair below 1,000 feet, but Dargue had elected to lead his flight up through the clouds, apparently hoping to break out on top. As the flight passed in and out of clouds, confusion reigned, with the second and third elements at times passing the first. After the flight had settled down "on top," Dargue spotted a lone steamer through a break below, and despite smoke issuing from its stacks and a white wake trailing it (the *Mount Shasta* would have neither since it was unmanned and adrift), he diverted the flight to investigate. When he attempted to return to course, he probably went beyond the *Mount Shasta*. With no reference from which to begin a search, he gave up and returned to Langley.

The Navy had a field day poking fun at the Army. Assistant Secretary of the Navy Ingalls wrote Hurley and in a "helpful spirit" offered to assist the Army Air Corps in finding and sinking the *Mount Shasta*. "Our materiel has been constructed and our personnel trained with that end in view. Therefore, the naval aviation service will be glad either to guide and convoy the Army bombers to and from the target, or, if necessary, even undertake the entire mission of finding and destroying by bombs said old hulk." In Ingalls's office, an unidentified Navy bard slipped to the press a poem about the "troubles of an imaginary Army airman who had ventured out to sea":

> Oh Navy take back your coast defense,
> For we find that the sea is too rough;
> We thought on one hand it would help us expand,
> We find we are not so tough.
> The sea is your right you hold it by might,
> We would if we could but we can't.
> It seems that the sea is entirely Navy,
> Army planes should remain o'er the land.[35]

Two days after their initial attempt to find the *Mount Shasta*, Dargue and his pilots tried again, with only slightly better results. Instead of flying in close formation, they flew in a giant V formation with two miles between each plane. This way they were certain not to miss. But such a flight was unwieldy and it was impossible to maneuver around a rainstorm encountered almost immediately after leaving shore. Again, there was confusion. Some planes lost the flight and returned to Langley. The remainder were able to rendezvous on the other side of the storm and continue on to bomb the *Mount Shasta*. Dargue scored a hit with a dud. There was one hit with a live bomb from another plane, and the remaining 48 bombs peppered the water around the old ship, showering it with shrapnel. When the bombing ended, the *Mount Shasta* was still afloat. Perhaps in time it would have sunk from the damage, but just to make sure, two Coast Guard cutters at the scene sent the *Mount Shasta* to the bottom with one-pound shells fired into its hull at the waterline.

The affair was a setback for both air supporters and budget-conscious Army leaders. The best of alibis and explanations were given. It was poor weather, bad luck, and lack of equipment and money for training. Mitchell added that all would have been different if there had been an independent, united air force.[36] But as Colonel Arnold, now air commander of March Field in California, wrote Maj Carl Spaatz, "Regardless of all the alibis and explanations . . . the two outstanding facts are that the bombers did not find the *Mount Shasta* on the first day and did not sink it three days later." He added, "I cannot help but feel that it will have a very detrimental effect on this newly assigned coast defense project. It is very easy for the Navy to take the stand before the next Congress that the Army has shown itself incapable of locating ships at sea and of sinking them after they do find them."[37] Arnold, of course, saw the problem from the point of view of an airman who wanted the largest possible share for the Air Corps in coming budgets. Leaders in the War Department shared Arnold's concern over the *Mount Shasta* fiasco but perhaps for slightly different reasons. They were contemplating curtailment of the Air Corps program—*stabilizing* the Air Corps was the term they used—and they had hoped for some transfer of funds from naval aviation to the Army to soften the blow. Now that would be less likely.

There would be no sugar to coat the pill that Secretary Hurley would serve the Air Corps in his budget proposal for FY 1933. Following the lines suggested in General Simonds's War Plans Division study, the budget for 1933 would slice off nearly $6 million from the Air Corps estimate.[38] The forthcoming budget battle in Congress, moreover, would center not on division of money between Army and naval aviation but on whether cuts in the Army budget should be in aviation and mechanization or in funds for personnel, particularly officers and training.[39] MacArthur, representing the Army position, would fight for personnel and training. It was no longer a question of how much of the Army's funds the Air Corps could spend; it was to the crisis point of which mattered more, men or machines.

In House appropriations hearings, MacArthur faced one of the War Department's toughest adversaries, Cong. Ross Collins (D-Miss.), who, as a result of the Democratic majority in the new Congress, had replaced William R. Wood (R-Ind.) as chairman of the Appropriations subcommittee. A cherubic-faced, quiet-mannered individual who spoke with a soft drawl, Collins was also, as one reporter noted, "a past master of political satire."[40] Generals did not awe him, neither with their impressive appearance in uniform nor with their jargon and technical expertise. He had read widely in the works of modern military writers and was an admirer of Billy Mitchell and the British military strategist and proponent of mechanized warfare, Basil H. Liddell Hart. A portrait of Liddell Hart hung over his desk. He refused to let generals "browbeat" him, and as one general put it, "He was poison to the War Department."[41]

When the appropriations bill for FY 1933 came up for consideration, Collins led a move to cut the Regular officer corps from 12 to 10 thousand and use the savings on airpower and mechanization of the ground forces.[42] MacArthur objected and was ridiculed by Collins for refusing to trade a few officers for tanks and planes. Collins's arguments were supported by Fechet's successor as chief of the Air Corps, General Foulois, and by Assistant Secretary Davison, who claimed that mobilization plans based on personnel were hurting the Air Corps. Foulois told the subcommittee that it would be a splendid thing if additional funds could be spent on heavy bombers rather than personnel.[43] With this sort of opinion backing him, Collins succeeded in attaching an officer-reduction amendment to the War Department bill. He told his fellow congressmen that "defense of this country lies in the utilization of science and warfare by a comparatively small army of trained experts," that what the Army needed was mechanization, and that money should be spent on planes, tanks, and modern guns. While other nations, notably Britain, were modernizing, in America we were "utterly unable to lift ourselves out of the rut and apply new principles to military science." He charged that the General Staff placed undue emphasis on pay and allowances and was either shortsighted or so dominated by the traditional combat branches that it was powerless to break the barriers of conservatism.[44] Other congressmen, including the chairman of the House Military Affairs Committee, John J. McSwain (D-S.C.), agreed with Collins's views that more money should be spent on weapons and equipment rather than on increases in pay and allowances. Within the bounds of "reasonable economy," McSwain favored placing the "highest emphasis upon the power of aviation."[45]

To MacArthur the attack on the officer corps was a thrust at the Army's heart. Tanks and planes were a matter of money. If

Congress would increase appropriations, the Army would purchase equipment with enthusiasm. The officers Congress seemed intent on sacrificing represented more than money to the Army. Loyal, experienced, and professional, these 2,000 men were the product of years of training, indoctrination, and experience. MacArthur and the General Staff could not agree with Collins's contention that his proposal would remove the deadwood that clogged the Army promotion system. There was no deadwood, MacArthur argued; it long since had been cut out by reductions in Army strength. From December 1931 to July 1932, "for seven long, dreary months," as the editor of the *Army and Navy Journal* put it, "General MacArthur fought the forces of destruction in Congress."[46] The bill passed the House by a vote of 201 to 182 despite MacArthur's testimony. It was, however, defeated in the Senate, and Collins's best efforts could not raise enough votes to override the decision. The officer corps was spared. Some observers said the deciding factor was the Army's influence with the Tammany Hall political organization of New York City, that the Tammany leader, John F. Curry, had sent instructions to the 21 Tammany members of Congress to save the Army, and they obeyed.[47] Whatever the tactics, they were successful. In jubilation, MacArthur sent a telegram to Assistant Secretary of War for Procurement Frederick H. Payne: "Just hog-tied a Mississippi cracker. House voted our way. . . . Happy times are here again. /S/ MacArthur"[48]

While this battle in Congress was at its peak, MacArthur was called upon by the State Department to give his position on disarmament. The World Disarmament Conference had opened in Geneva in February 1932. Disarmament had been a lively topic in diplomacy since the World War, and while statesmen tended to view it cynically, the Depression had made armaments more of a burden for all nations (ironically, the race to rearm in the late thirties would be credited by some observers with breaking the Depression). There was hope, if not conviction, that an acceptable disarmament formula might be found. Hoover was a strong supporter of disarmament, principally for economic reasons. He hoped that even the nervous French could be coaxed into an agreement that would allow reduction of armaments by one-third. It seemed so logical; together the great powers could save a billion dollars a year, and the savings for the American taxpayer would be over $200 million.[49] The appeal of disarmament to the public and the personal interest Hoover gave it made it impossible for MacArthur and other Army and Navy leaders to brush the issue aside.

One of the often suggested substitutes for arms limitation (the word *disarmament* was a misnomer; hardly anyone, even among the most ardent pacifists, saw much of a chance for total disarmament) was an agreement to abolish "aggressive" or "offensive" weapons, which included submarines and bombers. Submarines and bombers were not only burdens on the taxpayers of the great powers that maintained them, but there were unsettled moral questions regarding their use. Submarines had been used against ocean liners carrying noncombatants. Likely targets for bombers were cities and industrial areas. Suggestions to abolish these weapons had considerable appeal. MacArthur's analysis emphasized such points. While years later as an old man he would say, "Our ideal must be eventually the abolition of war"; in the early 1930s, he agreed with Aristotle that only the dead had seen the end of war. Still, as a harried chief of staff trying to keep an army together during the Depression, he could discern at least two worthwhile purposes for disarmament: "(1) to save on appropriations so that the nations' preparations for national defense would not eat too deeply into their budgets; (2) to make war, when it came, less destructive to private property."[50]

In a remarkably candid conversation, MacArthur, on 4 April 1932, told Norman Davis, the chief American delegate to the Geneva Conference, and Jay Pierrepont Moffat, chief of the Division of Western Europe Affairs in the State Department, that he could support a proposal to abolish military aviation. Then for three quarters of an hour, Davis and Moffat listened while the general expounded "his theories as to the future of the Army." After the meeting, Moffat, as was his habit, carefully recorded the conversation in his diary. He wrote that the "essential points" of MacArthur's argument were

(1) Aviation was the newest branch of the service and the most expensive. Between 25 and 35 per cent [sic] of our Army budget was already devoted to aviation and Trubee Davison, Assistant Secretary of War, was constantly coming back demanding an additional 15 to 20 million dollars each year. (2) Its value as an instrument of war was still undemonstrated. For instance, in the Shanghai fighting where the Japanese had had 100 planes in the air unopposed and were able to bomb constantly a limited area with impunity, they did remarkably little damage to the 19th Chinese Army although they succeeded in destroying four hundred million dollars worth of civilian property and dispossessing 10,000 noncombatants. (3) That the whole tendency of war, since the idea of the Prussian staff had become generally accepted was to regard it as a struggle between whole nations rather than between professional organizations. Effectively to arm all nations or to provide the Army and Navy with weapons that could subdue an entire nation was beyond the economic scope of any power and was more than any other factor driving the world to bankruptcy. It cost no more than it would decades ago to keep the same number of men under arms. It was the exorbitant cost of new auxiliary machines of war, such as heavy artillery, tanks, aviation, et cetera, that was making our defense cost so many times its prewar level. Money spent on aviation was money thrown away as when the equipment was used up, there was no salvage value left. If all nations of the world could agree to give up military and naval aviation, the effect upon budgets would be greater than it is possible to calculate. As it is, with the pressure of economy and decreased appropriations, he feared

that his Army would be destroyed, as in order to keep up a new and dramatic arm in which the public is interested and on whose retention it insists, the time may come when we will have to reduce the other branches below the point of safety. In his idea, our ultimate aim should be to obtain an agreement on the part of all nations that they would give no government support in any form to aviation. In other words, to give up military and naval aviation in their entirety and not to subsidize directly or indirectly civilian aviation. He admitted that this was too radical a solution but felt it should be the ultimate goal.[51]

Secretary Stimson was shocked at the chief of staff's "radical ideas of getting rid of military aviation."[52] MacArthur, he told Moffat, "was concerned with his budget and not thinking of all the occasions when aviation had been useful."[53] And the general's concerns were not ended with victory over Congressman Collins in the budget battle for FY 1933. To attract votes of hard-pressed taxpayers in the presidential election of 1932, Hoover promised two months before election day that he intended to cut the federal budget for FY 1934 by half a billion. For the War Department, this meant a budget of $277,700,000, which was $43,200,000 less than requested. The Republican Party platform declared that under Republican administration the Army had been reduced to the "irreducible minimum consistent with the self-reliance, self-respect and security of this country."[54] The Democrats promised even greater economies, and their victory at the polls in November must have seemed ominous to MacArthur and the General Staff.

That Same Old Chestnut

One of the delegates to the Democratic National Convention in 1932 and an ardent supporter of Franklin D. Roosevelt in the presidential campaign was none other than the irrepressible Billy Mitchell. His presence on the Roosevelt bandwagon raised speculation that the new administration would back proposals for that old idea that had been alternately criticized and touted for years—a department of national defense. In the previous Congress, several bills had sought to create such a department in the name of economy and efficiency. With virtually everyone in government supporting the need for reduced expenditures to counter the Depression, the promise of savings through reorganization of the military establishment was appealing. How much savings was the question asked by many, and the House Committee on Expenditures in the Executive Departments, better known as the Economy Committee, held hearings to find an answer. The committee reported that the consolidation of the War and Navy departments would save between $50 million and $100 million per year.[55] "Not so!" retorted Army leaders. "It would be inefficient, uneconomical, and uselessly cumbersome," said MacArthur.[56] Why reorganize what is already the envy of military men the world over. "In the truest sense of the word," said Secretary Hurley, we already have a department of national defense, "headed by the President as constitutional Commander in Chief."[57]

While Air Corps leaders generally disagreed with their War Department superiors, they were hesitant to support an immediate reorganization of the military. They apparently wanted first to secure their position against the Navy. In the Air Corps Plans Division, a young lieutenant named Thomas D. White wrote a study showing Navy duplication of Army aviation functions and the advantages of merging Army and Navy aviation. The implication was that all unnecessary duplications were those presently in the Navy budget.[58] In hearings before the House Committee on Military Affairs, General Foulois, testified against critics of an independent air force, not because he favored a department of national defense but because he was concerned by criticism that the present Air Corps was receiving about its effectiveness. Rep. Charles H. Martin (D-Ore.), one of the members of the committee, had said things "so derogatory to the Air Corps that I could not let them go unchallenged." Martin was a former assistant chief of staff of the Army and an outspoken opponent of a unified air force. He had told the press that "if you turn those air birds loose, you will have to organize something like the Veterans Bureau to take care of the appropriations to keep them going. They are the most extravagant, undisciplined people on earth. . . . Those fellows have no sense of economy."[59] Foulois told the committee that Martin's remarks showed "a pitiful lack of knowledge regarding the administration and operation of the Army Air Corps." No branch of the Army, he said, was more efficient than the Air Corps. As for a unified air force under a department of national defense, he suggested an "exhaustive investigation" of the Army and Navy air-expansion program before any legislation for a new military establishment. Congress made no exhaustive investigation in that session and neither did it pass legislation for reorganization of the Army and Navy.

The House vote on the most promising of the department of national defense measures in the spring of 1932 was 135 for and 153 against; in the new Roosevelt administration the vote could easily go the other way.[60] Roosevelt was evidently considering it. Mitchell's ideas impressed him. "You gave me so many tantalizing glimpses of a subject on which you are so well qualified to speak," he told Mitchell in a letter shortly after the election, "that I was tempted to set an immediate date for the talk you suggested."[61] The two men did meet in New York in early January 1933 and Mitchell gave the president-elect "a little diagram" in which he outlined his proposal for a department of national defense.[62]

It appeared that the odds might now favor united air forces as an equal arm with the Army and Navy under a department of national defense. Army leaders viewed the situation with alarm, and irony of ironies, some airmen, now that it appeared they might realize their dreams, were not so sure they were ready for consolidation with naval aviation. Arnold wrote to Maj W. G. Kilner in the Office of the Chief of the Air Corps: "I can think of nothing at the present time in such a consolidation which the Navy would not 'do us out of our teeth,' this mainly because they have more senior officers in their establishment than we have." The Navy Department, he argued, had always given its Bureau of Aeronautics far greater consideration than the War Department had given the Air Corps and now was in a much better position to take advantage of reorganization if the Democratic Party carried out its plans to establish a department of national defense. Arnold warned that the Navy was preparing for such an eventuality. Consider, he said, the West Coast air maneuvers planned for February 1933 in which the Navy "gracefully turns over to the Army Air Corps a large section of the West Coast for defense." This sudden display of cooperation by the Navy was out of character. More likely it was the intention to place the Air Corps "on the spot." Army airmen had embarrassed themselves with the *Mount Shasta* fiasco the previous summer, and they could embarrass themselves again if they did not find out "where the Navy has stacked the cards against us." And then, Arnold warned, "we will have our 'dear friend' Admiral Moffett make a statement that the Army has completely demonstrated its inability to cope with coastal patrol problems and must confine its activities to operations over land." It would be a major coup for the Navy. "Now I am not a hunter of trouble," he concluded, "but I believe that everybody in Washington should see and realize the serious side of these February maneuvers, particularly now that the Democratic party is in control."[63] Arnold's worries were unfounded, for the February 1933 maneuvers were cancelled as an economy measure and President Roosevelt eventually decided against putting his administration behind the proposal to reorganize the military. Arnold's attitude, however, spoke reams about the extent to which intraservice and intrabranch competitions over missions and budget dominated the thinking of Army and Navy officers.

Instead of debatable savings from reorganization of the War and Navy departments, the Roosevelt administration chose a more direct method of fulfilling the campaign promise to reduce federal spending, particularly for national defense. Huge armies, said the president in his message to Congress on 16 March 1933, "continually rearmed with improved offensive weapons, constitute a recurring charge. This, more than any other factor, today, is responsible for governmental deficits and threatened bankruptcy."[64] The president was speaking of a worldwide problem and his remarks were meant to condemn offensive rather than defensive weaponry. The United States Army was neither large nor, to the chagrin of Army and especially Air Corps leaders, armed with the most "improved offensive weapons." Nevertheless, strong sentiment in the new administration against military expenditure boded ill for the Army. On 28 March in what Public Works Administrator Harold L. Ickes described as the "saddest Cabinet meeting yet," Roosevelt's Director of the Budget Lewis Douglas outlined the president's plan for balancing the budget.[65] He would slash $90 million from Army appropriations for FY 1934. Included in the president's plan were provisions for putting three thousand to four thousand officers on furlough at half pay, discharging twelve thousand enlisted men, suspending or reducing flight pay for military aviators, and empowering the president to cancel contracts.[66]

"This was a stunning blow to national defense," MacArthur said in his annual report for 1933, and he fought it with everything he had, eventually coming into conflict with Roosevelt.[67] Exact details of the behind-the-scenes struggle between the two men may never be known. It was alleged that in a heated argument in Roosevelt's bedroom at the White House (the president often received visits from aides and conducted business from his bedroom in the forenoon), MacArthur threatened to resign and oppose the president publicly on the issue. After this confrontation, the general was so upset that he became physically ill and vomited on the White House lawn.

Whether Roosevelt changed his mind because of such a threat cannot be verified; nevertheless, he did change his mind. He directed the Budget Bureau to reconsider reductions in the War Department budget, and dropped the plan to furlough Regular officers. The War Department was allowed $225 million, still $45 million less than the sum originally appropriated.[68]

To get maximum benefit from the meager funds allowed by the administration, MacArthur laid down for the General Staff a set of principles to govern expenditures for FY 1934. With regard to the Air Corps, he declared that at least a fourth of the original estimate for aircraft should be spent, and that funds for operation of aircraft would have to be reduced below previously prescribed minimum amounts.[69] Foulois described them later as "the poverty days of the Air Service." The ground arms of the Army might have argued that they had been living in poverty for years.

One hope for relieving the poverty of all branches of the Army during the first years of the Roosevelt administration was the possibility of getting funds through the Public Works Administration

(PWA). One of the most important pieces of New Deal legislation, the National Industrial Recovery Act, provided $3.3 billion for public works. The General Staff prepared requests to be submitted to the PWA for projects totaling over $300 million, including $39 million to provide the Air Corps by the middle of 1936 with the 1,800 aircraft promised by the five-year program of 1926.[70] No one really expected that all the Army's requests would be approved, though there was optimism in Army circles that it might receive at least half of what was asked. In his personal appearance before the Public Works Board, Secretary of War George H. Dern outlined a plan to spend only $173 million.[71] Even this modest request from the Army irked Ickes, who had little sympathy for the War Department and contempt for MacArthur, who he believed was running the War Department. MacArthur, he said, "is the type of man who thinks when he gets to Heaven, God will step down from the great white throne and bow him into His vacated seat."[72] When Roosevelt approved much less than the Army requested, Ickes recorded the event in his diary with satisfaction:

> I lunched with the President today (Friday, October 20, 1933) to take up a number of matters with him, but he had so many things he wanted to talk about that I really didn't get through. However, he did scrutinize the list of public works that I submitted to. On the Army list that Secretary Dern got us to adopt yesterday on the theory that it had the prior approval of the President, he did just what he said he would do. He allowed $15 million for aviation for both the Army and Navy, and $10 million for motorization and mechanization of the Army. This was quite a contrast with the $172 million that Dern had us put through for the above. He also disapproved a considerable allocation for coast defense purposes.[73]

The $7,500,000 of PWA funds allotted the Air Corps would eventually be spent on 64 bombers and 30 attack planes.[74] In view of the short "useful" life of aircraft in its combat fleet, this would merely keep the Air Corps from slipping in strength. Expansion had stopped, and for how long was uncertain. Airmen were distressed. They had become used to expansion guaranteed by law (fig. 2). The five-year program, though it never reached its goal, ended de facto if not de jure. Since the program began, the Air Corps had increased in combat strength while other combat arms of the Army were shrinking. A total of 6,240 men were taken from other arms to fill Air Corps ranks. They came from Infantry, Cavalry, Field Artillery, Coast Artillery and Engineers as well as lesser branches—Ordnance, Finance, the Army Music School—even a man from the Indian Scouts (fig. 3). Now the flow of men and money from other branches had stopped, and it would not start again if Army planners had their way. The War Plans Division, said Brig Gen Charles E. Kilbourne (its new chief) to MacArthur, "does not recommend the initiation of a new Five-Year Program for the Air Corps at present. . . .

THE GREAT DEPRESSION

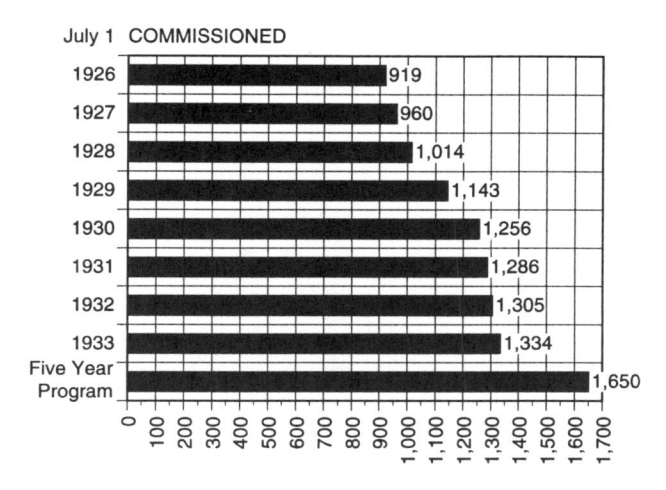

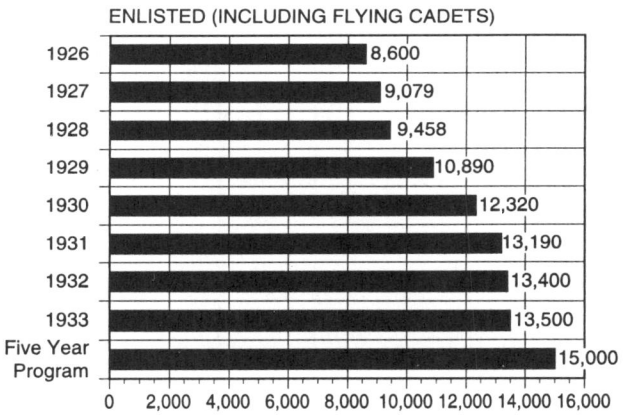

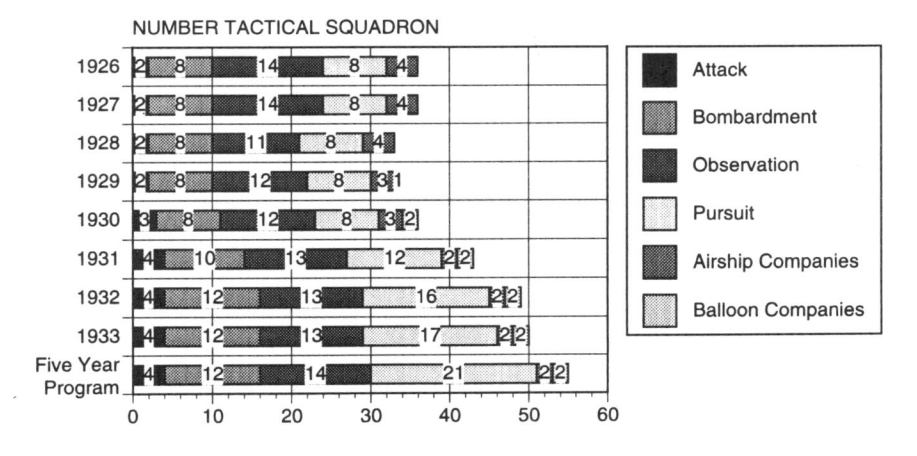

July 1 COMMISSIONED

Year	Value
1926	919
1927	960
1928	1,014
1929	1,143
1930	1,256
1931	1,286
1932	1,305
1933	1,334
Five Year Program	1,650

ENLISTED (INCLUDING FLYING CADETS)

Year	Value
1926	8,600
1927	9,079
1928	9,458
1929	10,890
1930	12,320
1931	13,190
1932	13,400
1933	13,500
Five Year Program	15,000

NUMBER TACTICAL SQUADRON

Year	Attack	Bombardment	Observation	Pursuit	Airship Companies	Balloon Companies
1926	2	8	14	8		4
1927	2	8	14	8		4
1928	2	8	11	8		4
1929	2	8	12	8	3	1
1930	3	8	12	8	3	2
1931	4	10	13	12	2	2
1932	4	12	13	16	2	2
1933	4	12	13	17	2	2
Five Year Program	4	12	14	21	2	2

Figure 2. Annual Strength of the Air Corps

THE ARMY AND ITS AIR CORPS

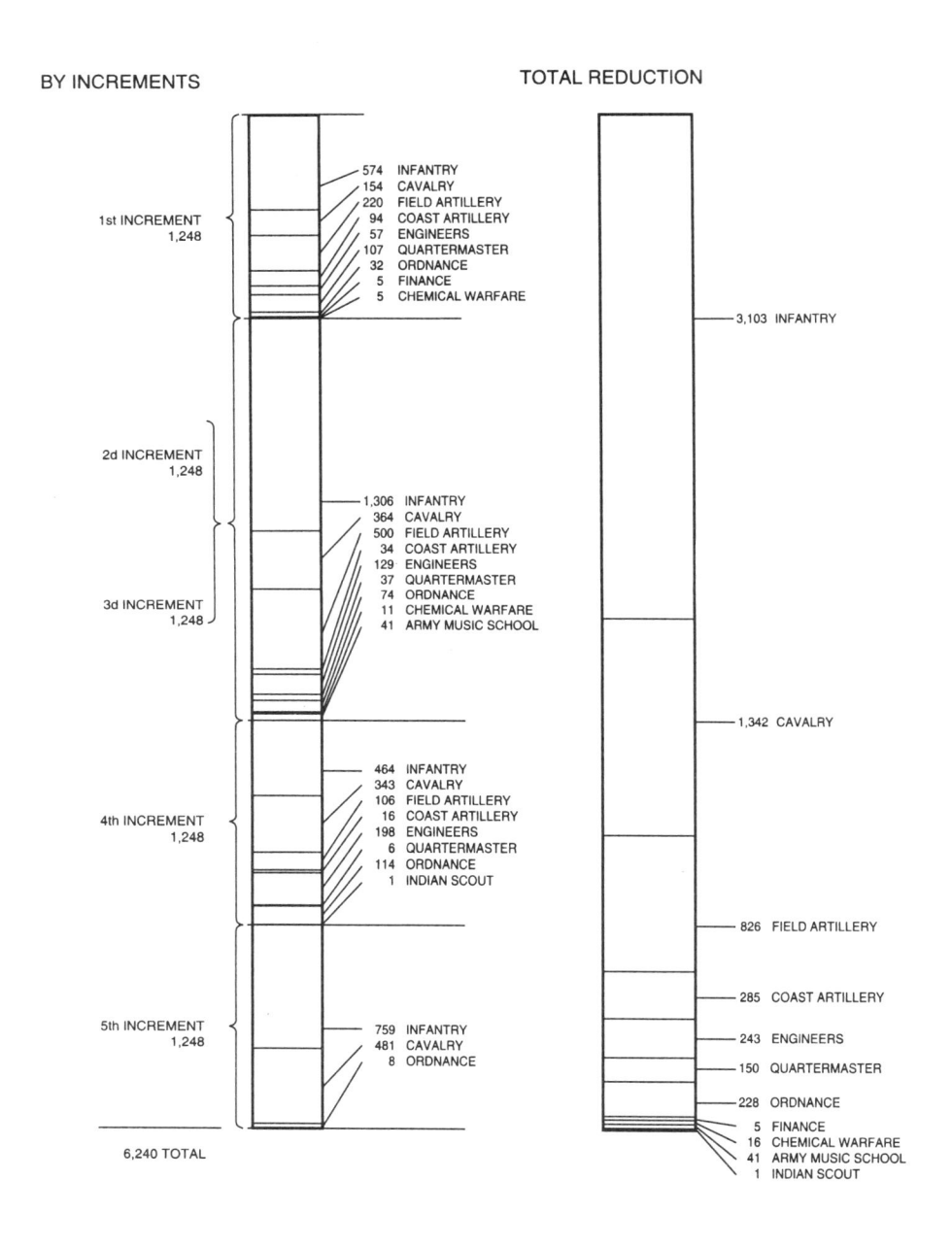

BY INCREMENTS

1st INCREMENT 1,248
- 574 INFANTRY
- 154 CAVALRY
- 220 FIELD ARTILLERY
- 94 COAST ARTILLERY
- 57 ENGINEERS
- 107 QUARTERMASTER
- 32 ORDNANCE
- 5 FINANCE
- 5 CHEMICAL WARFARE

2d INCREMENT 1,248

3d INCREMENT 1,248
- 1,306 INFANTRY
- 364 CAVALRY
- 500 FIELD ARTILLERY
- 34 COAST ARTILLERY
- 129 ENGINEERS
- 37 QUARTERMASTER
- 74 ORDNANCE
- 11 CHEMICAL WARFARE
- 41 ARMY MUSIC SCHOOL

4th INCREMENT 1,248
- 464 INFANTRY
- 343 CAVALRY
- 106 FIELD ARTILLERY
- 16 COAST ARTILLERY
- 198 ENGINEERS
- 6 QUARTERMASTER
- 114 ORDNANCE
- 1 INDIAN SCOUT

5th INCREMENT 1,248
- 759 INFANTRY
- 481 CAVALRY
- 8 ORDNANCE

6,240 TOTAL

TOTAL REDUCTION
- 3,103 INFANTRY
- 1,342 CAVALRY
- 826 FIELD ARTILLERY
- 285 COAST ARTILLERY
- 243 ENGINEERS
- 150 QUARTERMASTER
- 228 ORDNANCE
- 5 FINANCE
- 16 CHEMICAL WARFARE
- 41 ARMY MUSIC SCHOOL
- 1 INDIAN SCOUT

Figure 3. Reduction in Other Arms to Permit Increases in Air Corps under Five-Year Plan

The fact that our military aviation is second or third in the world, and the Army as a whole seventeenth, indicates the advisability of a balance in estimates so as to develop at least a balanced expeditionary force for the Army, and to carry forward many important projects now lagging for lack of appropriations, before further expansion of our air arm."[75]

In the way that victories sometime turn out to be less than anticipated, the men of the Air Corps had forced the creation of their own arm within the War Department and managed a five-year plan, only to see a chance event—the Great Depression—come along and turn the victory into at least a stalemate and maybe even a defeat. With technology moving ahead so rapidly, it was disheartening to see appropriations cut down, year after year—even if, relatively considered, the Air Corps was getting more than the other branches of the Army. Just when the inventions had brought the promises of the World War to fulfillment—when the airplane had become a serious instrument of war, developing along the lines that were becoming evident in the last year or two of the World War—the Depression had intervened. Too, an aircraft industry at last had been established in the United States, so that even a year or two of hard times within the Air Corps would not reduce the industry to nothing. The Depression had again raised the old budget problems, bringing allies to the leaders of the War Department who for their own reasons were not greatly in favor of the "wild blue" dreams of the Air Corps enthusiasts led by Mitchell and his coterie of visionary supporters.

By the beginning of the administration of President Roosevelt, the outlook for the Air Corps was bleak. Most Army leaders agreed with General Kilbourne of War Plans, and Army planning would reflect their attitude. But the Air Corps would not stay down. Events in 1934 would take over, most notably as in 1925–26, when the Mitchell affair forced creation of the Air Corps and its five-year program. Forces outside the Army again would push the Air Corps ahead.

Notes

1. Quoted in John W. Killigrew, "The Impact of the Great Depression on the Army, 1929–1936" (PhD diss., Indiana University, 1960), 147.
2. Ibid., 20–21.
3. *New York Times*, 26 and 27 August 1929.
4. Killigrew, 28–29.
5. Ibid., 20. See also "Notes on the Survey," 26 October 1929, in Summerall manuscripts (MSS), LOC. General Summerall penciled at the top of the first page: "Seen only by President Hoover and Secretary Good. They agreed on its conclusions."
6. "Notes on the Survey."
7. Ibid.
8. The report of Fechet's board is in the files of the Adjutant General (AG) 580 (1-20-30), Record Group (RG) 407, National Archives (NA). See also memorandum by Trubee Davison, 5 December 1929, Records of the Army Air Force, Central Decimal

Files 032, RG 18, NA. Both Fechet and Davison complained in their annual reports of shortages in the Air Corps because of lack of funds, *New York Times*, 18 and 28 November 1929.

9. Edwin H. Rutkowski, *The Politics of Military Aviation Procurement, 1926–1934: A Study in the Political Assertion of Consensual Values* (Columbus, Ohio: Ohio State University Press, 1966), 43–45.

10. Diary of Henry L. Stimson, 1 November 1930, Yale University Library, New Haven, Connecticut.

11. Killigrew, 55.

12. Ibid., 56–57.

13. See *Annual Report of the War Department, 1930* (Washington, D.C.: GPO, 1930), 139–40. The evolution of this report can be seen in "Notes Used for the Report" in Summerall MSS.

14. D. Clayton James, *The Years of MacArthur*, vol. 1, *1880–1941* (Boston: Houghton Mifflin, 1970), 355–56.

15. Ibid., 359–61; Killigrew, 118–19; Frazier Hunt, *The Untold Story of Douglas MacArthur* (New York: Devin-Adair Co., 1954), 140; and Douglas MacArthur, *Reminiscences* (New York: McGraw-Hill, 1964), 100.

16. Killigrew, 64–65.

17. James, 356.

18. *Army and Navy Journal*, 16 May 1930. Eventually there were 53 posts closed as a result of this decision.

19. Ibid.

20. President Herbert Hoover to secretary of war, letter, 15 May 1931; and President Herbert Hoover to secretary of Navy, letter, 15 May 1931, War Plans Division (WPD) 888-68, RG 165, NA.

21. Patrick Hurley to Gen Douglas MacArthur, letter, 20 May 1931, WPD 888-68, RG 165, NA.

22. Memorandum for record with the Proceedings of the Special Committee, undated, WPD 888-89, RG 165, NA.

23. Hurley to MacArthur; and David S. Ingalls to Adm William V. Pratt, letter, 20 May 1931, both in WPD 888-68, RG 165, NA.

24. Memorandum for the secretary of war, 7 August 1931, WPD 888-68, RG 165, NA.

25. Ibid.

26. Gen Douglas MacArthur to Adm William V. Pratt, letter, 24 July 1931, WPD 888-68, RG 165, NA.

27. Adm William V. Pratt to Gen Douglas MacArthur, letter, 1 August 1931; and Gen Douglas MacArthur to Adm William V. Pratt, letter, 1 August 1931. Both are filed in WPD 888-68, RG 165, NA.

28. Memorandum for the secretary of war, 7 August 1931.

29. Gen George S. Simonds to Maj Gen George V. H. Moseley, letter, 11 August 1931, WPD 888-68, RG 165, NA. Simonds suggests that MacArthur might want to take the matter up with the president. MacArthur and President Hoover were quite close. "There is on file in the War Plans Division," wrote Summerall, "an abbreviation of this study which I thought the Chief of Staff might want to use in case he wished to submit something to the President in response to his request for Joint Board action. There is also attached to it a draft of a covering letter to the President, explaining briefly the Joint Board deadlock."

30. Gen Douglas MacArthur to Col J. Clawson Roop, letter, 14 August 1931, AG 580 (8-14-31), RG 407, NA. Earlier in June, Roop had held a conference with Army and Navy representatives to "secure information for consideration in connection with the budget estimates as well as any supplemental or deficiency estimates which may be submitted to provide funds for the two aviation services and to try and get this information in such form and detail as may furnish equivalent, and where practicable,

comparable information from the two services." See "Army and Navy Air Conference," 17 June 1931, AG 580 (6-31), RG 407, NA.

31. Memorandum for the secretary of war, subject: The Needs of the United States in Air Forces, 14 August 1931, AG 580 (8-11-31), RG 407, NA. The original of this study with General MacArthur's signature and a handwritten note at the bottom of the last page, indicating he discussed it personally with Secretary Hurley, can be found in AG 580 (8-11-31), RG 407, NA. Other copies are available in WPD 888-68, RG 165, NA. Gen Benjamin D. Foulois, in his memoirs, claimed "MacArthur gave me the job of making an independent study showing both Army and Navy needs in aviation." Foulois quotes passages from his study that are identical to passages in the WPD study indicating that the WPD study incorporated inputs from an Air Corps study. Whether Foulois was actually the author of the Air Corps study might, however, be questioned since General Simonds indicated in a letter to General Moseley that Maj Horace Hickam was the source of Air Corps inputs into the WPD study. See Benjamin D. Foulois and Carroll V. Glines, *From the Wright Brothers to the Astronauts: The Memoirs of Benjamin D. Foulois* (New York: McGraw-Hill, 1968), 219–20; and Simonds to Moseley, 11 August 1931.

32. The maneuvers got a great deal of press coverage. For examples see *New York Times*, 2 May, 9 May, 12 May, 16 May, 17 May, 23 May, 24 May, 25 May, and 31 May 1931. For accounts and comments by participants, see Foulois and Glines, 212–15; and Henry H. Arnold, *Global Mission* (New York: Harper, 1949), 130–31. A lively account of the maneuvers is also available in Robert S. Allen and Drew Pearson, *More Merry-Go-Round* (New York: Liveright, Inc., 1932), 216–18.

33. Allen and Pearson, 216–17.

34. There are accounts of the *Mount Shasta* incident in Foulois and Glines, 215–18; and Allen and Pearson, 272–73. See also *New York Times*, 10 August, 12 August, 14 August, and 15 August 1931.

35. *Army and Navy Journal*, 15 August 1931.

36. *New York Times*, 30 August 1931. In the Simonds MSS, LOC, there is a folder on the *Mount Shasta* incident with a study blaming the poor bombing on the difficulties of crosswind bombing.

37. Col Hap Arnold to Maj Carl Spaatz, letter, 26 August 1931, Arnold MSS, LOC.

38. *Army and Navy Journal*, 12 October, 8 November, and 12 December 1931. See also *New York Times*, 20 December 1931.

39. One of the economy measures supported by MacArthur in the spring of 1931 was the disbanding of Maj Adna R. Chaffee's experimental tank force at Fort George G. Meade, Maryland. See James, 358. In a speech, Major Chaffee agreed that since the United States is a nation of automobiles and trucks, basic experimentation in the technology of mechanization can be left to private industry. See a copy of the speech in Simonds MSS.

40. James, 356–57, 426–27; and Allen and Pearson, 200–201, 221, 223–24.

41. "The Reminiscences of Benjamin D. Foulois," 1960, 43, Oral History Collection, Columbia University, 43 (hereinafter cited as Foulois, OHC).

42. Killigrew, 116–17; MacArthur, *Reminiscences*, 100; James, 359–60; and Hunt, 139–40. Rep. Ross Collins first announced that he was considering a proposal to cut the officer corps by four thousand rather than two thousand officers. This he claimed would result in a savings of $20 million. *Army and Navy Journal*, 3 October 1931.

43. Killigrew, 107–108. Foulois felt Collins was the Air Corps's best friend in Congress. Foulois, in his oral history interviews in 1960, told about his first experience with Collins:

> He [Collins] interrogated me on that first session from start to finish, on a great many subjects which had nothing to do with aviation but had a lot to do with the attitude of the General Staff and the War Department. I answered frankly and sincerely; since I was under oath, I just simply assumed I had to tell the truth, the whole truth, etc. . . . He took me to lunch that day, in the lunchroom

of the House of Representatives, and he finally said to me, "Now, tell me, why is it that you can come up here and answer any questions fully and quietly without reservation, and I can't get a single officer in the War Department to do that?"

. . . When that first bill came up for writing the final draft of the bill, Mr. Cowans [sic] called me up, told me to come on up there, they were in the process of writing the final draft there, and he asked me to go over it. I went over the aviation section of it, and he had boosted our appropriations that had been alloted [sic] to us by the War Department, taken away from the War Department and put it in our part of the bill. He did that every year while I was Chief. He, to me, was the man who defended those bills on the floor of the House, from that first bill, when he got up there and started talking about details and said, "Gentlemen, I got that from a man who faced God Almighty in the air for 25 years."

. . . Cowan [sic] had charge of the War Department appropriations. . . . The Appropriations Committee handled all the money, so he was in charge of the subcommittee to handle all the War Department money. All through our four years, our starvation period. . . .

I'll tell you what happened in 1929–30, right after Fouchez's [sic] administration and into mine—I handled it up until Mr. Roosevelt came in, and after—and you had a hard job to get those extra dollars anywhere then. He [Collins] just kept us alive. I give him more credit than any man in Congress during my days for keeping us alive financially. I had a lot of friends, both in the House and in the Senate; it was my policy to make friends there. But the man who did the valuable work on that, whether in committees or in the House, was Ross Collins. (43–45)

44. *Congressional Record*, 72d Cong., 1st sess., 9932–35.
45. *Army and Navy Journal*, 13 February 1932; and Killigrew, 130.
46. *Army and Navy Journal*, 16 July 1932.
47. Allen and Pearson, 204–5.
48. Quoted in James, 362, and in Killigrew, 122.
49. *Republican Campaign Textbook, 1932* (Washington, D.C.: Republican National Committee, 1932) 27.
50. Nancy Harvison Hooker, ed., *The Moffat Papers: Selections from the Diplomatic Journals of Jay Pierrepont Moffat, 1919–1943* (Cambridge, Mass.: Harvard University Press, 1956), 58–60, 68–69, 90–92. See also *Paper Relating to the Foreign Relations of the United States, 1932* (Washington, D.C.: GPO, 1932), vol. 1, 61–73, 213–14. In Great Britain Winston Churchill fought against so-called "qualitative disarmament" arguing that "almost every conceivable weapon can be used in defense or offense; either by an aggressor or by the innocent victim of his assault," Winston Churchill, *The Second World War*, vol. 1, *The Gathering Storm* (Boston: Houghton Mifflin, 1948), 71–73. General Simonds, who went to Europe with the US delegation, warned against a straight percentage cut in world armaments. "Based on length of coastlines and frontiers, population and total area," he said, "our Regular Army, including its air component if far smaller than those of our first class powers, including their air forces. . . . A 10% cut in budgets may easily destroy a small army as a well balanced fighting force, while a larger army will have much more freedom of action in making its reductions." Found in "Notes on Proposal to Reduce the Budget of the US Army for Purposes of Reduction of World Armaments," 23 November 1931, Simonds MSS.
51. Hooker, 63–64.
52. Stimson diary, 3 June 1932.
53. Hooker, 69–70.
54. *Republican Campaign Textbook, 1932*, 86–87.
55. Memorandum, Economy Committee, in AG 580 (8-4-34), RG 407, NA.

56. Report of the chief of staff, *Annual Report of the War Department, 1932*, vol. 1, 94–102. Quoted in James, 362–63. See also Killigrew, 141.

57. "Honorable Patrick J. Hurley in statement on H.R. 7012, January 14, 1932," in AG 580 (8-4-34), RG 407, NA.

58. Memorandum by Lt Thomas D. White, "Financial savings which would result from a unification of the Army Air Corps and Naval Aviation," 3 February 1932, Central Decimal Files 032, RG 18, NA.

59. Foulois, OHC, 222.

60. AG 580 (8-4-34), RG 407, NA.

61. Franklin D. Roosevelt to Billy Mitchell, letter, 19 November 1932, Mitchell MSS, LOC. Mitchell's answer is also in his papers, Billy Mitchell to Franklin D. Roosevelt, letter, 21 December 1932.

62. Billy Mitchell to Franklin D. Roosevelt, letter, 17 January 1933, Mitchell MSS.

63. Hap Arnold to Maj W. G. Kilner, letter, 10 November 1932, Arnold MSS. See also Maj W. G. Kilner to Hap Arnold, letter, 22 November 1932; and Hap Arnold to Brig Gen R. S. Pratt, letter, 14 December 1932, both in Arnold MSS.

64. *Public Papers and Addresses of Franklin D. Roosevelt*, vol. 2, *The Year of Crisis, 1933* (New York: Random House, 1938–1950), 192.

65. Harold L. Ickes, *The Secret Diary of Harold L. Ickes*, vol. 1, *The First Thousand Days, 1933–1936* (New York: Simon & Schuster, 1953), 10–11.

66. Killigrew, 231. See also *New York Times*, 19 April, 21 April, and 7 May 1933. The Air Corps reacted quickly to the threat to cut flying pay. Instead of reducing flying pay that was estimated to save $172,000 a year, General Foulois proposed dropping from the Air Corps 25 officers assigned from other branches, limiting the pay of flying cadets to $1,500 per year, cutting down on nonflying officers, and reducing administrative costs. Cutting flying pay, he argued, would destroy the morale of the Air Corps. See "MacArthur Cites Need of Officers," *New York Times*, 27 April 1933.

67. Report of the chief of staff in *Annual Report of the War Department, 1933*, 15; Hunt, 152; and MacArthur, *Reminiscences*, 110–11. That Roosevelt had a respect for the political potential of MacArthur was revealed in a conversation reported by Rexford G. Tugwell in *The Democratic Roosevelt: A Biography of Franklin D. Roosevelt* (Garden City, N.Y.: Doubleday, 1957), 349–50. Roosevelt described MacArthur as a potential "man on horseback," whose strong appeal among right-wing elements made him "one of the two most dangerous men in the country." The other was the Louisiana demagogue, Huey P. Long. When Roosevelt took office there was some question as to whether he would retain MacArthur as chief of staff. FDR settled the rumors. "The office of Chief of Staff is not a political office," he said, "it would be a sad day for the country were it to so become. General MacArthur is serving under a four year appointment and that appointment runs the full period of four years." *Army and Navy Journal*, 2 September 1933.

68. Killigrew, 237–38.

69. Ibid.

70. Ibid., 262.

71. Ibid., 264.

72. Ickes, 71.

73. Ibid., 111.

74. Killigrew, 276; and *New York Times*, 22 October and 25 October 1933. An interesting sidelight of the procurement of airplanes was that the contracts had to go to aircraft companies which had not agreed to accept the "Code of Fair Competition" and other provisions of the National Recovery Act (NRA). In buying equipment for mechanization of the ground arm, Ford Motor Company was prohibited from bidding because it had not signed the "certificate of compliance with the automobile code, submitted to the NRA by the Automobile Chamber of Commerce." Ford built airplanes also. The Air Corps was offered a fairly large amount of Public Works Administration funds in a bill proposed by Sen. Hiram Bingham to train 100,000 civilian aviators. A similar proposal was presented by the American Eagle-Lincoln

THE ARMY AND ITS AIR CORPS

Aircraft Corporation. The Air Corps and the War Department opposed such a plan because as Secretary of War George H. Dern put it, "The War Department believes that every effort should be concentrated toward rounding out effectively the five-year Air Corps program authorized by Congress, and that any dispersion of federal funds on less essential projects is unwarranted except for the primary purpose of fostering commercial aviation." Quoted in Killigrew, 181–82.

75. Memorandum for General MacArthur, 8 April 1933. On 12 April, Gen Charles E. Kilbourne sent General MacArthur another memorandum listing "important projects requiring development other than the Air Corps." Heading the list was the need for an increase in personnel, but he also cited the need for new equipment for the ground arms. "There are but twelve armored cars on hand," he said, "while three hundred and twenty-eight are required for initial mobilization." He noted shortages in ammunition, antiaircraft equipment, and gas masks among others. A year later, Rep. Ross Collins described the condition of the Army as pitiable. Collins, being a disciple of Basil H. Liddell Hart, was of course concerned with the lack of mechanization. "We have 13 worthwhile tanks," he said, "we have 4 armored cars; we have 80 automatic rifles; and that is about all." *Congressional Record*, 73d Cong., 2d sess., 3939.

The Army and Its Air Corps
PHOTO SECTION
Photos Courtesy of the US AIR FORCE

Maj Gen Charles T. Menoher, first chief of the Air Service, 1920–21. He was a former field artillery officer who had commanded the 42d (Rainbow) Division in France.

Maj Gen Mason M. Patrick, chief of the Air Service, 1921–26

Brig Gen William "Billy" Mitchell in his Thomas–Morse MB-3, Selfridge Field, Michigan, 1922

The captured German battleship *Ostfriesland* suffers a hit from Mitchell's bombers, July 1921.

The Barling Bomber was a six-engined behemoth capable of carrying a 10,000-pound payload. However, it did not even have enough power to fly over the Appalachian Mountains.

The Mitchell court-martial begins, 28 October 1925. *Left to right:* Rep. Frank Reid, one of the defense counsels (Col Herbert White, the chief defense counsel is not in the picture); Mitchell; his wife, Betty, behind him; Sidney Miller, his father-in-law; Mrs. Arthur Young (Mitchell's sister Ruth); and Mitchell's brother-in-law, Arthur Young.

The Morrow Board, made up of highly respected men chosen by President Calvin Coolidge, assured the nation that there was no danger of attack from the air and denied that strategic bombing could break the will of a "high-spirited people." It rejected the call for a separate air force but recommended that the name of the Air Service be changed to the Air Corps.

Mitchell and *left*, Will Rogers after a flight at Bolling Field, Washington, D.C., 24 April 1925

Three Douglas World Cruisers of the round-the-world flight prepare to land at Dallas, Texas, on their return to Seattle, Washington, to complete the first flight around the world on 28 September 1924.

President Calvin Coolidge and Secretary of War John W. Weeks greet some of the round-the-world flyers. In back are Maj Gen Mason M. Patrick and Brig Gen Billy Mitchell.

Lt Russell L. Maughan beside his PW-8, in which he flew from coast to coast in a dawn-to-dusk flight, 23 June 1924

President Calvin Coolidge and Secretary of War Dwight Davis honor *left*, Lt Lester J. Maitland and *right,* Lt Albert F. Hegenberger at an awards ceremony, 29 September 1927. Maitland and Hegenberger had recently completed the first nonstop flight from California to Hawaii in the *Bird of Paradise*, a Fokker C-2 trimotor transport.

In 1929, the Air Corps captured a new world endurance record with a Fokker C-2 transport, the *Question Mark,* which was commanded by Maj Carl Spatz (correct spelling before 1938). Also among the crew were Capt Ira C. Eaker, Lt Elwood R. Quesada, Lt Harry A. Halverson, and SSgt Roy Hooe. Using in-flight refueling techniques developed in 1923, they kept the *Question Mark* aloft for almost 151 hours.

Pilots of the famous 94th Pursuit Squadron pose before one of their P-12s at Selfridge Field, Michigan, just prior to their historic flight using liquid oxygen for the first time in extended formation flights. Among the pilots were two future Air Force generals—*1st row, fourth from left,* Lt Emmett "Rosie" O'Donnell and *2d row, fourth from left,* Lt Harry A. Johnson.

A formation of P-12 pursuit planes from the 94th Pursuit Squadron, Selfridge Field, Michigan

Left to right: Brig Gen Benjamin D. Foulois, Secretary of War for Air F. Trubee Davison, Maj Gen James E. Fechet, and Brig Gen H. C. Pratt during the maneuvers of 1931. The maneuvers were in the form of demonstrations to acquaint the American people with the Air Corps and to give them a clear idea of the Army's air effort.

The Air Corps was thwarted in its attempt to establish a role in coastal defense with the bombing of the freighter *Mount Shasta* in August 1931 off the Virginia coast. Much to the chagrin of the Army and its fledgling Air Corps, two Coast Guard cutters had to send the ship to the bottom with two volleys fired into the hull at the waterline.

Maj Gen Benjamin D. Foulois, chief of the Air Corps, stands before a map showing the airmail routes to be covered by Army Air Corps pilots, February 1934.

A Curtiss B-2 Condor over Airmail Route 4 (the Salt Lake City–Los Angeles mail)

The Douglas B-7, designed as a fast day bomber, had fabric-covered wings, an all-metal fuselage, and hydraulically operated retractable landing gear. It flew airmail over the Salt Lake City–Oakland route in early 1934.

Charles A. Lindbergh opposed the decision to use the Army Air Corps to carry the airmail as "unwarranted and contrary to American principles."

Maj Gen Henry H. "Hap" Arnold, seen here as a lieutenant colonel in 1931, was appointed chief of the Army Air Corps in September 1938.

The Boeing B-9 bomber, a low-wing, all-metal monoplane, was introduced in the 1930s. Although it still had open cockpits, it had the "big bomber" look that raised the hopes of airmen who believed in strategic bombardment.

The Martin B-10 represented a new generation of bombers. It featured enclosed cockpits, a power-operated turret, and retractable landing gear.

The Boeing 299 was unveiled in 1935 and began undergoing flight testing as the XB-17. It was to make history in World War II as the rugged B-17 Flying Fortress.

Although the Douglas B-18 Bolo was not exactly what proponents of strategic bombing desired, the General Staff felt it was adequate for the time.

The Douglas XB-19, which first flew in 1941. With a wingspan of 212 feet, a 132-foot fuselage, and a rudder 42 feet high, it dwarfed other aircraft of its day.

Designed to meet the increasing performance of the new bombers, the Boeing P-26 Peashooter was the first all-metal monoplane fighter built for the Army Air Corps.

Aviation cadets illustrate "pylon eights" by using model airplanes, chalk, and string at Randolph Field, Texas, November 1940.

The Seversky P-35, a forerunner of the Republic P-47, was the first single-seat, all-metal pursuit plane with retractable landing gear and enclosed cockpit when it entered Air Corps service in 1937.

Chapter 5

The Airmail Crisis and the Creation of the GHQ Air Force

Friday, 9 March 1935, dawned cold and gray in Patchogue, New York. Winter weather, the worst in years according to old-timers, had for more than two weeks dealt most of the nation a series of freezing blizzards, squalls, and ice and wind storms. Patchogue, like every place in the northeast, was under a blanket of snow.

A Western Union messenger shuffled through the cold to the front steps of No. 15 Baker Street, the home of Mr. and Mrs. Richard Wienecke. Mrs. Wienecke answered the knock and nervously signed for the telegram the messenger had brought. Her son was an Army flyer and she had always feared for his safety. The telegram confirmed her worst fears:

DEEPLY REGRET TO ADVISE YOU THAT YOUR SON, LIEUT. OTTO WIENECKE, DIED AT 5 A.M. MARCH 9, AS A RESULT OF AN AIRPLANE ACCIDENT AT BURTON, OHIO, WHILE FLYING THE AIR MAIL. NO DETAILS OF ACCIDENT AVAILABLE.

COL. JOHN HOWARD

"The Army Has Lost the Art of Flying"

Lieutenant Wienecke, an experienced pilot with 1,280 hours flying time to his credit, had taken off from the Newark, New Jersey, airport in an 0-39 Curtiss Falcon shortly before midnight. His destination was Cleveland, Ohio, and the weather en route was forecast to be "not good but flyable." At Kybertown, Pennsylvania, he landed, refueled, and took off again. The weather had grown worse. By the time he approached Cleveland, the clouds were thick and low and it was snowing. About 5 A.M., flying dangerously low, he passed over a farmhouse about a mile northwest of Burton, Ohio. John Hess, the farmer who lived there, heard Wienecke's plane crash. "I was up and ready to go out to my morning chores," Hess said, "when I heard the plane." He grabbed a lantern and ran out to investigate. In his cornfield he found the plane among the stubble, its nose buried in the ground and its tail in the air. "I looked inside the ship," he said, "and I saw the pilot huddled forward. I shook his shoulder." But Otto Wienecke did not respond. His neck was broken.

Three more men died that day in the Army's airmail operation. At Cheyenne, Wyoming, Lt F. L. Howard and Lt A. R. Kerwin took off to familiarize themselves with the route to Salt Lake City, Utah. They were carrying no mail. Immediately after becoming airborne in their 0-38E, a Curtiss Falcon like Wienecke's but an earlier model, they experienced engine failure. Howard, at the controls, attempted to circle and "dead-stick" the Falcon back to Cheyenne airport. That required delicate flying, particularly in the thin air at Cheyenne, where the elevation was over 6,100 feet. He made a mistake, over-controlled, stalled, and plunged to the ground about 500 feet short of the runway. The aircraft burst into flames, and crews later had to use hacksaws to remove the charred bodies from the wreckage. The fourth death occurred just outside of Daytona Beach, Florida. Private E. B. Sell, the crew chief on a B-6A Keystone bomber, was killed when a fuel system malfunction forced his pilot, Lt W. N. Reid, to crash-land the big two-engined plane in a cyprus swamp. Sell was trying to solve the fuel problem by transferring gasoline from one tank to another with a hand pump when the impact threw him forward, smashing his skull against a cross brace in the fuselage.[1]

The deaths of Wienecke, Howard, Kerwin, and Sell brought to 10 the number of Army flyers killed in three weeks of airmail operations. This toll raised a storm of criticism in the press and Congress. President Franklin D. Roosevelt was assailed because it was he who had ordered the Army to fly the mail. A month earlier, on 9 February, he had told Postmaster General James A. Farley to cancel all commercial airmail contracts. A Senate investigating committee headed by Hugo L. Black (D-Ala.) had charged that through "collusion and fraud" involving Farley's Republican predecessor, Walter F. Brown, all but three of the 27 federal airmail contracts had been awarded to three large commercial aviation holding companies. Farley had advised Roosevelt to wait until 1 June to cancel the contracts. That would have given the Post Office Department time to call for new bids and there would have been no interruption in service. The president could see no reason for delay, particularly after Farley told him the Army could carry the mail if it became necessary.[2] The Army had flown the mail for a short time after the First World War and the chief of the Air Corps, Maj Gen Benjamin D. Foulois, had told Farley's assistant, Harlee Branch, that it could do it again. Referring to Foulois's decision to commit the Air Corps to fly the mail, Hap Arnold wrote years later, "I think it is doubtful if any other air leader in his place would have answered differently."[3] The Air Corps took great pride in its "can-do" spirit. Nevertheless, Foulois's decision was unwise. The task required skills and equipment the Air Corps did not have. Army pilots had little experience in cross-country flying and only a few had done any actual weather flying. Except for a handful of test models, Army planes were not equipped for blind flying. "If the weather is bad there is no object in sending an Army plane up," explained Maj Clifford A. Tinker. "In war we must see our objective. When the Army took over flying the mail there was no time to equip planes with instruments . . . no time to train men for the work."[4] Of course, not all the crashes could be linked to what has since been called "supervisory error"—to the poor judgment of those who made the high-level decisions—but there was sufficient evidence of supervisory error to give critics an argument. "That's legalized murder," said Eddie Rickenbacker after the first crashes in the Army airmail operation, and the phrase became a slogan in the press and Congress among enemies of the administration or of the Army.[5]

The pressure on the president to stop this "useless sacrifice of life" became intense.[6] On the morning of 10 March, Roosevelt summoned MacArthur and Foulois. After giving Foulois the tongue-lashing of his life, the president showed the generals a letter addressed to Secretary of War George H. Dern. He declared in the letter that he had given the Army the airmail assignment "on definite assurance . . . that the Army Air Corps could carry the mail." He conceded that the weather was partly responsible for the crashes. Nevertheless, he said, "the continuation of deaths in the Army Air Corps must stop," and he told Dern to "issue immediate orders to the Air Corps stopping all mail flights except on such routes, under such weather conditions and under such equipment and personnel conditions as will insure, as far as the utmost care can provide, against constant recurrence of fatal accidents."[7]

After the letter was made public, there was some debate over precisely who in the War Department had given the president "definite assurance . . . that the Army Air Corps could carry the mail." Neither MacArthur nor his deputy chief of staff, Maj Gen Hugh A. Drum, had been consulted before the airmail contracts were cancelled on 9 February. It appears the only assurance was that given by Foulois to Assistant Postmaster General Branch only hours before Roosevelt issued his executive order cancelling the contracts. It was a bad move. There had been no study of the problem nor any consultation with War Department leaders and other airmen. It was hardly the high-level "definite assurance" implied in the president's letter. MacArthur learned of the president's order to carry the mail when reporters asked him for his opinion.[8] Thus, he and other Army leaders were spared blame for the decision.

This did little to remove the onus of failure from the Army and its Air Corps. "The Army has lost the art of flying," said Billy Mitchell. "It can't fly. If any army aviator can't fly a mail route in any sort of weather, what would we do in a war?"[9] On the surface at least, it appeared that Mitchell's charge was true. The Air Corps set out to do something about it. Foulois grounded the Army airmail flyers, ordered the installation and testing of two-way radios and blind-flying instruments on all planes used for night runs, and removed from the airmail operation all but the "most experienced pilots available." Until the first of June, when the Army returned the job to commercial contractors, Air Corps leaders intended to prove that the Army could fly. They would be reasonably successful. While they could not avoid two more fatalities, the accident rate for the last two months of airmail flying would not approach that of the first two weeks. During the operation, Army pilots flew more than a million and a half miles and carried 777,389 pounds of mail. With the new B-10 bombers, delivered to the Air Corps during the operation, they set speed records on some routes. But as Foulois would later admit, it was not their successes that were important. "It was the failures, because the failures focused public attention on the inadequacies in our training and equipment." He blamed inadequacies on the "lack of Congressional interest and funds."[10]

Some observers would have disagreed with Foulois. But as to his admission of inadequacies in the Air Corps, there would have been no disagreement. Mitchell's question as to what we would do in a war demanded an answer. And the search for an answer raised other questions. Should the Army air arm be reorganized? Should it be reequipped? If so, with what sort of airplanes?

An "Air Plan for the Defense of the United States"

When Assistant Secretary of War F. Trubee Davison left office to run on the Republican ticket for lieutenant governor of New York in the 1932 election, there was concern among airmen that the General Staff would try to extend its control over the Air Corps.[11] Since then there had been an almost constant battle between the War Plans Division and General Foulois's staff. The issue was the so-called General Headquarters (GHQ) Air Force and its place in the nation's war plans. The GHQ Air Force was defined as a general reserve of attack, pursuit, and bombardment aviation to be concentrated under direct command of General Headquarters during wartime rather than parceled out to army and corps commanders. The Lassiter Board in 1924 had endorsed General Patrick's contention that such a force was necessary, and it had been War Department policy since that time that a GHQ Air Force would be incorporated in the Army's wartime organization. In peacetime it had seemed neither necessary nor economically feasible, except for occasional maneuvers. All attack, pursuit, and bombardment units were assigned to the corps under the direct command of corps commanders.

Details of the organization and use of the GHQ Air Force became an issue as a result of the reorganization of the Army during MacArthur's term as chief of staff (1930–35). To increase combat readiness, he decided to establish the command organization necessary to conduct a war. He set up a General Headquarters and four field army headquarters. Dividing the country into four army areas, he designated the senior corps commander in each area as an army commander. Every Regular officer, in addition to his peacetime duties, was given an assignment in the wartime organization to be assumed upon mobilization. MacArthur would become commanding general of field forces. Taking his cue from MacArthur, General Foulois contended that just as the chief of staff would take the field in wartime, so should the chief of the Air Corps. Foulois argued that he should be designated wartime commander of the GHQ Air Force, and since peacetime training and organization of GHQ Air Force units (attack, pursuit, bombardment, and GHQ observation) should parallel wartime operations and organization as closely as possible, he should therefore be given direct command of tactical units in peacetime.[12]

Brig Gen Charles E. Kilbourne, head of War Plans, believed that instead of expanding Foulois's control over Army airpower, it was advisable to "curtail it."[13] MacArthur apparently shared that opinion. He believed the chiefs of the arms such as the Air Corps should restrict themselves to administrative duties and not attempt to "build up command functions with respect to their field establishments and troops."[14] Command of tactical units in the field should be in the hands of field commanders. There was also fear, perhaps not felt as strongly by MacArthur as other officers on the General Staff, that giving the chief of the Air Corps tactical control of field forces in peacetime "would virtually separate the Air Corps from the rest of the Army," making combined training of air and ground forces difficult if not impossible.[15] Furthermore, Kilbourne argued that such an extension of the duties of the chief of the Air Corps would be more responsibility than one man could handle. "My studies and your analysis of your duties," he told Foulois, "strengthen my conviction that you are already overloaded and that the overload would be increased in war. In brief, I feel that the Chief of the Air Corps should be relieved of tactical control in peace (provided a competent general officer can be found, and by 'competent' I include adherence to the doctrines you promulgate) and should devote himself entirely to Zone of Interior duties in war." He disagreed with Foulois's analysis comparing the position of chief of the Air Corps with that of chief of staff. MacArthur's responsibility, Kilbourne reminded Foulois, "is to be of a general nature while you as chief of an arm having also supply and technical responsibilities, must have many intricate details to decide." He added that the function of chief of the Air Corps was "supervision of technical development, supply program, personnel procurement, replacement training, etc."; it was the job of a specialist, too complicated to allow him "to turn over to a deputy and take the field."[16]

Thus, the recommendations of the chief of the Air Corps and of the General Staff for command arrangement of the GHQ Air Force within the four-army plan were different: the chief of the Air Corps recommended that the GHQ Air Force be under his command, and the General Staff recommended that command of GHQ Air Force be given to a "competent" general officer loyal to the doctrines promulgated by the chief of the Air Corps but responsible directly to the chief of staff.

There was also the problem of the GHQ Air Force's size. In June 1933, the General Staff asked the chief of the Air Corps for recommendations as to how the GHQ Air Force should be used in war plans Red, Red-Orange, and Green—plans for war with either Britain, a coalition of Britain and Japan, or Mexico—plans that were being revised to conform to the new four–army plan. The assistant chief of the Air Corps, Brig Gen Oscar M. Westover, supervised preparation of the Air Corps's answer to the General Staff request. Instructions from the General Staff were to base the plan on an Air Corps strength of 1,800 serviceable planes, the number authorized by the Air Corps Act of 1926.[17] Since the goal of the five-year plan had never been reached, the Air Corps did not have 1,800 serviceable planes. As of June 1933, the total was 1,570, and only 147 were bombers. There were 480 pursuit, 147 attack, and 542 observation planes. The rest were a hodgepodge of trainers, utility planes, transports, and experimental models. The Air Corps had no long-range bombers. The Lassiter Board had suggested a 60-20-20 ratio of pursuit, attack, and bombardment aircraft. Airmen now agreed that a balanced force would have equal portions of the three types. Air Corps leaders considered their arm weaker in airplanes than numbers would imply. In their minds, the Air Corps needed many more planes, particularly bombers. And while 1,800 serviceable planes would be an improvement, it was not at all adequate. With only 1,800 planes, they believed air defense would be hopeless in any war with a European nation, especially if that nation was aligned with Japan.

Westover and his planners based their study on a strength of 4,459 planes. That, they declared, was the minimum force capable of defending the United States against air attack. Air Corps planners began with the argument that because of its long coastlines and exposed foreign possessions, air defense for the United States was difficult. They divided the continental United States into seven "critical" areas that must be defended, they said, by the Air Corps. These were the areas of New England, Chesapeake Bay, Caribbean Sea or Florida, Great Lakes, Puget Sound, San Francisco, and Los Angeles–San Diego. A general aerial defense plan, they said, would have to include continuous observation by Air Corps patrol planes a distance of 250 to 300 miles off our shore and a strike force of bombardment and/or attack and/or pursuit planes distributed "among the most critical areas at the beginning or just prior to a war." The study members denied that they were contemplating a "cordon defense." It was "an area defense set up for the protection of each critical area until the location of the main effort is determined, when a concentration will be made against it from the air forces in neighboring areas."[18]

Westover and his planners admitted that their air plan made little reference to the adjutant general's instruction "to make recommendations for the use of the GHQ Air Force in each of the . . . [colored] plans." They explained that the "opinion that all Air Force operations must tie in definitely with ground operations" was in error. There was, they said, "a phase in the defense of the United States in which air power plays a distinct part operating either alone or in conjunction with the Navy. And in either case the plan for the use of air power initially will bear little relation to the details of any of the existing colored war plans."[19]

General Kilbourne was unimpressed. The Air Corps plan, he said, was of no value either for war planning or for a logical determination of the strength at which the Air Corps should be maintained. He could not understand how the chief of the Air Corps or any officer of long experience could endorse the idea that "any arm of the national defense should be used without reference to a general plan covering the employment of all forces." If Air Corps planners had found America's air defense situation hopeless, they did so only because they began their study with false assumptions. They ignored the capability of ground and naval forces to assist in the defense against air attack. Enemy air forces would have to have floating bases or land bases on the American continent within striking distance of critical targets within the United States. Land and naval forces could help prevent establishment of such bases. The proposal to distribute the GHQ Air Force in seven areas bordering the coastal frontiers "without regard to the situation, the enemy, specific war plans, or other Army and Navy forces" constituted a cordon defense. The Air Corps was violating its own doctrine of the offensive. He argued that "even though the country be forced to the strategic and tactical defensive," air operations should be offensive. The Air Corps should attack the enemy fleet, establish air superiority, assist the Army in occupying areas in Canada, Mexico, or the

United States coasts where an enemy might attempt to establish land bases. He declared that the Air Corps term *defensive air operations* implied "an attitude of mind which is unfortunate." As for the proposal to establish an outpost line of aircraft 250 to 300 miles off the coast, Kilbourne pointed out that the Navy already patrolled coastal sea-lanes. Coming back to money, as every issue seemed to do in those days, he warned that coastal patrol by the Air Corps would cost over $38 million annually.[20]

To Army leaders it appeared that the Air Corps again was making a bid for more than its share of War Department resources. Kilbourne suggested that the chief of the Air Corps should be told that the Air Corps proposals left the impression that Air Corps leaders were more concerned about securing an increase for their arm than they were about the national defense.[21] General Drum agreed. The chief of the Air Corps's plan, he told MacArthur, was based primarily on getting up an argument for an increase in the Air Corps for the Army. This plan failed to comply with the instructions to submit a plan based on the aviation contemplated by the five-year plan.[22]

MacArthur directed Drum to chair a committee to revise the plan. Foulois and Kilbourne were to be on the committee, as well as the commandant of the Army War College, Maj Gen George S. Simonds, and the chief of Coast Artillery, Maj Gen John W. Gulick.[23]

In its report to Secretary of War Dern on 11 October 1933, the Drum Board generally supported Kilbourne's position over that of Foulois, Westover, and the Air Corps planners.[24] The report began with the premise that air forces could not operate without bases, land or floating, and that this fact made the threat of air attack on the United States less menacing than airpower enthusiasts claimed. As proof, the board included an analysis of a recent flight of 24 Italian seaplanes from Rome to Chicago that demonstrated the impossibility of a sudden air attack by large air forces on the United States. Although the flying time for the 6,063 miles between Rome and Chicago was only 46 hours, the trip took 15 days. The flight required support from 11 surface vessels, weather services of four countries, and air bases in eight countries. As for the airmen's contention that certain phases of air defense would be independent Air Corps operations, the Drum Board in typically vague military jargon said, "Whether operating in close conjunction with the Army or the Navy, or at some distance therefrom, all these agencies [air forces] must operate in accordance with one general plan of national defense. This principle relates to the utilization of the financial and material resources of the nation as well."[25]

Since Air Corps planners had not seen fit to tailor their air plan to fit the colored war plans, the Drum Board did it for them. In addition to "organic corps and army aviation," detachments for overseas garrisons, and training and aircraft development programs, the board advised establishment in peacetime of "a GHQ Air Force adequate to meet effectively the requirements of any or all of our war plans." To defend against overseas invasion, the GHQ Air Force would be used both for "long-range reconnaissance offshore to detect the approach of enemy expeditions, and for the attack of such expeditions before they reach the shores [missions preserved for the Army Air Corps by the MacArthur–Pratt Agreement of 1931]." In support of land operations, the GHQ Air Force would be used strategically "for long-range reconnaissance, for interdicting enemy reconnaissance, for demolition of important installations, and for interdiction of enemy movements." Tactically, it would support ground forces by opposing enemy air forces engaged in reconnaissance, demolition, and interdiction, "during battle by actual participation, and after battle by exploitation of victory or minimizing enemy exploitation in event of defeat."[26]

The Drum Board's suggestions for "composition and initial dispositions of the Air Corps as a whole and the use of the GHQ Air Force" were based on the Red–Orange plan. The generals on the board could at that time conceive of no worse contingency than war with a coalition of Britain and Japan. To perform its functions in the Red–Orange plan, they concluded that the Air Corps would need 2,072 serviceable planes, 980 of them combat planes assigned to the GHQ Air Force. That was the desired strength for the Air Corps. A strength of only 1,800 serviceable planes would be risky but acceptable. The board explained that while "1,800 active planes permit . . . adequate air components for our overseas garrisons and give reasonable assurance of success in our missions at home under conditions deemed probable in our estimates, the number is insufficient should our estimates prove erroneous or should there be unforeseen developments." The possibility that estimates might change was reasonably high. "As the world situation becomes more tense," Drum and the other generals warned, "other nations are going to make preparations, secretly or otherwise. What they will have when M-day actually arrives is quite likely to be greatly in excess of what they have at the writing of this report."[27]

For all their concern over the increasingly tense world situation and the needs of the Air Corps, the generals of the Drum Board, with the exception of Foulois, assumed the traditional position of Army leaders toward Air Corps expansion. While they lamented the understrength of Army air forces, especially in bombardment and attack squadrons, they emphasized that "our primary weakness in meeting the requirements of the strategic plans . . . lies not in the Army Air Corps but in the ground troops of the Army." Plans should be made to meet the needs of the Army as a whole. "The Committee," they declared, "is most emphatically of the opinion that the War Department should take no action and Congress make no appropriations toward carrying out the recommendations contained herein for any increase in the Air Corps over 1,800 serviceable planes which will be at the expense of other arms and branches of the military establishment."[28]

No development of the air arm at expense of other arms had been the plea of Army leaders since the end of the First World War. In the twenties, when Army strength was being reduced in the name of economy, the "first principle" of good business, and during the initial years of the Great Depression, when it was cut even further, the opinion of Army leaders was that the air arm should, with due consideration for its special needs, accept its share of reducing. When the Army was reduced, they argued, all its combat arms should be reduced in like measure. The Army should remain, as far as its starvation diet would allow, a balanced force. In the winter of 1933–34, the Army was still being reduced. War clouds were beginning to gather. As yet they did not darken the sky, giving cause for alarm. They did increase the probability that "other nations are going to make preparations, secretly or otherwise," and that "we should make preparations likewise."[29] Soon Congress and the people might be willing to increase the size of the Army. If that happened, Army leaders were prepared to sing the song of the twenties in reverse. Just as a well-balanced Army should be the principle in time of reduction, so should it be in time of expansion.

Secretary Dern approved the Drum Board's report, and on 31 January 1934, MacArthur outlined for the House Committee on Military Affairs the War Department program for carrying out the board's proposals. War Department leaders would have preferred to delay presenting the Air Corps program until it could be worked into a general expansion program giving similar attention to the needs of other branches of the Army. Unfortunately, they were forced to act quickly. The Navy and the Naval Affairs Committee were, as one member of the Military Affairs Committee put it, threatening to "come in and steal the entire aviation program for the United States."[30] A bill had been introduced and had passed the House authorizing the Navy to increase its strength by 1,184 planes above current authorization. While the Navy argued that this increase was necessary to bring its forces up to "treaty strength," it caused concern on the General Staff. Kilbourne warned that if the bill became law, it would probably result in a shift of appropriations favoring naval aviation. He said it was necessary for the Army to present a program that would call for broad consideration of the two services at the same time.[31]

The program MacArthur described to the congressmen envisioned a GHQ Air Force of at least five wings, 200 airplanes per wing. There would be two bombardment and two pursuit wings and one attack wing. This would amount to a force of approximately 1,000 combat airplanes. To provide 1,000 planes for the GHQ Air Force, the airplane strength of the Air Corps would have to increase to at least the current legal limit of 1,800 serviceable planes. MacArthur made clear that the number of planes and men needed for the Air Corps might change. Referring to proposed increases in naval aviation, he reminded the committee that in 1926 Congress had, after considerable study, fixed the general ratio of airplane strength in the Army and Navy at 18 to 10. War Department policy at the time was, first, to bring the Air Corps up to the level authorized by the five-year program—1,800 serviceable planes; second, to increase the Air Corps to 2,072 serviceable planes as suggested by the Drum Board but only in conjunction with a general plan for expansion of the Army as a whole; and third, to eventually expand the Air Corps to approximately 3,900 planes, an "authorized strength" that would give the Army the flexibility to maintain parity with the Navy. Army leaders were not ready to ask for large increases in Army air, but neither did they want to fall behind the Navy. MacArthur said,

> What I am anxious to do is to get an authorization which will not limit us by the straight-jacket of numbers such as was written into the 1926 bill. It is quite possible that the future development of the air will demand much higher figures than any that have been considered. It is quite possible that the future development of the air will demand much higher figures than any that have been considered. It is quite possible on the other hand, that anticipated totals may not be reached. I believe there should be a degree of flexibility in the matter.[32]

He was concerned that the Army not be trapped again by what he called "appropriation law," a new name for the complaint that the Air Corps five-year plan of 1926 had nearly destroyed the Army. Congress had authorized increases in men and planes for the Air Corps but had failed to appropriate funds. Therefore, he explained, the Army, by "appropriation law," was forced to choose between stopping the growth of the Air Corps or reducing the established arms. The General Staff chose not to stop the growth of the Air Corps, and the result was that the rest of the Army was "starved and skeletonized." It was a familiar story, and in telling it MacArthur was repeating the old plea not to expand the Air Corps at the expense of something else.

When describing how the new GHQ Air Force would be used, the chief of staff revealed some understanding and appreciation of strategic bombing as proposed by airpower advocates. He said the

GHQ Air Force "could be used in independent missions of destruction, aimed at the vital arteries of a nation." Army air forces could be "a great deciding factor in . . . mass combat." His intent in proposing organization of the GHQ Air Force was to provide a mobile air force to support the defensive war plans. Speaking of requests for a thousand combat planes, he said,

> They are all to be primarily concentrated in the United States. I contemplate use of those planes, however, in any emergency wherever it might be necessary. I contemplate, in case of necessity, throwing the entire outfit into Panama, or over to Hawaii, as the practicability of getting them over there becomes more and more apparent, and their need more definite. I am not even sure you could not get them over to the Philippines. You might have to do it in jumps—to Hawaii, Guam and Luzon. But I would throw them to any place where necessity arose.[33]

Congressional hearings on the relative merits of a bill (H.R. 7553) incorporating the War Department proposal and two bills (H.R. 7601 and H.R. 7872) advocating more radical changes in Air Corps policy were under way in late February 1934 when the Army began the airmail operation. The War Department vigorously opposed H.R. 7601 and H.R. 7872. Both bills would give the Air Corps a separate promotion list, a separate budget, and planning functions presently performed by the General Staff. H.R. 7601 would set the strength of the Air Corps at not less than 4,834 planes. It would fix the personnel strength of the Air Corps at 17 general officers; 5,241 other officers; and 32,804 enlisted men. These increases were to be made "without regard to the total strength of the Regular Army." With experience as their guide, Army leaders calculated that this would mean reduction of the other branches of the Army by 3,990 officers and 17,322 enlisted men.[34] "The outstanding feature of this bill," Kilbourne said, "is its appeal to human selfishness. It will be supported, openly or sub rosa, in spite of the disastrous effect upon the national defense as a whole, by some because of its promise of special opportunities for rapid promotion and increased pay and privileges. Our aviators have been taken on a high mountain and shown the kingdom of the world—few men can resist such temptation."[35]

Something had to be done to stop the disturbing trend that the legislation represented. On 21 February, Secretary Dern sent a letter to Rep. John J. McSwain (D-S.C.), chairman of the Committee on Military Affairs, detailing War Department opposition to H.R. 7601 and H.R. 7872. He noted that at the beginning of its hearings, McSwain's committee had devoted itself "entirely to the constructive problem of increasing the authorization for the Army Air Corps in consonance with similar legislation for the Navy, and which would enable the Army to place into actual being the GHQ Air Force." He urged McSwain and his committee to turn away from the "destructive proposals" embodied in H.R. 7601 and H.R. 7872. Undoubtedly, the incentive for these bills was "the belief that the air plane will dominate future war, and that the possession of a powerful air force, alone, will make our country safe." While Army leaders agreed that the airplane was a powerful weapon, they could not allow perpetration of the idea that airpower alone could defend the nation. "Such a belief is romantic," Dern said. If it were allowed to influence military policy, he and many other Army leaders feared it would destroy any hope of getting funds for the development of other branches of the Army. Their view of what an air force was and what it could do reflected their concern for economy and a balanced Army. Dern expressed this beautifully:

> An air force is far too costly, in view of its limitations, to be considered an agency for general destruction. It is a weapon of opportunity. The most important contribution that an air force can make to success in war is to aid our armies or navies to win victories. Properly directed it is capable of delivering powerful blows, by surprise, at the crisis of an action. It is of utmost value as an agency for harassment, for localized destruction, and for general observation. It is not an economic substitute for any of the other arms and services of the Army. Regardless of cost, it cannot possibly substitute for the basic combat elements on the ground. It is a valuable agency for support of ground and sea forces in defense of our outposts, our coast lines, and our territory. Its true value as such can be obtained only when it operates as a member of the defense team, subordinated like all other elements, to whatever team it happens to accompany. Its true development cannot be obtained unless plans and concepts for its use are woven into the common cloth, with all of the adjustment and compromise necessary to create harmony.[36]

The GHQ Air Force Becomes a Reality

The concerns that led Dern and the General Staff to oppose these bills in Congress were not lessened when the crashes in the airmail operation created a crisis. The contrast between the apparent efficiency of civilian airmail flyers and the apparent inefficiency of Army flyers added to the argument that the War Department had neglected the Air Corps. It appeared that a situation might develop much like that in 1925, when Mitchell's exploitation of naval air disasters appeared to shift the debate on airpower in favor of radical airpower advocates. It could give congressional proponents of H.R. 7601 and H.R. 7872 more support, increasing chances that all or part of their proposals might become law. It would almost surely delay passage of an acceptable program that would protect the Army's share of aviation money from Navy pilfering.

The situation in 1925 had been brought under control by a blue-ribbon committee, the Morrow Board, which made a general investigation of aviation policy. When the airmail situation reached a crisis on 10 March 1934, Dern proposed a similar solution. He invited

Charles A. Lindbergh, Orville Wright, and the noted distance pilot Clarence D. Chamberlin to join Drum and the other generals who had been on his board in a review of the aviation issue. Lindbergh had interests in Transcontinental Air Transport and Pan American and had publicly opposed the president's decision to cancel the airmail contracts, and he declined to serve. He telegraphed Dern:

> I believe that the use of the Army Air Corps to carry the Airmail was unwarranted and contrary to American principle. This action was unjust to the airlines whose contracts were canceled without trial. It was unfair to the personnel of the Army Air [Corps] who had neither equipment designed for the purpose nor adequate time for training in a new field. It has unnecessarily and greatly damaged all American aviation. I do not feel that I can serve on a committee whose function is to assist in following out an executive order to the Army to take over the commercial air mail system of the United States.[37]

Lindbergh was the Lone Eagle who had fired American imagination and enthusiasm for aviation with his transatlantic flight; he was a national hero and his presence on the committee would have given it prestige and placated some of the War Department's critics. His refusal to serve was embarrassing for the War Department, and Dern asked him to reconsider. Again, Lindbergh refused. Orville Wright also declined, on grounds of ill health. Chamberlin who had supported the Army on the airmail issue accepted. He was a minor figure compared with Lindbergh and Wright.[38]

To offset the withdrawal, Dern appointed five civilian members, all of them men who had been associated with the development of aviation. They were former Secretary of War Baker; Karl Taylor, former Army aeronautical engineer and president of Massachusetts Institute of Technology; George William Lewis, director of aeronautical research for the National Advisory Committee for Aeronautics; James H. "Jimmy" Doolittle, aeronautical engineer, manager of the Aviation Department of Shell Petroleum Corporation, and a well-known racing pilot; and Edgar Gorrell, pioneer Army aviator, now president of Stutz Motor Car Company. Upon Drum's suggestion, Dern asked Baker to chair the committee, which became known as the Baker Board. Drum became the executive vice-chairman. At the board's first meeting, Dern said,

> It appears that the experience of the Army Air Corps in carrying the mail has raised doubts about the general efficiency of our Army Air Force. These doubts have been emphasized by the utterances of critics whose competence the public cannot evaluate. Many of our citizens are bewildered. They do not know whether we have a good military air force or not. If we have, the public ought to know it and be reassured. If, on the other hand, we are deficient in equipment, personnel, or training we want your best judgment as to what should be done to bring us up to a satisfactory standard.[39]

This was a broad mandate, but many cynics could argue with justification that the board to which it was given was "clearly a packed court."[40]

The military members of the Baker Board began preparing as soon as Dern announced its creation, and it is not surprising that the final report of the Baker Board echoed that of the Drum Board.[41] Baker and associates, with one exception, Doolittle, rejected proposals for radical reorganization of the air arm. They described as visionary the idea that a very large and independent air force is necessary to defend the country against air attack. They endorsed the General Staff's plea for development of a balanced Army. While they agreed that the Air Corps was not properly equipped, evidence submitted to the committee revealed that comparable deficiencies existed in the Army as a whole in the procurement of necessary tanks and automatic rifles for the infantry, antiaircraft equipment for the coast artillery, mechanized equipment for the cavalry, modernization and motorization of the field artillery, means of chemical warfare for the chemical warfare service, motor transportation for the Army as a whole, and certain types of ammunition for the whole service. During the past fiscal year, there had been no ammunition allowance for any of the combat troops for target practice. The board's report added that though the War Department had plans for modernizing the Army, Congress and the Bureau of the Budget had never allotted funds to carry them out. The Army was advised to go ahead with the GHQ Air Force and the expansion of Air Corps strength to the 2,072 planes recommended by the Drum Board (the board had determined that it would take a total of 2,320 planes to keep 2,072 serviceable). As for the airmail operation, the Baker Board advised increased training in night and instrument flying and more strict standards. Every rated pilot in the Air Corps should average at least 10 hours per month or risk going before a Flying Proficiency Evaluation Board.[42]

Doolittle took exception to the board's opposition to radical reorganization of the air arm and filed a short minority report. Airmen would hail him later as the only member of the board who had both an understanding of the potential of airpower and the courage to speak out. He said,

> I believe in aviation—civil and military. I believe that the future security of our nation is dependent upon an adequate air force. This is true at the present time and will become increasingly important as the science of aviation advances and the airplane lends itself more and more to the art of warfare. I am convinced that the required air force can be more rapidly organized, equipped, and trained if it is completely separated from the Army and developed as an entirely separate arm. If complete separation is not the desire of the committee, I recommend an air force as a part of the Army but with a separate budget, a separate promotion list, and removed from the control of the General

Staff. These are my sincere convictions. Failing either, I feel that the Air Corps should be developed and expanded under the direction of the General Staff as recommended above.[43]

Foulois later said he wished he had joined Doolittle, but he did not; he signed the majority report, which was approved by Dern in late July 1934.[44]

The General Staff analyzed the report and concurred in its proposals, though Kilbourne suggested that "the War Department should insist upon the necessary personnel and modern equipment for at least four infantry divisions, three cavalry divisions, and the mechanized brigade before beginning to increase the Air Corps to the Drum Board figures and that, with this increase, should be carried on simultaneously the provision of antiaircraft materiel and the essential war reserves for the initial mobilization." Aside from keeping the Army in balance, he argued that advocating immediate increase of the Air Corps to the authorized strength of 1,800 planes would strain the Army's relationship with the Navy. He stated,

> We are faced with the practical situation in which we are asking the Navy, at a time when the political situation is most favorable to themselves, to curtail their own demands in order to enable the Army to overtake them. Since it will take us two years to reach the strength of the Five Year Program, even if the present estimates are approved, it appears certain that a proposal to place in our first priority more than the Five Year Program, and ask the Navy to delay their development for two or three years, would result in an immediate deadlock.[45]

Implied in Kilbourne's argument was the concern, developed from experience, that Congress would not increase defense appropriations to pay for Air Corps expansion and if it did not come out of money earmarked for combined Army and Navy aviation, it, of course, would come out of funds for other branches.

Dern, in late August, sent Roosevelt a letter describing the Baker Board's recommendations. He enclosed three suggested responses for the president to sign and return. The first approved the Air Corps remaining an integral part of the Army; the second, the program for 2,320 airplanes; and the third, a program for reequipment and rearmament of the Army as a whole. FDR signed all the letters. The program for improvement of the Air Corps was to be put into effect as soon as funds became available.[46]

Army leaders hoped this would put the airpower issue to rest, that the Baker Board report might be accepted as "the basis for development of the Army Air Corps for the next 10 years and thus terminate the continuing agitation and uncertainty which has been so detrimental to harmonious development and improvement."[47] They were to be disappointed.

At the Air Corps Tactical School, young officers had been studying employment of bombardment aviation and developing a theory of airpower. They were outraged by the Baker Board's declaration that bombardment aviation, acting independently, could not produce decisive results in any general mission contemplated under national defense policy.[48] When given opportunity to appeal the judgment of the Baker Board, they would seize it.

President Roosevelt in June 1934, as part of his reaction to the airmail crisis, had appointed Clark Howell, editor of the *Atlanta Constitution*, to chair a Federal Aviation Commission "to go over the whole subject of commercial aeronautics." Howell was no expert on aviation affairs, and that suited the president. He did not want an expert but an impartial arbitrator. To Howell's admission of ignorance about airplanes, Roosevelt replied, "That makes you just the man I want for this job."[49] There were two aeronautical experts among the other four men the president picked for the commission. Edward P. Warner was an aeronautical engineer and former assistant secretary of the Navy for aeronautics. Jerome C. Hunsaker, also an aeronautical engineer, had designed the ill-fated dirigible *Shenandoah* and the first seaplane to fly the Atlantic, the NC-4; and he was a member of the National Advisory Committee for Aeronautics. The two other members were Franklin K. Lane Jr., and Albert J. Berres, motion-picture executive and former labor leader. As questions of civil aviation, especially aircraft manufacturing, related to military aviation, the Howell Commission made clear that its investigation would encompass questions relating to military aviation including "unification of the air forces of the nation."[50]

Having survived the Baker Board, War Department leaders were not anxious for another investigation, particularly by a commission solely of civilians, but they had no choice. To ensure strong presentation of War Department views, MacArthur appointed Kilbourne to coordinate War Department testimony. Kilbourne took his job seriously. He realized that "this Federal Aviation Commission will be the last board or committee reporting on the subject of aviation for some time, and that its recommendations will have great weight with the President and Congress."[51] If at all possible, he (and Drum, who was closely following the matter) wanted to avoid the old controversies.[52] He directed that General Staff officers would handle all questions relating to strategy, military requirements, and employment of military forces. The chief of the Air Corps, Foulois, was to limit his testimony to organization and function of the Air Corps, personnel management, the training system, and information relating to mobilization. If Kilbourne had his way, Foulois would prepare his own testimony. "I am afraid some of your officers," Kilbourne told the Air Corps chief, "have their minds too much centered on controversial questions to give you much constructive aid."[53]

Despite Kilbourne's efforts, he was not able to keep controversial questions out of the Howell Commission hearings. Upon the urging of Rep. J. Mark Wilcox (D-Fla.), Howell and his colleagues requested by name a number of Air Corps officers to testify in order to hear "the views of representative Air Corps officers, as well as those of the General Staff."[54] Among those requested were Maj Donald Wilson, Capt Robert Olds, and Lt Kenneth N. Walker, then students at the Command and General Staff School at Fort Leavenworth, Kansas, and captains Claire L. Chennault, Harold L. George, and Robert M. Webster from the Air Corps Tactical School.[55] With the exception of Chennault, who was the champion of pursuit at the school, all these men were bomber advocates.

Kilbourne relayed the invitations to the airmen along with War Department permission to testify. They were told, however, that they would not be reimbursed for travel expense. Some of the airmen took this as a not too subtle hint that the War Department did not want them coming to Washington.[56] But the next day, Kilbourne informed them they could use Army aircraft and the Howell Commission would pay them five dollars per diem. Apparently still concerned that Army leaders would be displeased if they accepted the invitation to testify, the airmen discussed the matter with each other by telephone before deciding to go.[57]

In their testimony, the six officers emphasized the long-range bomber and challenged the Drum and Baker boards. George led the attack. After informing the commission that his statement reflected his own views and not War Department policy, he declared that "the object of war is now and always has been, the overcoming of the hostile will to resist." Airpower, he argued, had at last provided "the means whereby pressure could be applied directly to break down the hostile will without first defeating or containing the hostile surface forces." In future wars, air forces would go into action long before ground forces. It was important to maintain the strength of the nation's air force during peace. Airpower was "the immediate ability of a nation to engage effectively in air warfare." It was important to give the air arm freedom:

> Air power . . . can only be realized when its employment as a new method of conducting warfare is understood and when it is given an opportunity to develop itself primarily for the waging of independent warfare instead of as an auxiliary of the other armed forces. I believe that our Navy requires Naval aviation as an integral part of that organization. I believe, however, that all other aviation should be organized into an independent Air Force.[58]

The other airmen seconded George's argument. Olds forecasted that a strong independent air force might be the best guarantee of peace. "A determined air armada," he said, "loaded with modern agencies of destruction, in readiness within range of our great [world] centers of population and industry, may eventually prove to be a more convincing argument against war than all the Hague and Geneva Conventions put together."[59] Wilson warned the board that world conditions were leading toward war and that the United States was vulnerable to air attack, particularly since its air defense relied on planes with limited range.

Walker took issue with those Army leaders who believed that the only value of an air force was "to cover the mobilization of the Army," although he agreed that modern war could be won or lost in the air before ground forces could be mobilized. "Gentlemen," he warned, "unless we create an adequate and separate Air Force, this next war 'will begin in the air and end in the mud'—in the mud and debris of the demolished industries that have brought us to our knees."[60]

Everything now seemed in flux. These young airmen, all instructors or former instructors from the Air Corps Tactical School, had built a strong case for an independent air force and in doing so placed themselves in opposition to established War Department policy that "no legislation should be recommended which would change the present organization of the Army and Navy, in which our aviation for national defense is divided between the two services and is an integral part of each, subject to control by the Chief of Staff of the Army and the Chief of Naval Operations of the Navy."[61] In lieu of an independent Air Force, other airmen, including Colonel Arnold, were willing to accept the limited autonomy offered by organization of the GHQ Air Force. Admiral Pratt's retirement as chief of naval operations on 30 June 1933 had negated the MacArthur–Pratt Agreement and reopened the coastal defense controversy between the two services. Apparently, there was some concern, as Arnold had indicated during the presidential election of 1932 that a consolidated independent Air Force at this time would give undue influence to ranking Navy flyers. The principal mission of the GHQ Air Force in peace was its role in coastal defense plans. Its organization into an active force gave the Air Corps a more credible claim to coastal defense. Still, that claim had been undermined by the Drum and Baker boards' acceptance of Kilbourne's argument that Air Corps planners had overemphasized the independent role of airpower in coastal defense and depreciated ground and naval forces.

The Howell Commission's report, submitted to Congress on 31 January 1935, endorsed the wisdom of giving the GHQ Air Force a try. "There is ample reason to believe," the report stated, "that aircraft have now passed far beyond their former position as useful auxiliaries. . . . An adequate striking force for use against objectives both near and remote is a necessity for a modern army, and the projected GHQ Air Force must be judged with reference to its effectiveness in this respect."[62]

In late December 1934, Dern had given the go-ahead for the GHQ Air Force; the new air organization became a reality on 1 March 1935. Tactical units previously scattered among the nine corps areas were brought into three wings at Langley Field, Virginia; Barksdale Field, Louisiana; and March Field, California. Headquarters for GHQ Air Force was established at Langley.

Command arrangement for the new organization reflected the views of the General Staff rather than those of Foulois. The commanding general, GHQ Air Force, reported directly to the chief of staff in peacetime and to the theater commander in war. He was in charge of organization, tactical training, and employment of the Army's air forces. The chief of the Air Corps controlled training, procurement, and supply. Administration of air bases, including such matters as court-martial authority, remained under corps area commanders. This division of authority never set well with Air Corps leaders, and there was another reorganization in March 1939—the commander of GHQ Air Force becoming responsible to the chief of the Air Corps rather than the chief of staff.[63]

Maj Gen Frank M. Andrews, first commander of the GHQ Air Force, was an ardent advocate of airpower, and as differences mounted between him and the General Staff, he became an increasingly outspoken proponent of autonomy. His methods and personality clashed with those of Westover, who replaced Foulois as chief of the Air Corps. A proponent of airpower but also a believer in discipline, Westover was a stickler for regulations. As acting chief of the Air Corps, he had informed the airmen a month before he formally took command that Gen Malin Craig, who had taken over as chief of staff from MacArthur, believed the Air Corps had suffered because its officers had failed to understand broader Army problems. He advised Air Corps officers to avoid criticizing unfavorable decisions on Air Corps issues.[64] His intention was to promote Air Corps projects through approved channels, and he did not want disruptive opposition. He demanded cooperation, but then that was Westover's way. Back in 1926, when he was commander of Langley Field, one of his subordinates said of him, "Westover's methods were Germanic in type—which resulted in orders being obeyed because they were orders rather than because he was a good leader. There was not a spirit among the officers of its being 'our Field'; it was rather Westover's Field."[65] Andrews by contrast was a good leader. Many airmen looked to him to champion airpower, and he did, even on issues that fell within Westover's responsibility.[66]

There seemed to be something essentially argumentative about those Air Corps officers; they did not know what the requirements of good organization were. Or so the Army leadership must have felt in the mid-1930s when boards followed boards with an almost mechanical regularity, their judgments repeating the arrangements of the past with similar regularity, only to have zealous Air Corps officers undertake some new project or other, usually with large attention to publicity. General Westover must have seemed a clever replacement for the enthusiasm of Foulois, for Westover looked like a disciplinarian. But there was something didactic and unattractive about him, and the spirited Air Corps officers simply turned to the attractive Andrews, who, because of the organization of the GHQ Air Force, was now of the same rank as the chief of the Air Corps. Andrews quickly proved as much of a zealot as the retired Foulois.

And a new issue was arising. While there was a lull in debate over how many airplanes the Air Corps should have, novel developments in technology challenged the imagination of airpower advocates, increasing their enthusiasm for long-range heavy bombers over pursuit and attack aircraft designed to support ground operations. Here was a contention that directly challenged the belief of the Army, that the Air Corps existed as an arm among the several other arms of the ground forces. Long-range bombers gave new strength to the argument that war could be won entirely in the air.

Notes

1. *New York Times*, 10 March 1934; *Newsweek* 3 (17 March 1934): 5–7; Benjamin D. Foulois and Carroll V. Glines, *From the Wright Brothers to the Astronauts: The Memoirs of Benjamin D. Foulois* (New York: McGraw-Hill, 1968), 253; Norman E. Borden Jr., *Air Mail Emergency, 1934: An Account of Seventy-eight Tense Days in the Winter of 1934 When the Army Flew the United States Mail* (Freeport, Maine: Bond Wheelwright, 1968), 108–9, is a very readable account but has some rather confusing errors in chronology; and Eldon W. Downs, "Army and the Airmail—1934," *Air Power Historian* 9 (January 1962): 35–51. The accident investigation of Wienecke's crash indicated that, in addition to the weather, a probable cause of the accident was the improper installation of the gyro artificial horizon and the gyrocompass. These instruments had been mounted below the instrument panel by the pilot's knees, so low that they were hardly visible in flight.

2. At a news conference shortly after the cabinet meeting on 9 February, President Roosevelt seemed most anxious to announce his decision to cancel the airmail contracts. "Well, I suppose somebody is going to ask me about air mail contracts," he said. "You took the words right out of our mouths," replied one of the newsmen. Whereupon the president stated that he expected to issue "almost immediately" an executive order directing the postmaster general to cancel all domestic airmail contracts, and directing the secretary of war to put at the disposal of the Postal Service "such airplanes, landing fields, pilots . . . and equipment" as necessary to fly the mail. See Paul Tillett, *The Army Flys the Mail*, the Inter-University Case Program: Cases in Public Administration and Policy Formation No. 24 (Tuscaloosa, Ala.: University of Alabama Press, 1955), 30–32. See also James A. Farley, *Jim Farley's Story: The Roosevelt Years* (New York: Whittlesey House, 1948), 46; and

THE ARMY AND ITS AIR CORPS

Arthur M. Schlesinger Jr., *The Coming of the New Deal* (Boston: American Heritage Library, 1959), 451.

3. Henry H. Arnold, *Global Mission* (New York: Harper, 1949), 143. See also Carroll V. Glines, *Jimmy Doolittle: Daredevil Aviator and Scientist* (New York: Macmillan, 1972); Benjamin B. Lipsner and Len Hilts, *The Air Mail: Jennies to Jets* (Chicago: Wilcox and Follett, 1951), 244–46; and Foulois and Glines, 237–42.

4. Maj Clifford A. Tinker was quoted in *Newsweek* 3 (3 March 1934): 9. See also Carroll V. Glines, *The Saga of Air Mail* (Princeton, N.J.: D. Van Nostrand, 1968), 130–31; and Alfred Goldberg, ed., *A History of the United States Air Force, 1907–1957* (Princeton, N.J.: D. Van Nostrand, 1957), 39–40. Hugh J. Knerr claimed airmen warned that the Air Corps could not do the job with what it had, "that disaster was certain to follow the use of military aircraft where highly specialized mail planes customarily operated." But most of the evidence indicates that such warnings by Army airmen began to surface after the accidents began to occur, not before. Diary of Hugh J. Knerr, 1925–34, unpaged, in the special collections at the United States Air Force Academy Library, Colorado Springs, Colorado. Oscar Westover, the commander of the airmail operation, said of the Army's readiness for the job: "It was not lack of experience, as such, that sent these men to their deaths. The men were experienced fliers. But they did not have sufficient experience flying those particular routes. They were unfamiliar with the conditions they had to meet. . . . When you consider how the job was dumped in our laps, how little warning we had, how little time for preparation, the men have done exceptionally well, particularly in our present equipment." Quoted in Cecil R. Roseberry, *The Challenging Skies: The Colorful Story of Aviation's Most Exciting Years, 1919–1939* (Garden City, N.Y.: Doubleday, 1966), 400.

5. Eddie Rickenbacker was not predisposed to praise the airmail policy since he was vice president of Eastern Air Transport, one of the companies that lost its airmail contract. On the last day the commercial companies were to fly the mail, Rickenbacker and Jack Frye, vice president of Trans World Airlines (TWA), staged a cross-continent mail flight which Benjamin Lipsner said was intended "to demonstrate the utter stupidity of the cancellation orders." In a new DC-1, the experimental forerunner of the DC-3 which was by general consensus the first airplane to support itself economically as well as aerodynamically, Rickenbacker and Frye set a new record of 11 hours and 31 minutes from Los Angeles to Newark. See Edward V. Rickenbacker, *Rickenbacker, An Autobiography* (Englewood Cliffs, N.J.: Prentice-Hall, 1967), 184–88; and Lipsner and Hilts, 247–48.

6. The phrase "useless sacrifice of life" was that of Sen. Simeon D. Fess (R-Ohio). Critics in both the House and the Senate "sounded off" against the administration's airmail policy. *Congressional Record*, 73d Cong., 2d sess., 2082–4092, 4100. Lipsner, who as a captain in the Army had been one of the pioneers in the Army airmail operation in 1918, claimed he called President Roosevelt personally on 8 March to protest. "I begged him to stop those airmail deaths." Lipsner and Hilts, 250. General Foulois made a radio broadcast in an attempt to assure the public that the Air Corps was doing everything possible to promote safe flying and to answer critics whose continual reference to those "young inexperienced Air Corps pilots" was galling to Army airmen. "Much has been said lately of the type of Air Corps officers now actually flying the mail," he said. "Some would have you believe them a bunch of rosy-cheeked young babies. On the contrary, they constitute a corps of highly intelligent, rugged, determined, loyal, and fearless young officers. . . . Our military pilots are not weaklings looking for sympathy! They should be treated like men and not children. If there is anything that the average red-blooded American military pilot resents, it is this recent twaddle about inexperienced, rosy-cheeked boys being sent to their deaths. They are proud that theirs is a man-sized job, and they have no desire to be coddled." Foulois and Glines, 246–47.

7. Foulois was bitter about this encounter with the president for the rest of his life. It particularly bothered him that the president was still in bed when he received the two generals. "There, propped up in the famous Lincoln bed, was my Commander

in Chief looking like a high potentate ready to receive prisoners who had committed crimes against his kingdom." Foulois and Glines, 253-57. Roosevelt's letter to George H. Dern was printed on the front page of the *New York Times* the next day. See *New York Times*, 11 March 1934.

8. Sen. Hiram Bingham led the attack on the president for not conferring with the Army. "So far as I have been able to learn," he said, "it was not General MacArthur, Chief of Staff of the Army; it was not General Foulois, Chief of the Air Corps. It appears true that the President did not consult any of the regular military authorities who by law or position should have been called upon to express their judgment." *New York Times*, 12 March 1934. Apparently Roosevelt tried to get General MacArthur to say publicly that he had given the assurance that the Army could fly the mail, but MacArthur refused to go along. Frazier Hunt, *The Untold Story of Douglas MacArthur* (New York: Devin-Adair Co., 1954), 139-60; and D. Clayton James, *The Years of MacArthur,* vol. 1, *1880-1941* (Boston: Houghton Mifflin, 1970), 433-39. See also the transcript of the testimony of General Foulois and General Drum before the Senate Appropriations Committee in George S. Simonds manuscripts (MSS), Library of Congress (LOC). Jim Farley was also used to divert criticism from Roosevelt. "I learned in the past," he said, "to take abuse and criticism, but when I was called a murderer, I began to look around frantically for help. I looked to the White House. No help came. I was hurt that the president had not seen fit to divert the wrath. Later I realized that it was part of my job to take as many blows for him as I could. Nonetheless, a kind word would have been a great help when the lashes were falling." Farley, 46-47.

9. Quoted in Schlesinger, 454-55.

10. Foulois and Glines, 259-60. Summaries of the Air Corps's accomplishments in the airmail crisis can also be found in Tillett, 57-58, 67-68; Robert Frank Futrell, *Ideas, Concepts, Doctrine: A History of Basic Thinking in the United States Air Force, 1907-1964* (Maxwell AFB, Ala.: Air University Press, 1974), 61-62; Glines, *The Saga of Air Mail,* 139-40; Lipsner and Hilts, 252-53; and Henry Ladd Smith, *Airways: The History of Commercial Aviation in the United States* (New York: A. A. Knopf, 1942), 257-58. Smith notes that the cost of the Army airmail operation was $3,767,355. That amounted to $2.21 a mile, rather expensive when compared to the average of $0.54 a mile paid to commercial airmail operators in fiscal year 1933.

11. In reviewing F. Trubee Davison's influence on the budgetary process, Lt Col Irving J. Phillipson, chief, Budget and Legislative Planning Branch, told General Drum that "Mr. Davison exercised a material influence in the preparation of War Department Budgetary Estimates. This influence was exercised frequently in cooperation with other agencies and at times in opposition thereto." In bureaucratic jargon, Phillipson was saying that Davison championed the Air Corps's budgetary cause. Memorandum for Gen Hugh A. Drum, 14 March 1934, War Plans Division (WPD) 888-88, Record Group (RG) 165, National Archives (NA). See also John W. Killigrew, "The Impact of the Great Depression on the Army, 1929-1936" (PhD diss., Indiana University, 1960); and James, 437. Hap Arnold was one of those airmen who feared that the General Staff was taking over the Air Corps. "I have some very disquieting bits of news," he wrote Carl Spaatz, "which indicate that the General Staff has taken upon itself the task of running the Air Corps without acquainting the Chief of the Air Corps with the action until after it has been taken. It looks to me as if the General Staff must then be taking full advantage of the absence of an Assistant Secretary of War for Air." Hap Arnold to Carl Spaatz, letter, 22 September 1933, Arnold MSS, LOC.

12. Memorandum for the Deputy Chief of Staff, 3 December 1932, WPD 3089-1, RG 165, NA. The WPD 3089-1 file includes a number of memoranda on the conflict between Foulois and WPD.

13. Brig Gen Charles E. Kilbourne, memorandum to Gen Hugh A. Drum, 31 March 1933, WPD 3089-1, RG 165, NA.

14. Gen Douglas MacArthur to the commanding generals of all Corps areas and departments, letter, subject: Jurisdiction of Corps Area Commanders over Military Units and Establishments, August 1932, WPD 3089-1, RG 165, NA.

15. Lt Col Irving J. Phillipson, memorandum to Gen Douglas MacArthur, chief of staff, 13 December 1932, WPD 3089-1, RG 165, NA.

16. Brig Gen Charles E. Kilbourne, chief, War Plans Division, memorandum to Gen Benjamin D. Foulois, chief, Army Air Corps, 7 April 1933, WPD 3089-1, RG 165, NA.

17. Adjutant general, memorandum to Gen Benjamin D. Foulois, chief, Army Air Corps, 3 June 1933, AG 580 (6-1-33), RG 407, NA.

18. Brig Gen Oscar M. Westover, commander, GHQ Air Force, to the adjutant general, letter, subject: Air Plan for the Defense of the United States, 13 July 1933, AG 580 (6-13-33), RG 407, NA (hereinafter cited as Air Plan for Defense of US). Much of the air war plan was based upon a study entitled "Air Corps Peacetime Requirements to Meet the Defense Needs of the United States," which Westover had sent to the adjutant general four months earlier, AG 580 (3-15-33), RG 407, NA. This earlier study, which was based on the results of spring maneuvers on the West Coast, caused a bit of a stir in the War Department when it appeared that the Air Corps intended to distribute copies of the study outside the department. The General Staff considered this an example of Air Corps "propagandizing." General Drum demanded that General Foulois stop immediately the distribution of the study and explain why it had been mimeographed for distribution in the first place. Hugh A. Drum, memorandum to the adjutant general, 5 August 1933; and adjutant general, memorandum to chief of the Air Corps, 8 August 1933, both filed in AG 580 (8-5-33), RG 407, NA.

19. Air Plan for Defense of US.

20. Gen Charles E. Kilbourne, memorandum to the chief of staff, 25 July 1933, WPD 888-75, RG 165, NA.

21. Ibid.

22. Gen Hugh A. Drum, memorandum to the chief of staff, 3 August 1933, WPD 888-75, RG 165, NA.

23. Gen Douglas MacArthur, memorandum to Gen Hugh A. Drum, 7 August 1933, WPD 888-75, RG 165, NA; and Gen Douglas MacArthur, memorandum to the adjutant general, subject: Detail of Special Committee of the General Council, 10 August 1933, AG 580 (8-10-33), RG 407, NA.

24. There is an outline of the conclusions of the Drum Board in AG 580 (8-4-34), RG 407, NA. See also Futrell, 67–68; and Goldberg, 39.

25. "Report of Special Committee, General Council, on Employment of Army Air Corps under Certain Strategic Plans," AG 580 (8-11-31), RG 407, NA (hereinafter cited as Drum Report).

26. Ibid.

27. Ibid.

28. Ibid.

29. Ibid.

30. "Statements and Hearings on Army Air Corps Bill," WPD 888-86, RG 165, NA (hereinafter cited as Statements and Hearings).

31. Gen Charles E. Kilbourne to Major Richards, letter, 6 February 1934, WPD 888-80, RG 165, NA.

32. Statements and Hearings.

33. Ibid.

34. Memorandum for the secretary of war, 15 February 1934, WPD 888-80, RG 165, NA.

35. Kilbourne to Richards.

36. George H. Dern to John J. McSwain, letter, 21 February 1934, AG 580 (2-8-34), RG 407, NA.

37. Charles A. Lindbergh to George H. Dern, telegram, 14 March 1934; and Charles A. Lindbergh to George H. Dern, telegram, 15 March 1934, AG 580 (3-13-34), RG 407, NA. Dern had had a meeting with Lindbergh on 10 March to discuss Air Corps problems. It was a cordial meeting and perhaps for that reason Dern felt he could convince Lindbergh to help the Army out of the airmail "mess." *New York Times*, 10 and 11 March 1934; *Newsweek*, 24 March 1934, 10–11; and the *Army and Navy Journal*, 17 March 1934.

38. Orville Wright to George H. Dern, telegram, 13 March 1934; and Clarence D. Chamberlin to George H. Dern, telegram, 13 March 1934, AG 580 (3-13-34), RG 407, NA.

39. War Department news releases, 10 and 17 April 1934, in Simonds MSS; Foulois and Glines, 260–61; and Borden, 118–19.

40. C. B. Allen, "Trouble Aloft!" *New Outlook* 163 (April 1934): 9–12.

41. Memorandum for Gen Hugh A. Drum, 13 March 1934, Simonds MSS.

42. Baker notified Dern in a letter of 12 July 1934 that the board had completed its work. The letter is in AG 580 (7-12-34), RG 407, NA. *Final Report of War Department Special Committee on Army Air Corps* (Washington, D.C.: GPO, 1934). Excerpts from the Baker Board Report can be found in a number of sources. See Glines, *Doolittle*, 116; Goldberg, 40; Borden, 138–41; Tillett, 64; and Foulois and Glines, 260–61.

43. Quoted in Glines, Doolittle, 115–17. See also Futrell, 71; and Foulois and Glines, 261.

44. Foulois and Glines, 261.

45. Memorandum for the adjutant general, 2 August 1934, WPD 888-89, RG 165, NA. The General Staff compared the conclusions of the Baker Board with those of the Morrow Board of 1924. See WPD 888-92, RG 165, NA.

46. For the first draft of this letter, which was prepared by the War Plans Division of the General Staff, see George H. Dern to President Roosevelt, letter, 7 August 1934, WPD 888-89, RG 165, NA. The final draft of the letter was personally delivered to the president by Secretary Dern on 24 August 1934. Copies of the final draft and of the president's replies are in AG 580 (7-15-34), RG 407, NA.

47. Memorandum for the adjutant general, 1 August 1934, AG 580 (7-20-34), RG 407, NA.

48. Baker Board Report.

49. W. B. Courtney, "The Wreck of the Air Mail," *Collier's* 95 (9 February 1935): 10–11.

50. See newspaper clipping entitled "Unify Our Air Forces" in Simonds MSS.

51. Douglas MacArthur to Clark Howell, letter, 2 August 1934; and memorandum for the chief of staff, 8 August 1934. Both of these documents are in WPD 888-92, RG 165, NA.

52. Gen Hugh A. Drum, memorandum to Gen Charles E. Kilbourne, 27 August 1934, WPD 888-92, RG 165, NA.

53. Memorandum for General Foulois, 27 October 1934, WPD 888-92, RG 165, NA.

54. J. Mark Wilcox to Clark Howell, letter, 18 November 1934, WPD 888-92, RG 165, NA.

55. Memorandum for the adjutant general, 19 November 1934, WPD 888-92, RG 165, NA.

56. Ibid. When the original requests for witnesses were sent out in October, General Kilbourne had taken the matter of travel expenses up with the finance officer of the Air Corps, who said that "they could not be paid from Army funds," Gen Charles E. Kilbourne to Col J. Carroll Cone, letter, 31 October 1934, RG 165, NA. See also Haywood S. Hansell Jr., The Air Plan that Defeated Hitler (Atlanta, Ga.: Higgins-MacArthur/Longino and Porter, 1972), 27.

57. Gen Charles E. Kilbourne to Clark Howell, letter, 20 November 1934, WPD 888-92, RG 165, NA; and Hansell, 27.

58. Quoted in Hansell, 28. For the entire transcript of these officers, see "Testimony Presented by Major Donald Wilson, Captain Robert Olds, Captain Harold Lee George, Captain Robert M. Webster, First Lieutenant K. N. Walker Before the Federal Aviation Commission," available in the USAF Academy Library, Colorado Springs, Colorado.

59. Quoted in Futrell, 73.

60. Ibid., 72.

61. Memorandum, subject: Recommendations to the Federal Aviation Commission on Legislation Deemed Advisable by the War Department, 7 November 1934, WPD 888-92, RG 165, NA.

62. Quoted in Futrell, 73. See also Wesley Frank Craven and James Lea Cate, eds., *The Army Air Forces in World War II*, vol. 1, *Plans and Early Operations, January 1939 to August 1942* (1949; new imprint, Washington, D.C.: Office of Air Force History, 1983), 30–31.

63. Goldberg, 40–41; Craven and Cate, 31–32; Futrell, 73–75; George E. Stratemeyer, "Administrative History of the US Army Air Forces," *Air Affairs* 1 (Summer 1947): 520–21; Knerr diary, 1925–39, unpaged; and Foulois, Oral History Collection (OHC), 52–54.

64. Jean H. DuBuque and Robert F. Gleckner, *The Development of the Heavy Bomber, 1918–1944*, USAF Historical Study 6, revised (Maxwell AFB, Ala.: USAF Historical Division, Air University, 1951), 17–18.

65. Maj W. H. Frank to General Patrick, letter, 21 July 1926, Patrick MSS, RG 18, NA. For other opinions of Westover, see Spaatz, OHC, 78–79; and Ira C. Eaker, OHC, 53–54.

66. Eaker, OHC, 73–74; and Eugene Beebe, OHC, 76–77.

Chapter 6

Preparation for War

"For 13 years," wrote MacArthur in his annual report for 1935, "the curve representing the Army's ability to perform its vital emergency missions has been trending continuously and dangerously downward."[1] That trend was about to reverse. The stable world order of the 1920s had been unbalanced by the actions of Japan, Germany, and Italy. The first reaction of Americans was to affirm with neutrality acts their intention not to become involved in foreign conflicts. But they could not ignore the threats that aggressive powers presented to the United States. Throughout the remainder of the 1930s, there would be increasing concern about the needs of the Army, with emphasis on the need of its air arm. As General Arnold put it in his memoirs, "The combination of technical advances and the state of international relations . . . gave 'air power' a chance for mushroom growth."[2] Improvements in range, speed, and firepower brought greater respect for the airplane both as a threat to the nation's security and as a weapon to defend against that threat. It had taken 20 years, but finally the goals of the airpower visionaries were becoming goals of the realists.

The Heavy Bomber

Procurement of bombers and pursuit aircraft during the 1920s had lagged behind purchase of observation aircraft. While some airmen, particularly those not privy to proceedings in high War Department councils, were quick to blame the General Staff for this imbalance, it is unfair to attribute it wholly to prejudice of Army leaders who allegedly refused to see any value of aviation other than as the "eyes of the Army." Such criticism, which often made its way into print in the twenties and thirties, was a gross exaggeration of the views of most Army leaders who believed the role of aviation included observation but also offensive operations in support of, or at least coordinated with, the operations of surface forces.

There were other reasons for the imbalance in favor of observation. An obvious reason was that pursuits and bombers were considerably more expensive than observation aircraft. Less obvious to the casual observer, procurement of bombers and pursuits was slowed because it was difficult to choose a production model. Consider the problem of choosing a pursuit model for production. While there were no revolutionary changes in pursuits during the twenties—the single-seat biplane with an open cockpit and fixed landing gear was standard—improvement in power plant and refinement in design steadily increased performance. It was hard to decide where to freeze development for production. Any design chosen would be obsolete by the time it reached the field. Choosing a bomber was just as difficult and perhaps more frustrating. Bomber development in the twenties was stymied by technological barriers. Large airplanes capable of carrying heavy loads presented designers with vexing problems, most of which revolved around weight or structural weakness of available building materials. Modifications that would add speed and performance to a small pursuit were either impossible or of negligible advantage in construction of big bombers. New design in biplane bombers often offered so little advantage over previous models that Air Corps leaders were tempted to wait for further development before requesting production. The Keystone B-3A, delivered to the Air Corps in 1930, had a maximum speed of 121 miles per hour and a range of 510 miles with a bomb load. It was not much better than the Martin bombers Mitchell had used to sink the *Ostfriesland* in 1921. The Martin bomber could do 98.5 miles per hour and its range with a bomb load was 600 miles.

Fortunately, the Keystone B-3A marked the end of the biplane era. A technical revolution was at hand in 1931. Developments in metallurgy made possible the construction of a light, all-metal monoplane. Military airplanes were to have a new look as well as higher limits of performance. In addition to metal construction of the sleek monoplanes of the thirties, such features as closed cockpits, retractable landing gear, and fully cowled engines were to become standard.

Airmen, making do with biplane bombers, were anxious to see development of multiengined monoplane bombers. Maj Hugh J. Knerr, commander of the 2d Bombardment Group at Langley Field, as early as May 1928 requested two types of multiengined monoplane bombers. His group was equipped with two squadrons of Keystone LBs and one squadron of aging Martin MB-2s. In maneuvers, his Keystones and Martins had proved inadequate to solve the tactical problems of modern warfare. "I had the vague feeling," he later wrote, "those bird-cages could not survive aerial combat."[3] What was needed was a short-range day bomber with great speed and firepower to protect itself and a long-range night bomber capable of heavy loads. With darkness as a defense, the night bomber could afford to sacrifice speed and defensive firepower for increased range and load. Knerr's suggestions received support from other airmen. Lt Col C. C. Culver, commander of the 2d Wing, said that trying to design a single airplane to do both jobs would result in "a mediocre all-purpose airplane rather than a first-class single purpose one."4 But General Fechet, then chief of the Air Corps, recognizing the unlikelihood of getting the budget-minded General Staff to approve two programs, ordered the Materiel Division to develop a single plane capable of performing the observation mission as well as day and night bombing. The result was the Douglas B-7, a gull-winged monoplane originally developed for observation as the XO-36, and the Fokker B-8, a modification of the O-27. The B-7 was powered by two 12-cylinder Curtiss V-1570s and could reach a top speed of 182 miles per hour. It was classified as a fast day bomber. The only real contribution of the B-8 was that its engine nacelles were built into the wings. That arrangement reduced drag, increasing performance. Neither airplane met the need for what Knerr had classified as long-range night bombers. Both were short-range aircraft and could carry no more than 1,200 pounds of bombs.5

Officers at the Air Corps Tactical School, in March 1930, reiterated Knerr's recommendation for two types of bombers. They argued, however, that the terms *day bomber* and *night bomber* were tactically inaccurate. The two bombers needed were light bombers and heavy bombers, with maximum loads of 1,200 and 2,000 pounds, respectively. These definitions were refined and became important as the Army debated the functions and needs of the GHQ Air Force in the thirties.6

Several aircraft manufacturers offered designs for monoplane bombers; and one of the most impressive was Boeing's XB-901, first flown in April 1931. It was later designated the YB-9. It was a mid-wing monoplane with retractable main gear and four open cockpits in its long narrow fuselage. Pilots called it the flying pencil. Its two Pratt and Whitney R-1860-11 Hornets supercharged delivered 600 horsepower each. At 6,000 feet, the YB-9 could do 186 miles per hour with a 2,260-pound bomb load. Its maximum range was 990 miles. It was a great improvement over the Keystones, but the Air Corps bought only six planes.7

The Martin B-10 outclassed the B-9 and would become the Air Corps's next first-line bomber. The test model, designated the XB-907, first appeared at Wright Field in the summer of 1932. Like the B-9, it was a mid-wing monoplane with retractable landing gear. It had three open cockpits and a position for a fourth crew member inside the fuselage. After impressive performance in its initial tests, the XB-907 was returned to the factory and rebuilt. The new version, the XB-10, had enclosed cockpits, a power nose turret, and larger wings; and it was powered by two 675 horsepower R-1820-F Cyclones. Its top speed was an amazing 207 miles per hour.8

In the summer of 1934, while the airmail fiasco was still a fresh and painful memory, General Foulois decided to show off the B-10s and in the process perhaps recover some of the Air Corps's reputation for flying skill. He sent Hap Arnold, in command of ten B-10s, on a flight from Washington, D.C., to Alaska. After a send-off with a lot of fanfare from Bolling Field on 19 July, Arnold and his men flew to Patterson Field, Ohio, then to Minneapolis, Winnipeg, Regina, Edmonton, Prince George, and Whitehorse, arriving in Fairbanks on 24 July.[9] They remained there for two weeks, mapping airways and photographing some 20,000 square miles of territory.[10] The only accident occurred on 3 August when a young lieutenant became confused in shifting fuel tanks and had to crash land in Cook Inlet, Alaska. The crew was rescued, and the airplane was recovered and repaired.[11]

In mid-August Arnold and his men began the return trip with a flight to Juneau, Alaska, where one of the airplanes was christened the *Juneau* with a "bottle of pop" (a pilot and a member of the welcoming committee had slipped behind the plane before the ceremony and drunk the champagne).[12] The remainder of the trip to Seattle, Washington, and then cross-continent to Washington was without incident. The 7,360-mile round-trip, without serious incident, was impressive. Arnold was awarded the Distinguished Flying Cross.[13]

The B-10 was the pride of the Air Corps. It was the most powerful bomber in the world, and its speed gave it advantage over the best pursuits of its day. The Boeing P-26, a little monowing, open cockpit pursuit dubbed the "Peashooter," was the "hottest" pursuit the Air Corps had. It was more than 25 miles per hour faster than the B-10, but General Fechet, former chief of the Air Corps and now national defense editor for the *Aero Digest,* felt that was not enough. "A twenty-five miles per hour advantage," he said, "is not really as effective in the 200 mile per hour range as it was when bombers did 100 and pursuiters [sic] 125 miles per hour."[14]

In maneuvers, the B-10 and B-12 (the latter a modification of the B-10) were able to penetrate pursuit defenses with little difficulty. Reporting on West Coast maneuvers of 1934, Arnold noted "that pursuit or fighter airplanes operating from frontline airdromes will rarely intercept modern bombers except accidentally. Such being the case, they can normally operate solely against other pursuit or observation and it is doubtful whether such operations justify their existence." While he seemed convinced that the speedy new bombers had made pursuit obsolete, he was careful to qualify his judgment. "Conclusions reached as a result of these tests, regardless of how positive the proof may seem, should be accepted only after being again proved by actual maneuvers and operations elsewhere."[15]

Arnold recommended that the Air Corps system of using separate pursuit, bombardment, attack, and observation boards to make procurement policy be abandoned in favor of a single air board. This, he said, would "prevent the over-enthusiasm of the advocates of one form of aviation from securing equipment that does not fit into the big picture."[16] It is not clear which overenthusiastic advocates prompted the suggestion. It is clear that he doubted the propriety of Air Corps policies regarding pursuit and attack. Arnold believed that development was toward bigger airplanes with greater performance. He advocated a multiseated fighter and replacement of attack airplanes by light and medium bombers. "I am convinced that the attack as we understand it now," he told a friend in 1932, "does little more than complicate an already too complicated system of procurement and supply. . . . Therefore, in my opinion, we should wipe out all ideas of special attack development and concentrate on the light bombing types and convert them into attack planes."[17]

Bomber advocates at the Air Corps Tactical School were less restrained than Arnold in enthusiasm for bombardment aviation. Even before the B-10, they were convinced that "a well-planned air force attack is going to be successful most of the time."[18] To them it seemed that the bomber was well-nigh invincible. They argued that pursuit was obsolete and attack an expensive luxury, since aviation was more effective when used for interdiction behind enemy lines and strategic bombardment to destroy the enemy's means and will to fight.

There were airmen who disagreed with the bomber-invincibility theories. Foremost were Capt Claire L. Chennault, who taught the pursuit course at the Air Corps Tactical School from 1932 until 1936, and Capt George C. Kenney, who taught the attack course from 1926 to 1929. Chennault was destined to lead the Flying Tigers in the China-Burma-India theater during the Second World War. Kenney would command the Southwest Pacific Air Forces under MacArthur.

Chennault believed that the rules in maneuvers involving bombers and pursuit aircraft had been "rigged" to favor bombers. Years later, he wrote in his memoirs:

> All sorts of fantastic and arbitrary restrictions were placed on fighters in maneuvers that were supposed to simulate honest conditions of actual combat. We were barred from having warning-net stations within sixty miles of the bombers' target. Interceptions had to be made at least twenty-five miles away from the target. One year we kept a fighter on patrol over Wright Field to radio warning when the bombers began to take off. Instead of recognizing the value of fighters for long-range reconnaissance and the need for defensive fighters to deny the enemy aerial intelligence, the bomber boys had maneuver rules changed to ban our patrol.[19]

After reading Arnold's report on the 1934 maneuvers, Chennault wrote a detailed rebuttal. He argued that maneuvers putting the

P-26 against the B-12 was not a contest between equally modern aircraft. While the B-12 was unquestionably the world's most advanced bomber, the P-26 could not compare to foreign pursuits. Maneuvers had demonstrated weakness in pursuit tactics and ineffectiveness of the P-26 against the B-12. Rather than suggesting as Arnold did that this left pursuit with no mission, Chennault contended it pointed to the need of a warning system, improvement in the training of pilots, and a superior single-seat pursuit.[20]

Chennault opposed the multiseat fighter. Such an aircraft, he said, would be too heavy, slow, and expensive, and unable to climb and maneuver. Experiments with multiseat fighters proved him right. In November 1935, the secretary of war approved the Bell XFM-1 (Experimental Fighter Multiplace), later designated "Airacuda." It was to be an all-purpose fighter, attack, bomber, and observation plane; but most important, it was to be an interceptor capable of "sustained attack of hostile aircraft in flight."[21] A heavily armed twin-engined plane with a crew of five, the XFM-1 aroused excitement when it first flew in September 1937. Eight months later, the Air Corps ordered six service test models at a cost of $3,168,265. The Airacuda was expensive, as Chennault predicted, and it was a failure. Unwieldy and slow, it was easy prey for single-seat pursuits.[22]

Chennault constantly recommended faster single-seat pursuits with more firepower and range. By 1936, the Seversky P-35 and Curtiss P-36 offered marked improvement over the P-26. The next year, the Air Corps ordered prototypes of the Curtiss XP-40, Lockheed XP-38, and Bell XP-39. These three planes would be standard American fighters for the first two years of the Second World War. They were not operational, however, when war began in Europe. In 1939, the Air Corps still had the best bombers in the world and lagged in pursuit. The best performing pursuit, the Curtiss P-37, was no match for the German Me-109.[23]

The Air Corps lagged behind foreign air forces, particularly the Germans, in development of attack aircraft. The German Junkers Ju-87 Stuka and Ju-83 completely outclassed the American A-17.[24] In the late twenties, Captain Kenney had received War Department support for his attack course at the Air Corps Tactical School. He wrote textbooks for the course and developed techniques and weapons such as fragmentation bombs with time-delay fuses, which would later prove themselves in combat. But after Kenney's tour ended in 1929, the Air Corps Tactical School neglected close support. The Air Corps was not interested in attack. Prior to appearance of the A-12 Shrike in 1933, the majority of attack aircraft had been modified observation types. The A-12 was a two-place monoplane built by Curtiss. It had a top speed of 186 miles per hour and was armed with two .30-caliber machine guns and an internally carried bomb load of 10 chemical or fragmentation bombs, or four 100-pound demolition bombs.[25] To bomber-oriented airmen such as Arnold, the A-12's bomb load was pitifully inadequate. The Northrop A-17, delivered to the Air Corps in 1936, had a load nearly 200 pounds greater than the A-12, but this was still considered inadequate. In tests at Barksdale Field in 1938, attacks by A-17s proved less effective than bombardment, and it was decided to replace attack aircraft with light bombers.[26]

Slow development of pursuit and attack aviation in the early and mid-1930s was clearly the result of preoccupation of Air Corps leaders with the heavy bomber. Later, critics would say that failure to push pursuit and attack aviation, especially pursuit, was the Air Corps's greatest mistake in the thirties.[27] Bombers were not as invincible as was imagined. High-performance, heavily armed interceptors guided by radar raised the odds against bombers penetrating air defense. Bomber advocates underestimated interceptors. Moreover, they did not know about the development of radar, a fact that was later judged a "fortunate ignorance" by one member of the bomber school. "Had this development been well known," said Maj Gen Haywood S. Hansell Jr. years later, "it is probable that theorists would also have reasoned that, through the aid of radar, defense forces would be massed against incoming bomber attacks in a degree that would have been too expensive for the offensive."[28] If not for that fortunate ignorance, the majority of airmen might not have supported strategic bombardment theories.

In the mid-1930s, airmen were ignorant of radar and, except for a few die-hard attack and pursuit enthusiasts, gave heavy bombers first priority. With the B-10 they were beginning to get the speed they wanted; now it was time to go for range. At Wright Field in 1933, the Materiel Division sought to determine if it was possible to build an aircraft capable of carrying a 2,000-pound bomb load 5,000 miles (five times the range of the B-10). A bomber with such range would solve the hoary problems of reinforcing the air forces in Hawaii, Panama, and Alaska. Designated Project A, the study received General Staff approval, and Boeing and Martin were asked to submit designs and engineering data. Range was very much a question of size. The plane had to be big enough, with a wing span wide enough to carry the fuel load for range. The Martin design (XB-16) was for a leviathan weighing 104,000 pounds, with a 173-foot wing span and six Allison V-1710-3 engines, 1,000 horsepower each. Boeing's proposal (the XB-15) called for a 70,000-pound plane with four of the 1,000-horsepower Allison engines and a wing span of 149 feet. The Boeing design was chosen for further study, and a prototype was completed in late 1937. Its performance failed to meet expectations. The Allison engines were not perfected in time, and Boeing engineers had to substitute 850-horsepower twin Wasps. It was a standing joke that if those engines had ever looked back to see what they were pulling, they would all four quit simultaneously. The B-15 had a range 1,600 miles short of the desired 5,000 miles.[29]

Meanwhile, the Air Corps was planning the next production bomber. To decide upon a model, a "fly-off" competition was held at Wright Field in the autumn of 1935. The design circular sent to manufacturers stated that the new bomber must carry a bomb load of 2,000 pounds and have a range of at least 1,020 miles and a top speed of at least 200 miles per hour. Desired range was 2,200 miles and desired speed was 250 miles per hour. The plans were to produce up to 220 planes. The three most promising entries were by Martin, Douglas, and Boeing. The Martin 146 was an enlarged B-10. It had Fowler flaps to improve landing characteristics and two Wright R-1820-G5 Cyclones that propelled it to a top speed of 234 miles per hour with a maximum range of 1,589. The Douglas DB-1, later designated the XB-18, was also a twin-engined design powered by two Wright Cyclones with a performance similar to that of the Martin. The Boeing plan was by far the most exciting entry—an impressive sleek four-engined giant, dubbed Model 299 by Boeing and XB-17 by the Air Corps.[30] Newspaper reporters, said the later author of a history of Boeing Airplane Company, "called it an aerial battle cruiser, a veritable flying fortress."[31] And the XB-17's performance matched its appearance. In the 2,000-mile nonstop flight from Boeing's Seattle plant to Wright Field, the Boeing test pilot pushed the big plane at an average speed of 233 miles per hour, arriving at Wright Field more than an hour early.

Here, in what became known after its acceptance as the B-17, was the most famous plane in the entire history of the Air Corps, and perhaps of American military aviation. What a gorgeous plane it was! With its sleek fuselage and huge rounded tail, the four big engines suspended lightly under the long, graceful wings, no airman could ever forget it. None of the later planes except possibly the B-36, which was memorable mostly because of its gigantic size and freakishly reversed engines, would so excite enthusiasts of the air.

It was, of course, just the sort of plane General Andrews wanted for GHQ Air Force. He had made clear that he believed that long-range large capacity airplanes were more efficient, economical and useful than short-range medium capacity airplanes. Such planes could reinforce Hawaii, Alaska, and Panama. They could do long-range reconnaissance and bombing missions up to 1,500 miles from their bases. While initial cost of the 3,000-mile bomber was approximately twice that of the 1,000-mile bomber, "it requires 4 short-range bombers to strike the blow of one long-range bomber." He recommended War Department purchase of "bombardment and L.R. observation airplanes of the greatest capacity and range available" and urged that "all future development of bombardment and long-range observation planes be directed toward still greater increase in range and bomb carrying capacity."[32] Air Corps officers in charge of procurement held similar opinions, and even before the competition was completed, they proposed that the Army buy 65 B-17s instead of 185 other planes previously authorized for FY 1936.

Then, on the morning of 30 October 1935, tragedy struck. On takeoff from Wright Field, the XB-17, piloted by Maj Ployer P. "Pete" Hill, went into a steep climb. Heading almost straight up, it stalled, fell off on one wing, and plummeted. As it approached crashing, it appeared for a second to pull out of the dive but did not make it. The big plane smashed into the ground and burst into flames. Hill and Les Tower, who had gone along as an observer, were dragged from the wreckage. Hill died that afternoon, Tower some days later. The remaining three crew members recovered.

It seemed that Army leaders had reason to be reluctant to produce the big plane. Critics declared the XB-17 "too much airplane for any one man to handle."[33] Investigation revealed, however, that pilot error had caused the accident. Hill had forgotten to remove the control surface locks, which were designed to keep the elevator from whipping in the wind when the plane was on the ground. With control surfaces locked, no one can handle any airplane, whatever size.

Although the accident did not diminish Air Corps enthusiasm for the B-17, the War Department refused to put it into production. The request for 65 of the big bombers was reduced to 13 for service testing. The B-18 was chosen for production, and 133 planes were ordered.[34]

While the cost of the B-17 was an important factor in the Army's decision, it was no longer the overriding factor it had been in previous years. In his final report as chief of staff, MacArthur optimistically declared,

> For the first time since 1922 the Army enters a new fiscal year [July 1935–June 1936] with a reasonable prospect of developing itself into a defense establishment commensurate in size and efficiency to the country's needs. Obstacles, which for thirteen years have impeded, if not inhibited, progress toward this goal, have recently either been swept aside by Congress or materially reduced in importance. The present year definitely marks the beginning of a long-deferred resumption of military preparedness on a scale demanded by the most casual regard for the Nation's safety and security.[35]

The appropriation bill for 1936 had provided for 46,250 additional men to fill out the "attenuated skeletons" of tactical units in the Regular Army and bring the Air Corps up to authorized strength.[36]

MacArthur declared that the Army's principal needs for additional legislative authorization involve air development and that the "first need of our Air Corps is for fighting planes."[37] A year later, General Westover would admit in his annual report that the year was "notable for the very substantial increase in appropriations for the Air Corps."[38]

At last there was money coming, and Army leaders were fully aware that some of it must be spent for greater air strength. Their concern was that this increased air strength contribute to a well-balanced army and support of the Army's defensive mission. Army leaders were concerned not only with how many planes the Air Corps should have, but what kind, and how they should be used. Actually the last issue, how the planes should be used, was pivotal. Use determined the kind and how many. Andrews in his argument for purchase of B-17s indicated that intended use for the airplanes was coastal defense of the continental United States and its possessions. The range and firepower of the long-range bomber allowed it to reinforce the possessions and to detect and destroy distant enemy forces before they could attack.[39] He avoided mention of strategic bombing doctrine, although he and his staff at Headquarters GHQ Air Force recognized strategic bombing as the most important use for the long-range bomber. But Army leaders were well aware of the relation of the long-range bomber to strategic bombing and that a decision to adopt the B-17 would in a sense be a decision on how the GHQ Air Force would be employed.

War Department Training Regulation 440-15, *Employment of the Air Forces of the Army*, had been under review since October 1934, when MacArthur, anticipating organization of the GHQ Air Force, had ordered a restatement of air doctrines "with a view to a broader understanding of the Air Corps's place in the scheme of national defense and in expectation of doing away with misconceptions and interbranch prejudices."[40] Debate on the new air doctrine revealed the difference between Air Corps and General Staff ideas of airpower. A draft to the new air doctrine was drawn by Kilbourne's War Plans Division, based on the findings of the Drum and Baker boards. It placed little emphasis on strategic bombing.[41] This raised a storm from the officers at the Air Corps Tactical School. While they prudently recognized that "national policy, geographic location of bases and the present range of planes" dictated an air defense role for GHQ Air Force, they made clear, as they had before the Howell Commission, that "the principal and all important mission of air power, when its equipment permits, is the attack of those vital objectives in a nation's economic structure which will tend to paralyze that nation's ability to wage war and thus contribute directly to the attainment of the ultimate objective of war, namely, the disintegration of the hostile will to resist."[42] In the final draft of Training Regulation 440-15, the General Staff conceded that in future war there would probably be an air phase before contact of surface forces and the outcome of that phase would have a serious effect upon subsequent operations. In the air phase and also in later phases of combat, the GHQ Air Force could conduct operations beyond the reach of ground forces. The implication remained in the General Staff's choice of words that wars would be decided on the ground. The General Staff was not ready to accept the strategic bombing doctrine and therefore the need for long-range bombers.

In April 1936, War Plans proposed an aircraft policy "limiting the range and capacity of the larger types of aircraft to those necessary for national defense purposes." Brig Gen Stanley Embick told the chief of staff that it was inadvisable to equip GHQ Air Force with long-range bombers "since this would give rise to the suspicion, both at home and abroad, that our GHQ Air Force was being maintained for aggressive purposes." While it was desirable to have some aircraft capable of reinforcing Hawaii, Alaska, and Panama, defense needs would be better served by many smaller planes. They were more flexible, could operate from less elaborate bases, and, since there would be more of them, more pilots could be trained. He suggested that the maximum military requirements for a bomber were a 2,200-pound bomb capacity and a 1,500-mile combat range. These limits were not to restrict experiment or service testing of planes of advanced design.[43]

General Andrews disagreed wholeheartedly with War Plans and campaigned vigorously to get the War Department to change its policy. The principal mission of the GHQ Air Force was coastal defense, which he contended meant defense of the Western Hemisphere. "Any serious threat against our defensive jurisdiction," he said, "must come across the water from overseas." GHQ Air Force must prepare to defend against seaborne invasion supported by aircraft carriers and against air attacks from hostile air bases in the Western Hemisphere. Bombers would have to find the enemy and attack. He denied that equipping the GHQ Air Force would be aggressive. "Whatever the modern bomber may be in the case of countries contiguous or near to each other," he said, "in the fortunate situation in which the United States finds itself, combined with our policy of defense, the modern bombardment airplane can be considered only as a powerful instrument of defense. To reach its maximum effectiveness as such it must be able to operate efficiently and safely over large areas of water."[44] The two-engined B-18 would not only be "at the mercy" of pursuits being developed abroad, but its range and low performance would make it hopelessly inadequate for over-water defense.[45]

Continued procurement of two-engined bombers was a serious mistake. "I strongly urge," Andrews said, "that contract awards be made only for four-engined bombers."[46]

Andrews made the most of every opportunity to prove the capabilities of the B-17. In maneuvers with the Navy in 1937, Lt Col Robert Olds found the battleship *Utah* in an area 100 by 300 miles off the California coast. The skipper of the *Utah*, feeling secure because of low clouds, had allowed his crew to work above deck. Olds saw the sailors on the *Utah*'s deck, but because he feared the Air Corps would not get credit for the find unless he carried out the planned attack with water-filled bombs, he gave the order to proceed. While no one was killed, several sailors were injured, one seriously. Instead of complaining, the captain of the *Utah* took responsibility for unpreparedness and radioed a "Well done!" to Olds's commander. The Air Corps hoped its success in the maneuvers would be made public, but it was not.[47] In February of the next year, they did have a very public demonstration of the B-17's capability. Olds led a Good Will Flight of six B-17s to Buenos Aires. With just one refueling stop at Lima, Peru, the planes made the 5,225-mile trip to the Argentine capital in 28 flying hours.[48] Three months later, on 19 May 1938, Andrews ordered a flight of three B-17s to intercept and make simulated attacks on the Italian liner *Rex* in the Atlantic inbound to New York. With Olds again in command, the B-17s located the *Rex* 725 miles from shore. Unfortunately, the Navy apparently protested the flight. Malin Craig, MacArthur's successor as chief of staff, telephoned Andrews to restrict Army flights to within 100 miles of the coast. The Navy had abrogated the MacArthur–Pratt Agreement after the end of Admiral Pratt's tour as chief of naval operations and now Craig, who believed strongly that the Army should concentrate on aircraft to support ground operations, was apparently willing to turn coastal defense over to the Navy.[49]

General Andrews's campaign for the B-17 brought him increasingly into conflict with Craig and the General Staff. When his tour as commander of GHQ Air Force ended, he was returned to his permanent rank of colonel and, like Mitchell, was "exiled" to San Antonio in 1926. Andrews's staff, according to his chief of staff, Col Hugh Knerr, was intentionally "broken up, scattered to the four corners." Knerr was retired for ill health after, again according to him, the Army tried to declare him psychologically disturbed, with a persecution complex.[50] Whether Knerr's charges were true or not is subject to debate; but it is true that Craig felt that many airmen had a narrow perspective, did not understand the situation of the Army, and were prone to exaggerate the weakness of the Air Corps. "Some of our officers in computing the strength of our air fleet," he said, "are prone to waive aside any planes that are not of the most modern type. These same officers may include in the strength of foreign air fleets, planes which are either not existent or which should long before have been delegated to a museum."[51]

While Andrews was leading his "fight for airpower" from his position as commander GHQ Air Forces, General Westover was working for the same goal through the Office of the Chief of the Air Corps. The two were often in conflict over prerogatives of their respective offices but were in agreement over the need for heavy bombers.

Several times approval was given for development and production of heavy bombers and withdrawn. Such was the case with the Air Corps program advanced by Secretary of War Harry H. Woodring. As the Air Corps approached its authorized strength of 2,320 aircraft in FY 1939, Woodring directed that a five-year aircraft replacement program be drawn up to begin with FY 1940.[52] Based on Air Corps studies for a so-called Balanced Air Corps program, and recommendations of Generals Westover and Andrews, the Woodring program was approved on 18 March 1938. It authorized a combat strength of 1,094 combat planes, 144 of them four-engined bombers, 266 twin-engined bombers, 259 attack aircraft, and 425 pursuit aircraft. Procurement of the four-engined bombers was to begin in FY 1940 with the purchase of 67. But in July 1938, only four months after approval of the program, it was withdrawn, and Westover was informed that "estimates for bombardment airplanes for the FY 1940 will be restricted to light, medium and attack types." Westover protested. He pointed out to the General Staff that the Woodring program, along with the Balanced Air Corps program on which it was based, represented two years of study and was the "first complete and balanced program approved by the War Department, General Staff and the Air Corps." He warned that disapproval of the Woodring program would set the Air Corps back five years. Westover did not get the chance to read the General Staff's reply to his protest because he was killed in an aircraft accident on 21 September.[53]

General Craig approved the reply on 30 September. Brig Gen George P. Tyner, who wrote it, explained that approval for the program was denied because it would require an increase in Air Corps personnel who would have to come from other combat arms. He implied that airpower had been overemphasized with the Woodring program, which raised the Air Corps to readiness above other combat arms. He noted that in recent wars in Spain, China, and Ethiopia, air forces had been unable by themselves to gain a decisive victory. As for influence of airpower short of war, he mentioned "recent events in Europe, wherein sovereign states have been completely or partially absorbed by stronger nations."

Subjected states had allies with powerful air forces but this did not deter the aggressor.[54]

Thus, the General Staff supported increases in the strength of the Air Corps but balked on production of heavy bombers. The original order of 13 B-17s was eventually delivered to the Air Corps. In 1937, the prototype of the B-15 was delivered. These 14 planes were the total of Air Corps heavy bombers through 1938. But the situation was about to change.

The Army Air Force

President Roosevelt in 1938 was receiving frightening reports from Amb. Hugh R. Wilson in Berlin regarding the Luftwaffe and the production capacity of the German aircraft industry. He held a White House conference with his military advisers on the afternoon of 14 November, and among those present were Secretary of Treasury Henry Morgenthau; Harry Hopkins, head of the Work Projects Administration; Assistant Secretary of War Louis Johnson; General Craig; Deputy Chief of Staff George C. Marshall; Adm Harold R. Stark; and Major General Arnold, the new chief of the Air Corps. Roosevelt reviewed the growing military might of Germany and proposed a large air force as a defense. He said that a well-equipped army of 400,000 men would not make much of an impression on Hitler. A large air force would. He suggested asking Congress for 20,000 airplanes and a production capacity of 24,000. Congress might give at least 10,000 planes and production capacity for 10,000 per year. The immediate goal would be 3,750 combat planes; 3,750 reserve planes; and 2,500 training planes. General Arnold was overjoyed.[55] Airpower enthusiasts now had a champion at the very top of the nation's political structure, something they had never had before. Presidents Coolidge and Hoover, and Roosevelt in his first administration, all had restrained military spending, reducing it to the bare minimum whenever and wherever possible. With their expensive needs and high expectations for airpower, airmen often had felt this policy was directed at them. Now a president was beginning to advocate expansion, with emphasis on the Air Corps. This gave not only priority but prestige to the airmen's needs. As Arnold put it, the Air Corps had achieved its Magna Carta.[56]

The president said he intended to ask Congress for $500 million to pay for this expansion of the Air Corps. The War Department began plans for the expansion. In addition to the purchase of 10,000 airplanes, War Plans included expanding Air Corps training programs and support facilities, and also an increase of 58,000 in the ground forces and 36,000 in the National Guard. The latter proportions angered President Roosevelt. The War Department, he complained, was offering him everything except airplanes. After much discussion, Craig and Marshall finally convinced the president to allot $200 million of the proposed $500 million for ground armament and $120 million of the remaining $300 million for non-plane air items, including more bases.[57]

On 12 January 1939, in a special message to Congress, Roosevelt declared that American air forces were so utterly inadequate that they had to be immediately strengthened. In response, Congress authorized $300 million for expansion of the Air Corps "not to exceed six thousand serviceable airplanes." The War Department initiated a "balanced" program to increase Air Corps strength to 5,500 planes; 3,203 officers; and 45,000 enlisted men. This meant purchase of 3,251 planes in the next two years. By 30 June 1941, the Air Corps hoped to have 24 combat-ready tactical groups.[58]

To the delight of Air Corps leaders, the principal mission of this expanded air force was defense of the Western Hemisphere. In his notes on the 14 November meeting, Hap Arnold wrote that the president had said that "the United States must be prepared to resist attack on the western hemisphere from the North Pole to the South Pole, including all of North America and South America, and that our national defense machine at the present time, while weak in other parts, was weakest in Army planes. When called upon for such a mission . . . we must have a sufficiently large air force to deter anyone from landing in either North or South America."[59] That was justification for procurement of long-range bombers, and 250 B-17s were included in the 5,500-plane program.[60]

Secretary Woodring in March 1939 appointed General Arnold to head an Air Board to determine how best to use aircraft in defense of the hemisphere. The study reached the desk of General Marshall, who had succeeded General Craig as the new chief of staff in August 1939, on the first day of September—the day the Nazis began their blitzkrieg against Poland. On 3 September, the British and French declared war on Germany. The Second World War had begun.

Two weeks later, Poland lay defeated, and the shock over its fall had an immediate effect on American policy. After heated debate, Congress enacted a new "cash and carry law" in November 1939, which allowed belligerents to buy arms in the United States provided they paid cash and transported the goods home in their own ships.[61] Since the British fleet had swept German shipping from the seas, the policy favored Britain and France, both of whom wanted American aircraft. By the end of 1939, they had ordered 2,500 planes from American manufacturers. By the end of March 1940, the figure was 8,200. This gave American planes a test in combat. But as Arnold and his staff feared, shipments of planes to the

British and French slowed deliveries to the Air Corps. Arnold's warnings against increasing shipments to the Allies brought him into conflict with the president who once allegedly had said that he considered "the Maginot Line our first line of defense."[62] In March 1940, Roosevelt let Arnold know that "there were places to which officers who did not 'play ball' might be sent, such as Guam."[63]

By late spring 1940, it appeared that the arms shipments to Britain and France had been in vain. The Germans had flanked the Maginot Line. The fall of France was imminent and there was doubt about Britain's ability to stand before the Nazi blitz. Faced with this disaster, Roosevelt appeared before a joint session of Congress to present proposals for strengthening America's defenses, again emphasizing airpower. There was a feeling of urgency in the chamber as the president spoke of the vulnerability of the Western Hemisphere to air attack. There should be, he declared, a program to provide and maintain 50,000 airplanes for the nation's Army and Navy air services (36,500 planes for the Army; 13,500 for the Navy) as well as an increase in the nation's manufacturing capability to build 50,000 planes a year to back up this program. The purpose in expanding aircraft production was twofold: to build America's air defense and to increase production of aircraft for the British and French. The Allies' needs were swamping American manufacturers with urgent orders for planes which General Arnold insisted the United States could ill afford to give up until its own air arm was adequate. The president ended his speech with a request for a billion dollars for Army and Navy aviation and an appeal for congressional cooperation.[64]

The emphasis was on airpower. Poland had "died on its air fields," with little doubt among war planners about the effectiveness of airpower.[65] Before the German victories, Gallup surveys had indicated that among Americans "nine in every ten favor a larger air force."[66] Now even the one in ten who opposed a larger air force must have had doubt. Henry L. Stimson, Roosevelt's new secretary of war, declared, "Air power has decided the fate of nations; Germany, with her powerful air armadas, has vanquished one people after another. On the ground, large armies had been mobilized to resist her, but each time it was additional power in the air that decided the fate of each individual nation."[67]

Despite efforts of the previous year to build the Air Corps, there was understandable concern that America's air forces were undermanned and underequipped. Frequently quoted was Eddie Rickenbacker's remark that the United States was 10 years behind Germany in the development of military aviation, the United States was producing only 402 military aircraft a month by April 1940, and a large part of that output was going to England.[68] The Air

Corps had assigned only 907 cadets to pilot training in early 1940. Only some 1,900 of its airplanes were combat craft, of which just a few had self-sealing gasoline tanks, armor, and heavy machine guns.[69]

Within two weeks after President Roosevelt's 50,000-airplane speech, Congress appropriated funds for any aircraft the Air Corps wanted. The total of money exceeded a billion and a half dollars, considerably more than the president had requested. "All you have to do is ask for it," said Sen. Henry Cabot Lodge Jr. (R-Mass.).[70] By early autumn, the total had risen to over two billion. Spending all this money kept Air Corps procurement officers working around the clock. Shortly after the speech, they let contracts for 10,000 airplanes, and by midsummer they were, as I. B. Holley Jr. has written in an Army study, "signing as many as 1,000 contracts a day . . . purchasing everything from flying boots to four-engine bombers."[71]

For all the bold talk of the president, unprecedented appropriations of the Congress, frenetic rushing about of procurement officers, the real results, which could only be measured in aircraft delivered to the Air Corps, were meager. Six months after the speech, during a low point in production, an entire week passed with only two tactical aircraft delivered.[72] Nor did the situation improve much for months to come. In the summer of 1940, Arnold reviewed the airplane situation and noted that total tactical strength of the Army's air forces was 523 airplanes. That number was a paper total, since nine of the tactical air groups were equipped with obsolete B-18s or P-36s, which were of little use against Japanese Zeros or German Messerschmitts.[73] Finally, in the autumn of 1941, when deliveries began to increase, time had almost run out. In November 1941, Arnold could see some improvement over the bleak conditions he had observed in his survey of the previous summer. Still, there was woefully little to show for the money and time spent since President Roosevelt had announced the goal of 50,000. Instead of 36,500 aircraft, the original Air Corps calculation of its share of the 50,000, the Army Air Corps on the eve of Pearl Harbor contained only 3,304 combat planes; of these 1,024 were overseas.[74] Noncombat types included another 7,024: 216 transports; 6,594 trainers; and 214 communications, of which only 98 were overseas. During the first month of the war, 412 combat planes were lost, and the Air Force could only replace half that loss at the time.[75]

The failure of procurement machinery was not due so much to human faults as it was to faults of the machinery. The president's demand for 50,000 airplanes and a billion dollars was as one writer put it, "a stunner, and it took the breath away; most noticeably, the breath of the Army Air Force, nothing in the Air Force's dreams having fore-shadowed anything like this."[76] Production capabilities were limited. American manufacturing was still a small-scale operation, 41st among American industries with annual output of less than 6,000 planes.[77] Neither the industry nor the procurement system was prepared for a 50,000-plane program. The Air Corps was already in the midst of a sudden expansion initiated in 1939 by Roosevelt's demand for 10,000 airplanes and Congress's appropriations of $300 million toward that goal. A sudden new goal meant not an orderly procurement but "guesses, makeshifts and temporary expedients, always subject to change."[78] In the jargon of military planners, it added a "confusion factor" to planning. It was a situation that would be repeated in the next two years; only as production goals were stabilized would production expand to meet the demand.

Plans changed so rapidly it was difficult to keep them in mind. For several months after the president announced his 50,000-plane proposal, the War Department studied its needs. On 26 June 1940, General Marshall approved the First Aviation Objective: 12,835 planes organized into 54 combat groups by April 1942. The 54-group program had hardly been initiated when planning began for an even larger force, 84 groups to be combat ready by 30 June 1942. Dubbed the Second Aviation Objective, the 84-group plan was approved in March 1941. By then the possibility that the United States would be drawn into the war was becoming greater with each day. On 9 July 1941, President Roosevelt directed the secretaries of war and the Navy to prepare an estimate of "overall production requirements required to defeat our potential enemies." Responsibility for preparing the section dealing with the needs of the Air Corps was given to Lt Col Harold L. George and his newly created Air War Plans Division of the Office of the Chief of the Air Corps.[79]

At last, with George's designation as head of Air War Plans, came some clear thinking. In a week's time, George and three other officers from his division—Lt Col Kenneth N. Walker, Maj Laurence S. Kuter, and Maj Haywood S. Hansell Jr.—prepared what proved to be an amazingly accurate estimate of the requirements for war against Japan and Germany. Known as Air War Plans Division—Plan 1 (AWPD-1), their war plan of July 1941 declared that the Air Corps would need 201 combat groups without the proposed B-36-type bomber and 251 with the B-36. The latter force would be equipped with 60,799 operational aircraft, including 3,740 B-36s. It would be manned by 179,398 officers and 1,939,237 enlisted men, for a total of 2,118,635. The estimate was very close. Wartime peak strength was 2,400,000 men and approximately 80,000 aircraft organized into 243 combat groups.[80]

Building a massive air force brought altogether different problems than air planners had faced during the years of budget cuts. When mobilization at last got underway, the coffers were open wide. The question now was how to mobilize and train on a massive scale, for most American military leaders a unique problem.

President Roosevelt had made realistic training programs difficult for the Air Corps at the outset by insisting that the money be spent for planes and nothing but planes. Hitler would not be impressed "with barracks, runways, and schools for mechanics."[81] But even Arnold, the staunchest of supporters for increased airplane production, insisted that money for planes was of no use without operating bases, pilots, and crews, and that the president's program would require a ground force of about a million men.[82]

It was obvious that as aircraft expansion programs spiraled, so would the necessity for pilots and navigators, mechanics, and bases. One of the first changes made to increase the number of trained pilots was to relax eligibility requirements. Originally, eligible men had to have two years of college, not because it was necessary in pilot training but because all graduating cadets became commissioned officers and commissioned officers had to have some college education. By mid-1939, a high school graduate could be accepted for flight training as a noncommissioned officer if he was unmarried and of good character, between 18 and 22 years of age, in the upper half of his high school class with a minimum of one and one-half mathematics credits, met the physical requirements, and passed the Army General Classification Test.[83] On the eve of Pearl Harbor, more than 9,000 pilots had received their wings under this program. Meanwhile, some 59,000 mechanics and technicians had graduated from training schools. The number of officers and men in the Air Corps had risen to 354,000.[84]

One reason pilot training could be accelerated so quickly and effectively was the use of civilian flying schools and personnel. Arnold in 1938 had recruited some of the best-known civilian flying school people to house, feed, and train flying cadets.[85] The instructors were trained by the Air Corps, and Army training planes furnished the schools.[86] Until the huge expansions of 1941, graduates going on active duty received final training at Randolph and Kelly Fields in Texas. Use of civilian training facilities and people helped build a reserve of pilots who could be called upon when war came, and it also meant no delay in expanding the training program. Expansion plans were on the board, however, and by the end of 1941 pilots were in advanced training not just in Texas but all over the southern half of the United States.

Texas, the location of good flying weather and Bermuda grass runways, had been headquarters for primary and advanced flying training until the expansion of 1940. The Air Corps Training Center at San Antonio had been established in 1926 under command of Brig Gen Frank P. Lahm, the first military passenger in an airplane and long known as one of the Air Corps's inner circle of pilots. Under the direction of Lahm, the San Antonio facilities were expanded considerably in the late 1920s, and on 20 June 1930, were dedicated as the "West Point of the Air" and named Randolph Field for Capt William M. Randolph, a native Texan and member of the Site Selection Board who had been killed in a crash in 1928. The spot chosen, 23,000 acres known as the Cibolo Site, was ideal because of good weather, level ground, and the nearness of Fort Sam Houston. Concentric circles of quarters designed by local architects reached out from the headquarters buildings, with bedrooms on the windward side for coolness. Originally, the only paved ground was the warming-up area in front of the hangars; paved runways were added later with the use of higher-powered engines. The only difficulty seemed to be finding enough water; many wells had to be dug before there was an adequate water supply. Planners did manage to put in an oval swimming pool behind the Officers Mess, described for authorization purposes as an auxiliary fire reservoir. When one congressman inspecting Randolph Field asked why an auxiliary fire reservoir had underwater lighting, the explanation was that "if a fireman should happen to fall in it at night, we wouldn't be able to locate him without the lighting." The amused congressman proceeded to authorize three more "fire reservoirs," provided no other congressmen were told about it.

The land for Randolph Field had been donated by the citizens of San Antonio, anxious to have the Air Corps training headquarters because of the large payroll and expenditures for supplies. At the time the Air Corps was looking for an agreeable location, General Patrick had said that government fields were available in Florida with its favorable climate and that the government was not paying for any land. The burghers of San Antonio had arranged to buy the Cibolo Site using funds from back taxes.[87]

During the Depression's enforced economies, as few as 150 cadets a year graduated from the facility, but among this small group came many of the men who would lead the Air Force a decade later: Curtis E. LeMay, Edwin W. Rawlings, Joseph H. Atkinson, Elwood R. Quesada, Thomas S. Power, and Donald L. Putt.[88] This picture of a small select group of cadets changed drastically by 1941 when the objective became 30,000 pilots by the end of the year, eight other training bases were in operation besides Randolph and Kelly Fields, and 20 more were under construction or just completed.[89] In the continental United States in 1939, there had been only 17 Army air bases and four depots. Most of the bases were in need of repair. Housing varied from good to poor. Some airmen were living in permanent brick buildings. Others, like the men at Chanute Field, Illinois, were living in overcrowded, run-down "temporary" barracks constructed during the buildup for the First World War. Chanute had such a bad reputation that when an airman erred it was sometimes suggested in jest, "Don't shoot'em, Chanute'em."[90] Repairing these old bases and building new ones to meet Air Corps demands was a gargantuan task. Tens of thousands of workmen were engaged and by December 1941 there were 114 Army air bases in the United States.

The Air Corps was also expanding old bases and establishing new ones outside the continental United States. Extension of hemisphere defense into the Atlantic and Pacific required bases. In the Pacific, the problem, as one later account put it, "was essentially one of extending facilities in our own territories." In the Atlantic, it meant agreements with foreign powers for use of their territory.[91]

The two most probable routes for a German attack on the Western Hemisphere were from Dakar in French West Africa to the eastern coast of Brazil in the South Atlantic, and via the island chain formed by Iceland, Greenland, and Newfoundland in the North Atlantic. Because of lack of fortifications, the Caribbean was vulnerable to German raiders. The first step toward extending Atlantic defenses was the "destroyers for bases deal," announced by Roosevelt on 3 September 1940. The agreement gave the United States 99-year leases on bases in Newfoundland, Bermuda, the Bahamas, Jamaica, Antigua, Saint Lucia, Trinidad, and British Guiana in exchange for 50 US destroyers. Air Corps units were stationed on four of the Caribbean sites and at Gander Lake, Newfoundland. In the spring of 1941, after US agreement with the Danish government, Air Corps bases were established in Greenland. Several months later, American forces joined British forces on Iceland, which had declared independence from Denmark. In November 1941, a base was established in Dutch Guiana by agreement with the Dutch government in exile.[92]

In the spring of 1941, American forces in the Caribbean area were organized into the Caribbean Defense Command, largely air units stationed at Puerto Rico and Panama as well as at the leased bases. General Andrews, whom General Marshall earlier had retrieved from "exile" in San Antonio, became the commander.[93]

The anchor of Pacific defense was Hawaii, and on 1 November 1940, air units there were organized into the Hawaiian Air Force. It had only 117 obsolete aircraft but was steadily reinforced, and by 6 December 1941, there were 231 Army planes in Hawaii, half of them modern, including twelve B-17Ds.[94] Great faith was put in the ability of the B-17s and the 99 P-40s stationed in Hawaii to defend the islands. When President Roosevelt opposed transfer of the fleet from Hawaii to the Atlantic in April 1941, believing it was needed to protect the islands, General Marshall assured him that with the B-17s and "our fine new pursuits, the land force could put up such a defense that the Japs wouldn't dare attack Hawaii, particularly such a long distance from home." Secretary of the Navy Frank Knox agreed with Marshall that Hawaii was impregnable.[95]

Prior to the summer of 1941, the Philippines were considered outside of American defenses. In June, partly because of faith in the B-17, a decision was made to defend that remote outpost. The Philippine army was mobilized and General MacArthur, who was in the Philippines, was recalled to active duty to organize and command the United States Army Forces in the Far East. Plans were made to reinforce the air force under MacArthur's command with a substantial number of B-17s. The first contingent of nine airplanes, under the command of Maj Emmett "Rosie" O'Donnell Jr., flew from Hawaii to Clark Field in the Philippines in early September. Twenty-six more bombers arrived in November. Maj Gen Lewis H. Brereton, commander of the Far East Air Force, had 265 combat planes at his disposal.[96] But in his diary Brereton complained, "There were no spare parts of any kind for P-40s, nor was there as much as an extra washer or nut for a Flying Fortress."[97] By December only two revetments were ready for the B-17s and the air-warning net was "pitifully inadequate."[98]

Preparation of air defenses in Alaska also began late. Work on Elmendorf Field, Alaska, commenced in the spring of 1940. In December 1941, there were only 32 obsolete aircraft in Alaska.[99]

The whirlwind expansion of airpower put a great strain on the three-way relationship between GHQ Air Force Headquarters, the Office of the Chief of the Air Corps, and the War Department. The fragmented chain of command caused by the side-by-side arrangement of GHQ Air Force and the Air Corps hindered the effectiveness of the Army's air arm. In the words of Robert A. Lovett, who was the special assistant for all air matters to Secretary of War Henry L. Stimson, "It was a perfectly screwball arrangement."[100] There were several adjustments before the problem was solved. On 1 March 1939, General Arnold as chief of the Air Corps was given authority over the commander of GHQ Air Force. A year and a half later, in November 1940, Arnold was designated acting deputy chief of staff for air, retaining his position as chief of the Air Corps. His dual role, plus his close working relationship with Marshall, was supposed to bring some unity and direction to air policy, but as the tempo of mobilization increased and delays and confusion plagued the efforts of the war planners, it was apparent the organization was not working. Eventually, Gen George H. Brett was appointed chief of the Air Corps, and both he and the commander of GHQ, Gen Delos C. Emmons, reported, at least technically, to Arnold. Further changes had to be made. The first was to create in 1941 a virtually autonomous air arm; it was called the Army Air Forces, consisting of both the GHQ and its air forces in the field and the Army Air Corps under one boss, Arnold. It had its own budget, although the force's housekeeping was still done by the Army. Its chief sat on both the Combined and Joint Staff meetings, although he was rarely consulted except in air matters.[101] The other change was to appoint Lovett to the post of assistant secretary of war for air, a job that had been vacant for eight years. Stimson's assistant and already an ally of airpower, Lovett had come to Washington partly as a result of a report he wrote as a private citizen in 1939 after visiting aircraft plants.[102] His new job was to study all questions involved in procurement of airplanes, including purchase and production. The working relationship between Arnold and Lovett was good, Arnold later recalling Lovett as "a man who possessed the qualities in which I was weakest, a partner and teammate of tremendous sympathy, and of calm and hidden force."[103]

Ironically, with this move in 1941 toward autonomy, agitation practically ceased for a separate Air Force. In any event, there was no longer time for it. As Lovett remarked, "You can't, in the face of war, so to speak, have reorganization. It's like trying to operate on a man for some serious internal disorder while at the same time you ask him to carry on his daily work—particularly if it's manual labor."[104]

The end of agitation saw a more measured appreciation of the Army. Arnold would suggest in his memoirs that being kept with the Army structure all those years may have resulted in the "best rounded, best balanced air force in the world."[105] Air Corps planners in the 1930s would have liked a single-minded commitment to strategic bombardment, but they were forced to give some attention to "tactical" ground-support operations. And though they had to share a budget with ground forces, the money they did have went for planes and not for housekeeping. In contrast, the Royal Air Force (RAF), autonomous since 1918, had to pay not only for planes but for materiel, training, and housing for not only pilots but all the people in auxiliary services—the "cook, the baker, medics, signal personnel, etc."[106] In 1940, the RAF still did not have bombers that had been designed in 1935–36.[107]

Notes

1. Annual Report of Chief of Staff for the Fiscal Year Ending 30 June 1935, in the *Annual Report of the Secretary of War, 1935* (Washington, D.C.: GPO, 1935), 42.

2. Henry H. Arnold, *Global Mission* (New York: Harper, 1949), 158.

3. Diary of Hugh J. Knerr, 1925–1934, unpaged, in the special collections at the United States Air Force Academy Library, Colorado Springs, Colo.

4. Quoted in Jean H. DuBuque and Robert F. Gleckner, *The Development of the Heavy Bomber, 1918–1944*, USAF Historical Study 6, revised (Maxwell AFB, Ala.: USAF Historical Division, Air University, 1951), 8–9.

5. Ray Wagner, *American Combat Planes* (Garden City, N.Y.: Hanover House, 1960), 101–2; and Lloyd S. Jones, *U.S. Bombers, B1–B70* (Los Angeles: Aero Publishers, 1962), 21–26.

6. DuBuque and Gleckner, 10.

7. Wagner, 101–2; Jones, 27–29.

8. Wagner, 104–7; and Jones, 30–32.

9. Benjamin D. Foulois and Carroll V. Glines, *From the Wright Brothers to the Astronauts: The Memoirs of Benjamin D. Foulois* (New York: McGraw-Hill, 1968), 270–71.

10. Martin Caidin, *Air Force: A Pictorial History of American Airpower* (New York: Rinehart, 1957), 64–67; Arnold; and Historical Office of the Army Air Forces, *The Official Pictorial History of the AAF* (New York: Duell, Sloan and Pearce, 1947), 78–79. In the Arnold papers in the Library of Congress (LOC) there is a scrapbook on the Alaska flight.

11. Arnold had made the same mistake on one of his flights but fortunately he had enough altitude to correct the mistake and get his engines restarted before crashing. Knerr diary.

12. Ibid.

13. According to Knerr, Gen Oscar Westover had indicated that every member of the flight would be awarded the Distinguished Flying Cross. "The General congratulated us and said we had earned the Distinguished Flying Cross by our performance, and by bringing all the airplanes home. Not long after, I was informed General Arnold [sic] had taken the award himself for the entire flight." Ibid.

14. Quoted in the *New York Times*, 16 April 1933.

15. Henry H. Arnold to the chief of the Air Corps, letter, 26 November 1934, records of the Adjutant General (AG) 580 (11-26-34), Record Group (RG), 407, National Archives (NA).

16. Ibid.

17. Henry H. Arnold to Brig Gen H. C. Pratt, letter, 26 September 1932, Arnold manuscripts (MSS), LOC.

18. Maj W. H. Frank, assistant commandant Air Corps Tactical School (ACTS), report to Brig Gen Benjamin D. Foulois, D/AC Ohio Maneuvers, subject: Report on Maneuvers, 30 August 1929. Quoted in Robert Frank Futrell, *Ideas, Concepts, Doctrine: A History of Basic Thinking in the United States Air Force, 1907–1964* (Maxwell AFB, Ala.: Air University, 1974), 33. On the same page, Futrell also states that Lt Kenneth N. Walker coined a phrase that expressed the bomber doctrine: "A well organized, well planned, and well flown air force attack," he said, "will constitute an offensive that cannot be stopped." Capt Robert M. Webster repeated Walker's words almost verbatim before the Howell Commission. Ground officers, he asserted, "were not aware of the fact that a properly organized attack, once launched in the air, cannot be stopped." Testimony presented by Maj Donald Wilson, Capt Robert Olds, Capt Harold Lee George, Capt Robert M. Webster, and 1st Lt K. N. Walker before the Federal Aviation Commission, Washington, D.C.

19. Claire L. Chennault, *Way of a Fighter: The Memoirs of Claire Lee Chennault*, ed. Robert Hotz (New York: G. P. Putnam's Sons, 1949), 26. See also Robert T. Finney, *History of the Air Corps Tactical School, 1920–1940*, USAF Historical Study

100 (Maxwell AFB, Ala.: USAF Historical Division, Air University, 1955), 38–39; and Thomas H. Greer, *The Development of Air Doctrine in the Army Air Arm, 1917–1941*, USAF Historical Study 89 (Maxwell AFB, Ala.: USAF Historical Division, Air University, 1955), 47–66.

20. Chennault, 59.
21. Greer, 66.
22. Wagner, 202–4. The idea of an "air cruiser," an airplane that could handle both bombardment and air combat missions was suggested by the Air Corps Board in 1940. Gen George Marshall liked the idea but, according to Futrell, General Arnold felt it was then more important to emphasize production of existing planes than to begin research and development on entirely new planes. Futrell, 98.
23. Wagner, 194–224; Alfred Goldberg, ed., *A History of the United States Air Force, 1907–1957* (Princeton, N.J.: D. Van Nostrand, 1957), 44–45; Martin P. Claussen, *Material Research and Development in the Army Air Arm, 1914–1945*, USAF Historical Study 50 (Maxwell AFB, Ala.: USAF Historical Division, Air University, 1946), 28–29; and Futrell, 77.
24. Goldberg, 45; and Wagner, 62. Air Corps officers conceded that the Ju-87 Stuka dive-bomber was an effective weapon when operating under conditions of nearly complete air superiority. They pointed out, however, that it was likely that the Stuka could not defend itself against fighters. Futrell, 96.
25. Greer, 66–67; and Wagner, 56–60.
26. Wagner, 61–62; and Ronald R. Fogleman, "Mitchell on the Development of the USAAC," in Robert C. Ehrhart, *Modern Warfare and Society* (Colorado Springs, Colo.: US Air Force Academy, 1975), 19.
27. Bernard L. Boylan, *The Development of the Long Range Escort Fighter* (Ann Arbor, Mich.: University of Michigan Press, 1955), 242–46.
28. Quoted in Futrell, 100–101. See also Haywood S. Hansell Jr., *The Air Plan that Defeated Hitler* (Atlanta, Ga.: Higgins–MacArthur/Longino and Porter, 1972), 22.
29. Wagner, 108–14; Futrell, 78–83; and DuBuque and Gleckner, 14–15.
30. Wagner, 108–13.
31. Harold Mansfield, *Vision, the Story of Boeing: A Saga of the Sky and the New Horizons of Space* (New York: Duell, Sloan and Pearce, 1966), 120. See also Foulois and Glines, 231.
32. Gen Frank M. Andrews to the adjutant general, letter, 22 July 1935, War Plans Division (WPD) 3748, RG 165, NA.
33. Quoted in Foulois and Glines, 231–32.
34. Ibid., 323; Futrell, 86–87; Goldberg, 42; and Mansfield, 124.
35. *Annual Report of the Secretary of War*, 1935, 41.
36. Ibid., 44.
37. Ibid., 65–66.
38. *Annual Report of the Chief of the Air Corps.* A copy is located in File Number 319.1D from January 1932 to August 1936, Central Decimal Files 1917–38, RG 18, NA.
39. Gen Frank M. Andrews to the adjutant general, letter, 1 June 1937, records of the Office of the Chief of Staff (OCS) 17480-99, RG 165, NA.
40. Quoted in Wesley Frank Craven and James Lea Cate, eds., *The Army Air Forces in World War II*, vol. 1, *Plans and Early Operations, January 1939 to August 1942* (1949; new imprint, Washington, D.C.: Office of Air Force History, 1983), 48.
41. Ibid.
42. Ibid., 50.
43. Gen Stanley Embick, memorandum to the chief of staff, April 1936, WPD 3748-1, RG 165, NA.
44. Gen Frank M. Andrews to the adjutant general, letter, 1 June 1937, AG 452.1 (6-1-37) (1), RG 407, NA.
45. Quoted in DuBuque and Gleckner, 28.
46. Frank M. Andrews to the adjutant general, letter, 1 June 1937, AG 452.1 (6-1-37) (1), RG 407, NA.

47. William Bradford Huie, *The Fight for Air Power* (New York: L. B. Fischer, 1942), 95–102.
48. Arnold, *Global Mission*, 177; and Pictorial History of the AAF, 84.
49. Arnold, *Global Mission*, 176; and Futrell, 87.
50. Knerr diary. Knerr later returned to active duty.
51. Memorandum by Gen Malin Craig, 17 March 1938, OCS 14110-21, RG 165, NA.
52. Futrell, 84–85.
53. Adjutant general to chief of the Air Corps, letter, 29 July 1938, AG 580 (7-29-38); and Gen Oscar Westover to adjutant general, letter, 31 August 1938, AG 580 (8-31-38). Both are in RG 407, NA.
54. Memorandum for the chief of staff, 26 September 1938, AG 480, NA.
55. Arnold's notes on the White House conference can be found in Chief of Staff, Misc. Conferences, 1938–1942, RG 165, NA. See also William Frye, *Marshall: Citizen Soldier* (Indianapolis: The Bobbs-Merrill Co., 1947), 249–50; John Morton Blum, *From the Morgenthau Diaries*, vol 2, *Years of Urgency, 1938–1941* (Boston: Houghton Mifflin, 1965), 47–49; Futrell, 91; and Arnold, *Global Mission*, 179–80.
56. Arnold, *Global Mission*, 179. Arnold notes the date of the White House meeting as 28 September in his memoirs. All other sources including Arnold's notes from the meeting set the date at 14 November.
57. Mark S. Watson, *Chief of Staff: Prewar Plans and Preparations* (Washington, D.C.: Historical Division, Department of the Army, 1950), 136–43; Russell F. Weigley, *History of the United States Army* (New York: Macmillan, 1967), 417–18; Frye, 249–52; and Futrell, 92.
58. Craven and Cate, 104–5; Goldberg, 43–44; and *Legislation Relating to the Army Air Forces Training Program, 1939–1945*, USAF Historical Study 7, revised (Maxwell AFB, Ala.: USAF Historical Division, Air University, 1951), 4–6.
59. Arnold's notes on the 14 November 1938 meeting, Chief of Staff, Misc. Conferences, 1938–1942, RG 165, NA.
60. General Marshall argued the airmen's case for the B-17 before General Craig. See Futrell, 92.
61. A "cash and carry" clause in the Neutrality Act of 1937 had expired in May 1939, and up until this time President Roosevelt had been unable to get Congress to enact a new "cash and carry" law.
62. Blum, 68–69. See also John M. Haight, *American Aid to France, 1938–1940* (New York: Atheneum, 1970), 82–83, 98–99.
63. Arnold's record of a conference in the White House, 13 March 1940, is filed under Aircraft Production, 1939–1941, Arnold MSS. Quoted in Haight, 204. See also Blum, 117.
64. For the text of the president's speech, see the *Congressional Record*, 77th Cong., 3d sess., 60244. See also I. B. Holley Jr., *Buying Aircraft: Materiel Procurement for the Army Air Forces* (Washington, D.C.: Office of the Chief of Military History, Department of the Army, 1964), 226–28; and Bruce Catton, *The War Lords of Washington* (New York: Harcourt, Brace, 1948), 21–65.
65. Arnold, *Global Mission*, 191. Although the German airpower in the Polish operation had been used mainly to support ground forces, Lt Col Donald Wilson, one of the "bomber boys" at the Air Corps Tactical School, declared that the Luftwaffe had "voluntarily undertaken the job of demonstrating our theories." The Luftwaffe had, as the bomber enthusiasts had advocated, destroyed the Polish air force on the ground. Quoted in Futrell, 96.
66. *Legislation Relating to the Army Air Forces Training Program*, 6.
67. Quoted in Arnold, *Global Mission*, 199.
68. Eddie Rickenbacker quoted in *Legislation Relating to the Army Air Forces Training Program*, 10–11.
69. Blum, 39.
70. Goldberg, 148.

71. Holley, 423.
72. There were almost 40 small trainers delivered that week but even that, according to Holley, was far below schedule.
73. Holley, 244–45.
74. Cy Caldwell, "The US Air Force, 1909–1948," *Aero Digest*, September 1948, 70.
75. Arnold, *Global Mission*, 271.
76. Catton, 21.
77. For the financial problems of the aircraft industry, see John B. Rae, *Climb to Greatness: The American Aircraft Industry, 1920–1960* (Cambridge, Mass.: Massachusetts Institute of Technology Press, 1968), 112.
78. Holley, 233.
79. Hansell, 49; Craven and Cate, 231–32.
80. Hansell, 88; and Carroll V. Glines, *The Compact History of the United States Air Force* (New York: Hawthorn Books, 1963), 149.
81. Frye, 254.
82. Ibid., 249–50.
83. *Legislation Relating to the Army Air Forces Training Program*, 72–73. One source of pilots was intentionally not tapped by the Army Air Corps. The Air Corps resisted efforts to open pilot training on an equal basis to Negroes. Negro leaders established a private school for Negro pilots outside of Chicago in 1940. Rep. Everett M. Dirksen (R-Ill.) supported the Negroes' cause in Congress, but to no avail (36). A War Department memorandum declared that "the very intimate association between pilots and mechanics in the operation and maintenance of aircraft and the dependence of such personnel on each other for safety of life is such that the introduction of a racial problem may very well destroy the morale and effectiveness of Air Corps units." OCS Emergency Planning File, RG 165, NA.
84. Goldberg, 51.
85. Arnold, *Global Mission*, 181–82.
86. *Legislation Relating to the Army Air Forces Training Program*, 15–16.
87. From a speech by Gen Frank P. Lahm, quoted in Glines, *The Compact History of the United States Air Force*, 123–25.
88. Goldberg, 37.
89. Ibid., 50.
90. Robert F. Futrell, *Development of AAF Base Facilities in the United States, 1939–1945*, USAF Historical Study 69 (Maxwell AFB, Ala.: USAF Historical Division, Air University, 1947), 6.
91. Craven and Cate, 120.
92. Ibid.
93. Ibid., 160.
94. Ibid., 120.
95. Diary of Henry L. Stimson, 23 and 24 April 1941 (vol. 33, 181–83).
96. Craven and Cate, 175–78.
97. Lewis H. Brereton, *The Brereton Diaries: The War in the Pacific, Middle East and Europe, 3 October 1941–8 May 1945* (New York: W. Morrow and Co., 1946), 22.
98. Ibid., 22; and Craven and Cate, 186.
99. Craven and Cate, 166.
100. Reminiscences of Robert A. Lovett (1959–1960), Robert A. Lovett Oral History Collection (OHC), Columbia University (hereinafter cited as Lovett, OHC).
101. Arnold, *Global Mission*, 209.
102. Lovett, OHC, 3–4.
103. Arnold, *Global Mission*, 195.
104. Lovett, OHC, 22.
105. Arnold, *Global Mission*, 167.
106. Ibid., 161.
107. Ibid., 160.

Chapter 7

Conclusion

The period from the Armistice in 1918 to the beginning of frantic rearmament in the late 1930s was no time for soldiers. This well-known fact set the limits to Army thinking and to the attitude of Army leaders toward the Air Corps and vice versa.

In the 1920s, success in business was the measure of character. Even Jesus Christ was admired for the skillful way in which he "picked up twelve men from the bottom ranks of business and forged them into an organization that conquered the world."[1] The principles of business became the moral code. Economy, the first principle of business, was nothing but idealism in its most practical form. As the antithesis of economy, war was abhorred by businessmen as well as pacifists. The business-oriented Republican administrations of Warren Harding, Calvin Coolidge, and Herbert Hoover proposed to put a check on militarists and other "nasty nice" advocates of "arrogant military preparedness," which made competition in armaments and the waste of war inevitable.[2] Republican administrations advocated disarmament to reduce the risk of war and applied the principles of business to the War Department to reduce the cost of such military forces as were absolutely necessary. By convention time in 1924, the Republicans could boast that "our standing army is now below 125,000 men, the smallest regular military force maintained by any great Power."[3] By the last year of the Republican era, 1932, they could claim that the American army had "through successive reductions . . . reached the irreducible minimum consistent with self-reliance, self-respect and security."[4]

The Great Depression of the 1930s discredited the business cult but did not relieve budget pressure on the military; on the contrary, the pressure intensified. The crash of the stock market had proved vastly disillusioning. Only a month before the panic on Wall Street, the president of the New York Stock Exchange had announced, "We are apparently finished and done with economic cycles as we have known them."[5] When the market then crashed, the reaction at first was not to disbelieve the principles but to apply them more vigorously. President Hoover economized on the federal budget. The military establishment was called upon to begin successive reductions to its "irreducible minimum."

By 1932, the defense budget was reduced from 20 percent of the total budget to 15, but the deepening of the Depression made even the irreducible minimum seem high and prompted the search for further reductions through disarmament.6 Hoover took active personal interest. At the Geneva Disarmament Conference in 1932, he tried to coax other nations into an agreement that would allow reduction of armaments by a third. In the meantime, he promised Americans that "we shall enter no agreements committing us to any future course of action or which call for the use of force to preserve the peace," allowing the nation to maintain its military force at the minimum until disarmament reductions were possible.7

The first Roosevelt administration proved even less friendly to the military than its Republican predecessor. In the campaign of 1932, Roosevelt pledged to reduce government expense and balance the budget. Almost immediately, in 1933, he set out to fulfill his pledge. War Department requests were slashed first by the Bureau of the Budget and then by Congress. Defense expenditure amounted to approximately 9 percent of the federal budget. This pattern of the budget being cut by both the Budget Bureau and Congress was normal from 1931 through 1935. Defense expenditure remained at less than 15 percent of the federal budget until FY 1940.8

Defense appropriations were cut in the 1920s and 1930s because planners felt the government could not afford anything but a skeleton organization for the military, and also because few Americans, even the military, saw any threat to national security. The shadow of Hitler was not apparent until the late 1930s, and the great oceans were a barrier to invasion from Asia. Besides, there was in the United States, indeed throughout most of the world, an indisputable peace psychology. This did not mean that Americans had accepted the dream that all war had ended with the Great War. The attitude was a mixture of optimism and resignation about the future. The optimism was expressed in attempts to prevent war through collective security, disarmament, and a multilateral peace pact. The resignation was reflected in the continued commitment to isolation, which implied that if war could not be prevented, the United States need not participate. And so, Army leaders had to remember "the military supremacy of the peacetime dollar" first and military needs second.9

War Department responses were of three sorts. The initial response to budget restriction was to spread the reduced funds evenly, keeping all elements of the establishment alive if not efficient. This led to a conservative attitude toward expensive projects that might favor one member of the military family over another. While Army leaders could not stop competition, they did attempt to suppress such "radicals" as the airpower advocates, whose demands they felt were excessive and threatened survival of other branches. (It is interesting that the Air Corps leadership also had radicals to suppress—the advocates of fighter and attack aviation whose demands threatened development of the long-range bomber.) Second, during prolonged periods, stabilization of the budget became the goal. Budget estimates were based on what had been approved by the Budget Bureau and appropriated by Congress. This arrangement intensified the conservatism of the Army leaders who came to believe it futile to ask for substantially more than had been allowed in the recent past. Third, when severe budget pressures forced Army leaders into priorities, they sought to preserve the corps of professional officers. This was true even in the Air Corps. When the leaders of its professional officers advocated a sacrifice of personnel for equipment in the 1931–32 budget battle between General MacArthur and Representative Collins, the personnel they envisioned sacrificing were officers of other components of the Army, not the airmen who would be needed to operate the equipment the personnel sacrifice would buy.

All the while, a 20-year war between the Army and Navy occurred within these tight budgetary arrangements. When the Army Air Corps began talking about long-range bombers that could be based on land but meet the enemy offensively miles out to sea, the Navy felt that its mission, in particular the money they received for that mission, was in jeopardy. When the Navy began to buy land-based bombers of its own, the Army felt its coastal defense mission, and thereby its own budget, was threatened. The possibility that an Army–Navy controversy might bring congressional and public attention to claims and complaints of the Air Corps, combined with the natural tendency of bureaucracies to resist change, explains in part why the Army fought to keep the dispute out of Congress and why Army leaders sometimes seemed to take the Navy's side in the coastal defense controversy. Particularly in peacetime, policy was the result of the pull and tug of many interests, inside and outside the military. A drastic change in the influence of one or another could throw the machinery of policy out of balance. A sudden decision in favor of the Air Corps over the Navy as the "far-flung" line of defense would greatly increase the influence of radical airmen and other aviation interests, and not just on the issue of coastal defense. The momentum of an Air Corps victory over the Navy could carry the airmen to victory over the Army on the issue of independence, which would further increase air power vis-à-vis ground and sea power.

Within the Army it was the conflict over budget as much as anything else that fueled the Air Corps drive for independence. There is considerable evidence that if this issue had been resolved quickly and efficiently—or had the military not been in a period of austerity during the early development of the air arm—doctrinal differences between the airpower enthusiasts and the Army and the Navy would never have become as large as they did. But the issue was not resolved; and air enthusiasts, feeling they had no choice, agitated for independence, bringing them into prolonged conflict not only with established military policy but with much of American domestic and foreign policy.

The budget fight engendered many feelings on the part of the aggrieved airmen, some legitimate and some not. Air Corps leaders believed they must keep abreast of technological development in aviation. Army leaders originally had been sympathetic. Very early in the air controversy, they agreed that all possible effort should be made to keep the Air Corps in modern aircraft and to keep the aircraft industry healthy so that it could rapidly equip a greatly expanded Air Corps in case of mobilization. But when the budget crunch was really on, when it came to a showdown between men and machines, Army leaders would choose men, not machines. To them it did not seem sensible to risk survival of the entire Army for survival of a single component.

The Air Corps had troubles other than its budgetary difficulties, and no historian should think that money alone was the root of everything. The visionaries in the Air Corps were constantly fighting against the sheer boredom that afflicts all military forces in time of peace. They felt that if they were not careful, their own military arm would attenuate simply through the routines, the convenient and even attractive routines, of military life. If the Army, and the Air Corps within it, was "an unfinished and unassembled machine," and for most of the era there was no threat to the nation, there was little urgency to finish and assemble the machine. Military life was good—cheap and easy. While pay was low, there was at least a paycheck. And it went far. A second lieutenant received $125 a month, $187.50 if a flyer. Prices at the post exchange were 25 to 40 percent cheaper than in town. Liquor in the officers club was available at less than two dollars a quart; mixed drinks cost 15 cents. Fifteen dollars spent at the post commissary could purchase enough canned fruit, vegetables, and other supplies to feed the average family for a month.

There was great danger that laziness would infect the Air Corps. No one expected much of a young officer. Duty normally ended at 1530 "to allow time for recreation," and Wednesday was a half-holiday.[10] Airmen found themselves under little pressure. There was lots of talk about advanced techniques in instrument and night flying, but little practice.[11] As Curtis LeMay wrote of the Air Corps of the 1930s, "There's a little ground school and a little flying, and little of this and a little of that, and [if] you're not on your toes . . . you haven't even got any toes to be on." It was only the constant hazard inherent in flying, he wrote, that "kept us from becoming completely la-di-da country club people."[12] Perhaps it was memory of this situation that prompted LeMay to fight so diligently to keep a credible mission for the Air Force in the 1960s.

For most of the interwar years, airmen—however easy the life, and inexpensive—felt that they had little voice in the future of their Air Corps. The visionaries believed that they had few supporters among ranking military men. In this belief they were right. For the most part, the visionaries were officers of junior and middle rank. In the Air Service days prior to 1926, there were only two generals— the chief and one assistant. The Army Air Corps Act authorized only four general officers, a major general as chief and three brigadier generals. During the first years after the war, only a handful of young Air Service officers had the rank, seniority, and service school requisites for General Staff assignments. During the Harding, Coolidge, and Hoover administrations, their influence in the War Department was almost nil. The same was true during the first Roosevelt administration. The Army Air Corps Act created an Office of Assistant Secretary of War for Air, filled by the energetic and air-minded Trubee Davison. His influence was at the pleasure of the secretary of war, and the budget squeeze of 1933 eliminated the office, which was not to be filled again for eight years. Only with the mobilization prior to the Second World War did the Air Corps obtain a champion at the top level of the executive branch when the president became an airpower advocate. Then appeared other allies such as Robert Lovett, who was appointed to the reinstated Office of Assistant Secretary of War for Air, who became for practical purposes secretary of the Air Corps.

With their influence through channels drastically reduced by their low position in the bureaucratic hierarchy, airmen were tempted to go around the chain of command, taking their case to the people, as the politicians would say. They had several choices. They could testify in hearings before Congress, a legitimate forum for military men. Or they could give public demonstrations of the capabilities of aircraft, a legitimate activity if done with restraint. Or they could express their opinions in speeches, in the press, and in articles and books, again a legitimate activity if done with restraint. Each of these choices carried a different combination of benefits, limits, and risks.

Air Corps visionaries did find willing but not measurably effective allies in Congress, especially in the military affairs committees. Constantly on the spot to make intelligent criticisms of War Department policy and actions, congressmen were eager for the sort of expert opinion airmen had to offer. When congressmen could refer, as did the Frear Committee in 1919, to having heard the testimony of "America's greatest living ace, Eddie Rickenbacker," it gave an air of credibility to their judgment and they were not quite so much at the mercy of War Department experts. They could challenge War Department proposals with counterproposals, such as the many bills submitted in the 1920s to create a unified department of national defense or a separate department of air. But when issues came to a vote, congressional allies of the Air Corps never had the strength to favor the Air Corps over objections of the War Department. Congress, like the bureaucrats in the executive branch, preferred gradualism to precipitous change, especially when there was no consensus among experts on the issue, as was the case in the airpower controversy.

The fact that Congress held authority to reorganize the military in the manner desired by the airmen had something to do with the decision of Billy Mitchell and his allies to carry their argument to the public. Congress, many people assumed, more than any other organ of the government, felt the pressure of public opinion. Legislators were elected and their future depended, or so it was believed, on their moving in line with what they believed to be the wishes of their constituencies. "The Air Force, in all those years between the wars," Ira Eaker said, "was always trying to think up things that would bring aviation before the public, make headlines in the newspapers and interest the public, therefore interest the Congress."[13]

The Air Corps did its best to stage dramatic demonstrations of airpower, but the results were disappointing. With full support of the Air Corps, Army aviators like Jimmy Doolittle earned a good fame for themselves and attention for the Air Corps by competing in air races, repeatedly breaking world records for speed, altitude, and distance. To dramatize the potential of bombers and the need for air defense, Air Corps flyers staged mock bombing attacks on targets such as Times Square in New York City. The effect of this sort of activity on public opinion is impossible to measure. It does seem safe to conclude that the demonstrations had no determining influence on the nation's air policy. Even the most spectacular demonstration, the sinking of the battleship *Ostfriesland*, caused no immediate change in air policy. There were times when the accomplishments of Army flyers appeared a liability to air enthusiasts. Often in congressional hearings their antagonists would point out the apparent contradiction in the airmen's warning that the United States was a fifth- or sixth-rate power in air strength with the fact that American flyers held most of the world's flying records. Paradoxically, demonstrations of weakness in the Air Corps, such as the failure to measure up to the airmail crisis in 1934, proved more of a catalyst for change than did demonstrations of strength.

Equally frustrating for air enthusiasts were the results of verbal campaigns to influence public opinion. It was a Mitchell axiom that "changes in military systems come about only through the pressure of public opinion or disaster in war."[14] In accord with this principle, Mitchell and his followers raised the pressure of public opinion almost, it appeared, to the point of explosion in 1925–26, during the publicity attending the opening of the court-martial. Yet the changes in the military system incorporated in the Army Air Corps Act of 1926 were largely superficial. Neither the president nor the bureaucrats in the War Department nor even Congress gave in to the public clamor in favor of Mitchell. They stood firm because of President Coolidge's handling of the situation, and also because the respected Morrow Board had reassured the nation that it was safe from air attack. There is a great difference between public pressure developing out of a widely felt concern over a vital issue and clamor as a result of a sensational event.

As the years passed, the airmen began to acquire something of a persecution complex. Because the federal government, and within it the Army bureaucracy, would not capitulate to the air visionaries, the latter saw the bureaucracy as hostile toward airpower. From the beginning, many leaders in the Army bureaucracy were willing to accede importance to the new air arm, but then counseled caution or delay for reasons mostly related to the budget and to a feeling that there was no great urgency in the matter. They wanted to maintain the potential for airpower without engaging in development. The higher-ranking officers in Washington also developed a cautious restraint resulting from experience of operating with the bureaucracies of the other government departments. They appeared to be more concerned with the problems that any change might raise than with the opportunities for change. They believed in gradual change; only through change by increments could they have a stable, balanced military and time to test the change as they proceeded with it. In crises such as those caused by the sinking of the *Ostfriesland*, there seemed agreement among all Washington bureaucrats, Army bureaucrats of course included, that the first goal was to defuse the crisis; then if change was necessary, the bureaucracy would slowly gather its forces in a sometimes painful process, debate the situation in Congress, the White House, and the newspapers, and finally, perhaps, still not come up with any change. Some of the resistance to change was likely due to the attachment that senior officers and veterans in Congress, and elsewhere in government, had to the arms they had served during their youth. Marshal Ferdinand Foch once suggested that military men imagine the next war will be fought in much the same way as the last. The American military, having accepted the idea that the infantry was the queen of battle and accepted the axioms of Alfred T. Mahan in naval matters, found it difficult to give up these ideas. Tradition dies hard.

The Air Corps visionaries were officers of middle rank, senior enough to have developed a service-wide perspective, but not so senior as to have developed the restraint that characterized the ranking officers. They welcomed change, and perhaps because of the nature of their profession, considered restraint to be a sign of ignorance or worse. They not only frequently risked charge of insubordination from their superiors, but seemed to thrive on it. There was the "Mitchell group"—Arnold, Spaatz, Milling—and the generation of flyers they indoctrinated, all of whom refused to make the decisions and commitments that would be easily approved by their War Department superiors.

That the air visionaries were willing to risk their careers by supporting policies unpopular with superiors needs some explanation. Perhaps any one of the radicals standing alone might not have taken such a risk. But in the Air Corps, the more trouble you were in with your superiors in the Army, the higher your status among your own group. Air Corps pilots were the elite, and if they were the "out" group, it was still a privilege to be a part of the fraternity. Until 1935, few Air Corps officers attended the Army's Command and General Staff College. Airmen, according to K. B. Wolfe, considered it a waste of time and had to be forced to go. Wolfe related in an interview years later that "Marshall told Arnold he was no longer going to put up with this business of the Air Force not going to Command and Staff College. So he swept up a whole crowd of us, just under the age of 40, and we had to go there. . . . We didn't want to go, and there was damn near mutiny . . . if you didn't get a good rating out of there, you weren't recommended for increased rank or command. Nobody in the Air Force gave a hoot about that."

It must be remembered that promotion within the Air Corps, other than the choice of the chief of the Air Corps and his assistant, was decided by Air Corps, not Army, people. A man was promoted on the basis of what his Air Corps superiors thought of him as an officer and as a member of the flying fraternity.

They were convinced that they were the orphans in the fairy tale. "Someone Away Up There didn't like them."[15] But as in all good stories, the orphan was destined to become the princess in the late 1930s, and by some standards, the queen herself by the end of the Second World War.

Notes

1. From the preface of Bruce Barton's *The Man Nobody Knows: A Discovery of Jesus* (Indianapolis: Bobbs–Merrill Co., 1925).

2. William A. White, *Forty Years on Main Street* (New York: Farrar & Rinehart, 1937),180–83; and Howard H. Quint and Robert H. Ferrell, eds., *The Talkative President: The Off-the-Record Press Conferences of Calvin Coolidge* (Amherst, Mass.: University of Massachusetts Press, 1964), 162–63.

3. *Republican Party National Committee Campaign Textbook, 1924,* (Washington, D.C.: Republican National Committee, 1924), 363–64 (hereinafter cited as Republican Campaign Textbook).

4. Ibid.

5. Winston Churchill, *The Second World War,* vol. 1, *The Gathering Storm* (Boston: Houghton Mifflin, 1948), 134–35.

6. *Republican Campaign Textbook, 1924,* 203.

7. Nancy Harvison Hooker, ed., *The Moffat Papers: Selections from the Diplomatic Journals of Jay Pierrepont Moffat, 1919–1943* (Cambridge, Mass.: Harvard University Press, 1956), 56, 68–71; and *Republican Campaign Textbook, 1932,* 27.

8. *Republican Campaign Textbook, 1940,* 203; and John W. Killigrew, "The Impact of the Great Depression on the Army, 1929–1936" (PhD diss., Indiana University, 1960), 431.

9. Quoted in the *Army and Navy Journal,* 4 September 1926.

10. Norman E. Borden Jr., *Air Mail Emergency, 1934: An Account of Seventy-eight Tense Days in the Winter of 1934 When the Army Flew the United States Mail* (Freeport, Maine: Bond Wheelwright, 1968), 25–27.

11. Curtis E. LeMay, *Mission with LeMay: My Story* (Garden City, N.Y.: Doubleday, 1965), 76, 97.

12. Ibid., 76.

13. Ira C. Eaker, Oral History Collection, Columbia University, 87–88.

14. William Mitchell, *Winged Defense: The Development and Possibilities of Modern Air Power—Economic and Military* (New York: G.P. Putnam's Sons, 1925), xviii.

15. LeMay, 77.

Essay Bibliography

Bibliographical Aids

The United States Air Force has published several very useful guides for the study of Air Force history. Mary Ann Cresswell, staff archivist, and Carl Berger, chief of the Histories Division of the Office of Air Force History, compiled *United States Air Force History: An Annotated Bibliography* (Washington, D.C.: Office of Air Force History, 1971). In 1972, the Office of Air Force History cooperated with the Historical Research Division of the Air University to publish *United States Air Force History: A Guide to Personal Collections in Public and Private Depositories* (Washington, D.C.: Office of Air Force History, 1972), compiled by Gloria Atkinson and Lawrence J. Paszek. This was followed shortly by Paszek's excellent *United States Air Force History: A Guide to Documentary Sources* (Washington, D.C.: Office of Air Force History, 1973).

Other useful bibliographical aids include *Bibliography of Aeronautics, 1909-1932*, 14 vols. (Washington, D.C.: National Advisory Committee for Aeronautics, 1921-1936); and R. Earl McClendon, *A Checklist of Significant Documents Relating to the Position of the United States Army Air Arm in the System of National Defense, 1907-1945* (Maxwell AFB, Ala.: Documentary Research Division, Air University, 1969). A survey of dissertation literature is provided by Allan Reed Millett and B. Franklin Cooling III, *Doctoral Dissertations in Military Affairs: A Bibliography* (Manhattan, Kans.: Kansas State University Library, 1972).

General Works

There is no comprehensive history of the Army air arm between the World Wars. The best coverage of the subject is Wesley Frank Craven and James Lea Cate, eds., *The Army Air Forces in World War II*, vol. 1, *Plans and Early Operations, January 1939 to August 1942* (1949; new imprint, Washington, D.C.: Office of Air Force History, 1983), chapter 2. There is also good information in Alfred Goldberg, ed., *A History of the United States Air Force, 1907-1957* (Princeton, N.J.: D. Van Nostrand, 1957). Less satisfactory for the interwar period is Carroll V. Glines, *The Compact History of the United States Air Force* (New York: Hawthorn Books, 1963). Cecil R. Roseberry's *The Challenging Skies: The Colorful Story of Aviation's Most Exciting Years, 1919-1939* (Garden City, N.Y.: Doubleday, 1966) is an effectively illustrated survey of civilian and military aviation during the period. *A History of the Air Force* (Chicago: University of Chicago Press, 1967) by Wilbert H. Ruenbeck and Philip M. Flammer is accurate, but quite brief. The interwar period is given short shrift (only two pages) in Monro MacCloskey, *From Gasbags to Spaceships: The Story of the U.S. Air Force* (New York: R. Rosen Press, 1968).

Pictorial histories of US military aviation are numerous. *Flying Squadrons: A Graphic History of the U.S. Army Air Forces* (New York: Duell, Sloan and Pearce, 1942) by S. Paul Johnston describes the reorganization of the air arm for the Second World War. After the war, the Historical Office of the Army Air Forces published *The Official Pictorial History of the AAF* (New York: Duell, Sloan and Pearce, 1947), which included a good collection of photography from the interwar period. Martin Caidin's *Air Force: A Pictorial History of American Airpower* (New York: Rinehart, 1957) also has good photos well presented. "History Written in the Skies," *National Geographic* 112 (August 1957): 272–94, is a pictorial survey of the first 50 years of military aviation. Of excellent quality is *The American Heritage History of Flight*, ed. Alvan M. Josephy Jr. et al., with introduction by Ira C. Eaker and Carl Spaatz (New York: American Heritage Publishing Co., 1962).

There is still much to be written on the Army between the World Wars. A provocative analysis that frames the major questions of the period is Walter Millis, *Arms and Men: A Study in American Military History* (New York: G.P. Putnam's Sons, 1956). For a reliable administrative history of the Army, consult Russell F. Weigley, *History of the United States Army* (New York: Macmillan, 1967).

Special Works

Monographs

A logical approach to Air Force history is to trace the organizational changes that ultimately resulted in an independent United States Air Force. Chase C. Mooney and Martha E. Layman, *Organization of Military Aeronautics, 1907–1935*, Army Air Forces Historical Study 25 (Washington, D.C.: Army Air Forces Historical Division, 1944); Chase C. Mooney, *Organization of Military Aeronautics, 1935–1945: Executive: Congressional and War Department Action*, Historical Study 46 (Washington, D.C.: USAF Historical Division, 1946); and Chase C. Mooney, *Organization of the Army Air Arm, 1935–1945*, USAF Historical Study 10 (Maxwell AFB, Ala.: USAF Historical Division, Air University, 1956) describe the controversy over the appropriate place for aviation in the defense establishment and the efforts to find an organization acceptable to both the War Department and Congress. Much of the same territory is covered by R. Earl McClendon, *Autonomy of the Air Arm*, rev. ed. (Washington, D.C.: Air Force History and Museums Program, 1996). Harry H. Ransom's "The Air Corps Act of 1926: A Study of the Legislative Process" (PhD diss., Princeton University, 1953) is an excellent account of the political repercussions of the Mitchell affair in 1925–1926. A summary of the organizational changes in the Army air arm is available in George E. Stratemeyer, "Administrative History of U.S. Army Air Forces," *Air Affairs* 1 (Summer 1947): 510–22.

The most comprehensive study of the evolution of airpower doctrine is Robert Frank Futrell, *Ideas, Concepts, Doctrine: Basic Thinking in the United States Air Force, 1907–1984*, 2 vols. (Maxwell AFB, Ala.: Air University Press, 1989). (Quoted material from *Ideas, Concepts, Doctrine* comes from the earlier textbook edition: *Ideas, Concepts, Doctrine: A History of Basic Thinking in the United States Air Force, 1907–1964* [Maxwell AFB, Ala.: Air University, 1974]). James Lea Cate's "Development of Air Doctrine, 1917–41," *Air University Quarterly Review* 1, no. 3 (Winter 1947) is succinct and well written. Thomas H. Greer, *The Development of Air Doctrine in the Army Air Arm, 1917–1941*, USAF Historical Study 89 (Maxwell AFB, Ala.: USAF Historical Division, Air University, 1955) describes the development of tactical and strategic doctrine with good coverage of the controversy in the Air Corps Tactical School between the bomber and fighter advocates. Strategic air doctrine was refined at the Tactical School, a brief history of which is available in Robert T. Finney, *History of the Air Corps Tactical School, 1920–1940*, USAF Historical Study 100 (Maxwell AFB, Ala.: USAF Historical Division, Air University, 1955). Ronald R. Fogleman's "The Development of Ground Attack Aviation in the United States Army Air Arm: Evolution of a Doctrine, 1908–1926" (master's thesis, Duke University, 1971) discusses the early development of attack aircraft and of a doctrine governing their use. *Pursuit* (Langley AFB, Va.: Air Corps Tactical School, 1926) was the textbook used by the Air Corps Tactical School. It includes a section on the "Historical Development of Pursuit Tactics."

A number of the leading airmen wrote about the air arm and the evolution of airpower. William Mitchell's writings were by far the most influential. In addition to his memoirs of the World War and numerous articles, he wrote *Our Air Force: The Keystone of National Defense* (New York: E. P. Dutton and Co., 1921); *Winged Defense: The Development and Possibilities of Modern Air Power—Economic and Military* (New York: G. P. Putnam's Sons, 1925); and *Skyways: A Book on Modern Aeronautics* (Philadelphia: J. B. Lippincott Co., 1930). Other books by airmen include Mason M. Patrick, *The United States in the Air* (Garden City, N.Y.: Doubleday, Doran and Co.,

1928); Henry H. Arnold and Ira C. Eaker, *This Flying Game*, 3d rev. ed. (New York: Funk and Wagnalls, 1936); Henry H. Arnold, *Winged Warfare* (New York: Harper and Brothers, 1941); and Arnold and Eaker, *Army Flyer* (New York: Harper and Brothers, 1942). William Bradford Huie's *The Fight for Air Power* (New York: L. B. Fischer, 1942) includes long sections written by Hugh J. Knerr, who preferred to remain anonymous at the time of publication.

For the General Staff's perspective of the organizational and administrative problems of the Air Corps in the late 1930s, the best secondary source is Mark S. Watson, *Chief of Staff: Prewar Plans and Preparations* (Washington, D.C.: Historical Division, Department of the Army, 1950). For an understanding of the organization and function of the General Staff itself, consult Otto L. Nelson, *National Security and the General Staff* (Washington, D.C.: Infantry Journal Press, 1946). Robert W. Kranskopf, in "The Army and the Strategic Bomber, 1930–1939," *Military Affairs* 22 (Summer 1958): 83–94, traces the Air Corps effort to justify the purchase of strategic bombers. Fred Greene's "The Military View of American National Policy, 1904–1940," *American Historical Review* 69 (January 1964): 354–77, is excellent.

Problems of the budget were inescapable for military leaders in the twenties and early thirties. The implications of stringent budget policies on aircraft procurement for the Air Corps are addressed in I. B. Holley Jr., *Buying Aircraft: Materiel Procurement for the Army Air Forces* (Washington, D.C.: Office of the Chief of Military History, Department of the Army, 1964). See also Edwin H. Rutkowski, *The Politics of Military Aviation Procurement, 1926–1934: A Study in the Political Assertion of Consensual Values* (Columbus, Ohio: Ohio State University Press, 1966). An excellent analysis of the Army's reaction to the Great Depression is John W. Killigrew, "The Impact of the Great Depression on the Army, 1929–1936" (PhD diss., Indiana University, 1960). Also excellent is Elias Huzar, *The Purse and the Sword: Control of the Army by Congress through Military Appropriations, 1933–1950* (Ithaca, N.Y.: Cornell University Press, 1950). The budget concerns of the Air Corps usually caused similar concerns in the aircraft industry. For the financial problems of the aircraft industry, it is helpful to consult John B. Rae, *Climb to Greatness: The American Aircraft Industry, 1920–1960* (Cambridge, Mass.: Massachusetts Institute of Technology Press, 1968).

The airmail crisis of 1934 has inspired several studies. Paul Tillett, *The Army Flys the Mail*, the Inter-University Case Program: Cases in Public Administration and Policy Formation No. 24 (Tuscaloosa, Ala.: University of Alabama Press, 1955) is detailed and well documented. Carroll V. Glines, in *The Saga of Air Mail* (Princeton, N.J.: D. Van Nostrand, 1968), gives a popular account.

Written with flare but marred by annoying minor errors is Norman E. Borden Jr., *Air Mail Emergency, 1934: An Account of Seventy-eight Tense Days in the Winter of 1934 When the Army Flew the United States Mail* (Freeport, Maine: Bond Wheelwright, 1968). See also Eldon W. Downs, "Army and the Airmail—1934," *Airpower Historian* 9 (January 1962): 35–51; and William M. Crabbe Jr., "The Army Airmail Pilots Reports! An Account of the 1934 Experiences of the Eastern Zone Officers," *Airpower Historian* 9 (April 1962): 87–94, 128.

The literature is extensive on the development of aircraft in the interwar period. Research and development is treated in *Comparative History of Research and Development Policies Affecting Air Material, 1915–1944* (Historical Division, Assistant Chief of Air Staff, Intelligence, June 1945); and Martin P. Claussen, *Materiel Research and Development in the Army Air Arm, 1914–1945*, USAF Historical Study 50 (Maxwell AFB, Ala.: USAF Historical Division, Air University, 1946). Douglas J. Ingells tells the story of the research and development center at Wright Field, Ohio, in his *They Tamed the Sky: The Triumph of American Aviation* (New York: D. Appleton–Century Co., 1947). For evolution of aircraft types, consult Ray Wagner, *American Combat Planes* (Garden City, N.Y.: Hanover House, 1960). The development of strategic bombers is treated in Jean H. DuBuque and Robert F. Gleckner, *The Development of the Heavy Bomber, 1918–1944*, USAF Historical Study 6, revised (Maxwell AFB, Ala.: USAF Historical Division, Air University, 1951). Recounts of the fascinating story of the B-17 can be found in Harold Mansfield, *Vision, the Story of Boeing: A Saga of the Sky and the New Horizons of Space* (New York: Duell, Sloan and Pearce, 1966); and Steve Birdsall et al., *Winged Majesty: The Boeing B-17 Flying Fortress in War and Peace* (Tacoma, Wash.: F. A. Johnsen, 1980). Fighter development is in K. S. Brown et al., *United States Army and Air Force Fighters, 1916–1961* (Letchworth, Herts, England: Harleyford Publications, Ltd., 1961); and Bernard L. Boylan, *The Development of the American Long Range Escort Fighter* (Ann Arbor, Mich.: University of Michigan Press, 1955). I. B. Holley Jr., *Evolution of the Liaison-Type Airplane, 1917–1944*, USAF Historical Study 44 (Washington, D.C.: Army Air Forces Historical Division, 1946), analyzes the conflicting views of air and ground officers toward observation aircraft designed for direct support of ground forces.

There are many monographs on mobilization for the Second World War. The Air Force Historical Office has sponsored such works as Robert R. Russel and Martin P. Claussen, *Expansion of Industrial Facilities under Army Air Forces Auspices, 1940–1945*, Air Force Historical Study 40 (Washington, D.C.: Army Air Forces

Historical Division, 1951) and Tom Lilley et al., *Problems of Accelerating Aircraft Production during World War II* (Cambridge, Mass.: Harvard Graduate School of Business Administration, 1946). A good analysis of the sale of military aircraft to France and its effect on the mobilization of the Air Corps is John M. Haight, *American Aid to France, 1938–1940* (New York: Atheneum, 1970). Haywood S. Hansell Jr., *The Air Plan that Defeated Hitler* (Atlanta, Ga.: Higgins-MacArthur/Longino and Porter, 1972) is written by one of the authors of AWPD-1, the basic American air war plan for the Second World War.

Biographies and Autobiographies

The most accurate and scholarly biography of Mitchell is Alfred F. Hurley, *Billy Mitchell: Crusader for Air Power* (New York: F. Watts, 1964), which was reprinted in 1975 by the University of Indiana Press, Bloomington, Indiana. Other biographies of Mitchell include Emile Gauvreau and Lester Cohen, *Billy Mitchell: Founder of Our Air Force and Prophet without Honor* (New York: E. P. Dutton and Co., 1942); Isaac D. Levine, *Mitchell: Pioneer of Air Power*, rev. ed. (New York: Duell, Sloan and Pearce, 1958); and Roger Burlingame, *General Billy Mitchell: Champion of Defense* (New York: McGraw-Hill, 1952). See Burke Davis, *The Billy Mitchell Affair* (New York: Random House, 1967), for a detailed account of Mitchell's court-martial. William Mitchell's *Memoirs of World War I: From Start to Finish of Our Greatest War* (New York: Random House, 1960) was published from the manuscript version in the Mitchell Papers in the Library of Congress.

There are three biographies of Newton D. Baker: Frederick Palmer, *Newton D. Baker, America at War*, 2 vols. (New York: Dodd, 1931); Clarence H. Cramer, *Newton D. Baker, A Biography* (Cleveland: World Publishing Co., 1961); and Daniel R. Beaver, *Newton D. Baker and the American War Effort, 1917–1919* (Lincoln, Nebr.: University of Nebraska Press, 1966). Palmer's work was written in close collaboration with Baker and has the characteristics of a memoir. Cramer's book is the only full-scale biography of Baker. Beaver's is a scholarly account of Baker's career as secretary of war. Willis Thornton's *Newton D. Baker and His Books* (Cleveland: World Publishing Co., 1954) was written from the comments Baker wrote in the margins of the books in his private library. The notes Baker wrote in his books provide interesting insights into his mind. For a highly critical assessment of Baker's performance as secretary of war, consult Ernest W. Young, *The Wilson Administration and the Great War* (Boston: Houghton Mifflin, 1922).

Aside from Mitchell, only a few of the leading airmen have inspired biographers. There is no biography of Mason M. Patrick, nor James E. Fechet, nor Oscar M. Westover, nor Frank M. Andrews. Henry H. Arnold's *Global Mission* (New York: Harper, 1949) is an interesting memoir, full of quotable phrases. A biography of Arnold was initiated more than a decade ago but is yet to be published. Benjamin D. Foulois and Carroll V. Glines's *From the Wright Brothers to the Astronauts: The Memoirs of Benjamin D. Foulois* (New York: McGraw-Hill, 1968) suffers from the unfortunate lack of objectivity that one often finds in memoirs. Brief sketches of Charles T. Menoher, Patrick, Fechet, Foulois, Westover, and Arnold are available in Walter T. Bonney, "Chiefs of the Army Air Force, 1907–1957," *Airpower Historian* 7 (July 1960): 129–42. Edward V. Rickenbacker, *Rickenbacker, An Autobiography* (Englewood Cliffs, N.J.: Prentice-Hall, 1967), includes an account of his participation in the airmail controversy. Jimmy Doolittle's air racing exploits and his opinions on the Baker Board of 1934 are treated in Quentin J. Reynolds, *The Amazing Mr. Doolittle: A Biography of Lieutenant General James H. Doolittle* (New York: Appleton-Century-Crofts, 1953); and Carroll V. Glines, *Jimmy Doolittle: Daredevil Aviator and Scientist* (New York: Macmillan, 1972). There is a short but candid comment on the argument between fighter and bomber advocates in Claire L. Chennault, *Way of a Fighter: The Memoirs of Claire Lee Chennault*, ed. Robert Hotz (New York: G. P. Putnam's Sons, 1949).

The best biography of Douglas MacArthur is D. Clayton James, *The Years of MacArthur*, vol. 1, *1880–1941* (Boston: Houghton Mifflin, 1970). Frazier Hunt's *The Untold Story of Douglas MacArthur* (New York: Devin-Adair Co., 1954) is good for the Roosevelt–MacArthur quarrel. Douglas MacArthur's *Reminiscences* (New York: McGraw-Hill, 1964) is openly self-serving. For an excellent biography of MacArthur's naval antagonist, see Gerald E. Wheeler, *Admiral William Veazie Pratt, US Navy: A Sailor's Life* (Washington, D.C.: Naval History Division, 1974).

Forrest C. Pogue's *George C. Marshall* (New York: Viking Press, 1963) is a four-volume study of Marshall's life: vol. 1, *Education of a General, 1880–1939*, contains reference to Marshall's early attitude toward aviation; vol. 2, *Ordeal and Hope, 1939–1942*, describes Marshall's increasing acceptance of the idea of airpower.

Newspapers and Periodicals

The *New York Times* is very useful for the study of aviation in the 1920s and 1930s. In addition to its excellent coverage of events such as the Mitchell court-martial, the newspaper had a regular Sunday section on developments in military and civil aviation.

Annually there was an article by the chief of the Air Corps on the state of the service.

Also very useful, particularly for the 1920s, was the *Army and Navy Journal*. Coverage of the legislative battles over reorganization of the air arm was very good. Interviews with congressmen, leading airmen, and War Department officials were often published in the *Journal*, and the letters to the editor gave some understanding of the opinions of soldiers in the field.

More recent periodicals containing articles on the history of the Air Corps and on military airpower include *The Air Power Historian*, later *Aerospace Historian*, and now *Air Power History*; and the *Air University Review* and its successor, *Airpower Journal*.

Printed Sources

Congressional involvement in the airpower controversy made the *Congressional Record* a prime source for this study. The *Record* offered more than just the debates in Congress. For example, it printed the full text of the Joint Board Report on the sinking of the *Ostfriesland* in 1921.

The *War Department Annual Reports* (Washington, D.C.: GPO) are a good source for the official Army position. They include the reports of the chief of staff and the secretary of war.

Published personal papers which were useful include Howard H. Quint and Robert H. Ferrell, eds., *The Talkative President: The Off-the-Record Press Conferences of Calvin Coolidge* (Amherst, Mass.: University of Massachusetts Press, 1964); Nancy Harvison Hooker, ed., *The Moffat Papers: Selections from the Diplomatic Journals of Jay Pierrepont Moffat, 1919–1943* (Cambridge, Mass.: Harvard University Press, 1956); and John Morton Blum, *From the Morgenthau Diaries: 1928–1945*, 3 vols. (Boston: Houghton Mifflin, 1959–1967).

Manuscript Sources

Archives

The records of the War Department in the National Archives are voluminous. A researcher must be selective. For this study, research was limited to Record Groups (RG) 18, 165, and 407. RG 18 is the Records of the Army Air Forces (1914–1947), which include records of the chief of the Air Service and the chief of the Air Corps. Also in RG 18 are personal papers of generals Patrick, Fechet, and Andrews. The Patrick papers include personal correspondence and copies of addresses given by Patrick. Although not extensive, these papers were rich in useful material. The Fechet papers were skimpy and of little value. The Andrews papers offered nothing for this study. RG 165 is the Records of the War Department and Special Staff (1903–1947). The records of the Office of the Chief of Staff and the records of the War Plans Division were consulted for this study. Policies concerning the Air Corps were worked out by War Plans and approved or disapproved by the chief of staff. RG 407 is the Records of the Adjutant General's Office (1917–1958). It includes reports, studies, war plans, budget and fiscal records, and general correspondence.

Personal Papers

The William Mitchell manuscripts (MSS) (Library of Congress) include correspondence, unpublished writings, speeches, reports, and other materials. These manuscripts are very important to the history of Army aviation.

The John J. Pershing MSS (Library of Congress) contain correspondence relating to his attitude toward an independent air force and his opinion of the Mitchell court-martial and conviction. Gen Fox Connor wrote Pershing (who was in Chile at the time) detailed letters describing the proceedings of the Morrow Board and of the Mitchell trial.

The Newton D. Baker MSS (Library of Congress) consist of 265 boxes, 16 of which pertain to his activities as secretary of war. Baker was an excellent letter writer, and his correspondence contains many insights into the events of his time.

The Hazel Lewis Scaife MSS (Library of Congress) are a collection of papers relating to the aircraft scandal probe that resulted in the congressional investigation of the Air Service in 1924–1925.

The Charles P. Summerall MSS (Library of Congress) have materials that help explain the relationship of the budget to General Staff attitudes toward the Air Corps.

The Henry H. Arnold MSS (Library of Congress) are a large collection of 85,000 items. These include material of great importance to the history of the Air Corps. In Arnold's correspondence with other airmen, there are candid discussions of controversial issues.

The George S. Simonds MSS (Library of Congress) include an aircraft file (1930–1933); correspondence on the proper size of the Air Corps in the early thirties; a report on the *Mount Shasta* incident; and a collection of fascinating correspondence with Gen Malin Craig, who was at the time the Army commander in Panama.

The Hugh J. Knerr MSS (US Air Force Academy Library, Special Collections) contain personal correspondence, scrapbooks, the manuscript of an autobiography, and 15 volumes of Knerr's diary (1887–1949). The diary was particularly useful.

The Benjamin D. Foulois MSS (Library of Congress) are a collection of correspondence, records, diaries, and copies of official documents.

The George H. Dern MSS (Library of Congress) are a disappointing collection of news releases and speeches.

The Ross Collins MSS (Library of Congress) have no materials concerning his close relationship with Foulois or his battle with MacArthur over the strength of the Army officer corps.

The Laurence S. Kuter MSS in Special Collections of the US Air Force Academy Library are mostly related to the Second World War. There are, however, some materials from Kuter's activities at the Air Corps Tactical School and on the Air War Plans Division (which wrote AWPD-1).

Other manuscripts consulted include those of Harry Stewart New (Indiana State Library), Henry L. Stimson (Yale University Library), William V. Pratt (Library of Congress), John L. Hines (Library of Congress), and Payton C. March (Library of Congress).

Oral Histories

Oral history interviews are very useful for acquiring a flavor of the times. But the "facts" drawn from oral history interviews are unreliable unless tested. I consulted the interviews of Benjamin D. Foulois, Ira C. Eaker, Eugene Beebe, Leroy T. Lutes, Thomas De W. Milling, Carl A. Spaatz, Frank P. Lahm, and Robert A. Lovett. These are in the Oral History Collection at Columbia University.

Index

Adams, Charles F.: 70–71, 75–76, 78
Air Board: 171
Air Corps: 99, 133–34, 139, 144, 148, 159, 161–62, 166, 170, 173–76, 187–89, 190–92
   budget problems: 60–61
   expansion: 170, 173–75
   five-year plan: 138, 141
   pilot training: 175–76
   Plans Division: 99
   Tactical School: 148, 159, 161–62, 166,
   Training Center: 176
air demonstrations
   against battleships: 15–17
   bombing of the *Mount Shasta*: 92–94
   maneuvers of 1931: 92
Air Force: 144
Air Service, US: 2, 4, 6, 11–12, 14–16, 18–19, 27–28, 30–33, 39, 44–45, 61, 64, 101, 144
   budget priorities: 1–2
   deplorable state of: 35
   personnel shortages: 33
   research and development: 33–35
Air Service Act of 1920: 19
Air Service/Air Corps units
   1st Surveillance Group: 14
   1st Air Division: 92
   1st Day Bombardment Group: 14
   1st Provisional Brigade: 16
   1st Pursuit Group: 14
   1st Army Observation Group: 14
   2d Bombardment Group: 158
   2d Observation Group: 14
Air War Plans Division: 174
Air War Plans Division-Plan 1 (AWPD-1): 174
Aircraft. *See also* entries for individual aircraft
   choosing production models: 157
   developing bombers: 159–70
   pursuit (fighter) aircraft: 161–63
   radar: 163
Airmail crisis of 1934
   accidents: 131–33
   Baker Board findings: 145
   cancellation of commercial contracts: 132–33
   equipment: 133–34
   Lindbergh opposition: 144
   personnel: 134
Aisne-Marne campaign: 6

Alaska: 163, 164–67
Alaska flight: 160
Allen, Robert: 92
Allied Expeditionary Force (AEF): 1, 4, 6
Allison V-1710-3 engine: 163
American Aircraft Commission: 9
American Society of Mechanical Engineers: 41
Andrews, Frank M.: 150–51, 164, 167–69
Argentina: 28
Armistice (1918): 2, 28, 185
Army Air Corps: 1, 3, 59, 65–66, 83–86, 88–89, 90–94
Army Air Corps Act of 1926: 61, 64, 189, 191
Army and Navy Journal: 17, 42
Army Command and Staff College: 192
Army War College: 138
Arnold, Henry H. "Hap": 5–6, 12, 18, 45, 94, 132, 149, 160–62, 170–73, 178–79, 192
Atkinson, Joseph H.: 176
Atoka Coal and Mining Company: 72

B-10: 134, 160–61
B-12: 160, 162
B-17: 165–66, 168, 171, 178
B-18: 165, 167
B-36: 164
Baker Board: 144–47, 149, 166
Baker, Newton D.: 3–6, 9, 13, 16, 17, 60
   description: 3–4
   view of airmen: 4–5
   view of airpower: 5
Balanced Air Corps Program: 169
Barbour, Henry E.: 73
Barksdale Field, La.: 150, 163
Barling Bomber (XNBL-1): 33–35
Bettis, Cy: 59
Bingham Committee: 69
Bingham, Hiram: 41, 68–69, 70–71
Black, Hugo L.: 132
Boeing 299: 164
Boeing Airplane Company: 164
Bolling Field, D.C.: 76
bombing tests: 15–17
Borah, William E.: 16
Boston and *Boston II* (aircraft): 28
Boston, Mass.: 92
Bowley, Albert J.: 43
Branch, Harlee: 132
Brereton, Lewis H.: 178

Brett, George H.: 179
Brown, Walter F.: 132
Brownsville, Tex.: 14
Budget and Accounting Act of 1921: 30
Buenos Aires, Argentina: 168
Bureau of Aeronautics: 64
Bureau of Efficiency: 74, 77–78
Bureau of the Budget: 30, 73–74, 88–89, 186–87, 101

Caribbean Defense Command: 177
Carrier Division One: 77
Chamberlin, Clarence D.: 144
Chaumont, France: 1
Chemical Warfare Service: 36, 89
Chennault, Claire L.: 148, 161–62
Cheyenne, Wyo.: 131
Chicago (aircraft): 28
Chicago, Ill.: 138
Chief of Naval Operations: 149
China: 27, 169
Cibolo Site: 176
Cleveland, Ohio: 131
Coast Guard: 94
coastal defense: 62–67, 69–79, 167, 187
Coco Solo (Panama): 66, 73, 75, 77
Coe, Frank W.: 10
Coffin, Howard E.: 41
Collins, Ross: 95–96, 98, 187
colored war plans: Red, 136; Red-Orange, 136, 139; Green, 136
Command and General Staff School: 148
Committee on Naval Affairs: 41
 committee report: 41–42, 45
 composition: 19
Conner, Fox: 31
Coolidge, Calvin: 28–31, 33, 39, 41, 44, 59, 61, 185, 189, 191
Craig, Malin: 68, 72, 74–75, 150, 168–69, 170–71
Crissy Field, Calif.: 27
Crowell, Benedict: 9
Crowell Commission: 9, 11
Culver, C. C.: 158
Currituck Light: 92
Curry, Charles F.: 9, 10–13, 45
Curry, John F.: 96
Curtiss Jennies (airplane): 14

D'Oisy, Peltier: 28
Daniels, Josephus: 15, 76
Dargue, Herbert H.: 18, 93–94
Davis, Norman: 97
Davison, F. Trubee: 59, 69–70, 75, 88–89, 97

Dayton, Ohio: 35
Daytona Beach, Fla.: 132
DB-1 (later B-18): 164
Denby, Edwin: 31, 64
Denison, Arthur C.: 41
Department of National Defense: 76
Depression (Great Depression): 185
 effect on the Air Corps five-year plan: 83–87, 89, 102, 105
 effect on disarmament: 96–97
 effect on military budget: 83
Dern, George H.: 102, 133, 138, 140, 142–46
destroyers-for-bases deal: 177
DH-4: 14–15, 33
Dickman Board: 6–7, 10, 12
 members: 7
 report: 7, 12
Dickman, Joseph T.: 6
Doolittle, James A. "Jimmy": 59, 144, 190
Douglas, Lewis: 101
Drum Board: 138–40, 148–49, 166
Drum, Hugh A.: 7, 37, 133, 138–39, 147
Duffy, Father Francis: 6
Durand, William F.: 41

Eaker, Ira C.: 45
84-group plan: 174
Elfrey, G. E.: 27
Embick, Stanley D.: 67, 167
Emmons, Delos C.: 179
Evans, Donald P.: 77

Fairfield, Ohio: 15
Far East Air Forces: 178
Farley, James A.: 132
Fechet, James E.: 67, 75, 84–86, 89, 95, 159–60
First Aviation Objective: 174
Fletcher, Frank F.: 41
Flying Tigers: 161
Foch, Ferdinand: 191
Fokker B-8: 159
Fort Bliss, Tex.: 14
Fort Leavenworth, Kans.: 148
Fort Sam Houston, Tex.: 38
42d (Rainbow) Division: 6
Foulois, Benjamin D.: 8–9, 11–12, 45, 76, 95, 99, 132–35, 138–39, 147–48, 150–51, 159–60
 airmail commitment: 132
 Alaska flight: 159–60
 Drum Board member: 138
 reaction to Menoher testimony: 8–9

France Field, Canal Zone: 14
Frear Committee: 6, 8, 189–90

GA-1: 32
GA-2: 32
General Headquarters (GHQ) Air Force
  air defense plans: 136–39
  command structure: 135–36
  establishment: 135, 150
  organization: 135, 150
  planes: 136–37, 141
  size: 136
General Schofield: 92
General Staff: 6, 9, 15, 31, 36, 45, 60, 62–64, 67–68, 73, 83–84, 89, 95–96, 101–2, 134, 140–41, 143, 147, 150, 166–68
Geneva Conference: 96–97, 149, 186
George, Harold L.: 148, 174
Good, James W.: 70–73
Good Will Flight: 168
Gorrell, Edgar Stanley: 44, 144
Greely, J. N.: 66
Guam: 172
Gulick, John W.: 138

Haan, William G.: 10
Hague Convention: 149
Hansell, Haywood S., Jr.: 163, 174
Harbord, James G.: 40
Harvey, Alva L.: 27
Hawaii: 29, 33, 59, 63, 77, 88, 163–67
Hawaiian Air Force: 177
Hegenberger, Albert F.: 59
Henderson: 16
Hess, John: 131
Hill, Ployer P. "Pete": 165
Hines, John L.: 7, 30, 60
Hitler, Adolf: 186
Holley, I. B., Jr.: 173
Hoover, Herbert C.: 68, 73, 77, 84–85, 87, 89–91, 96, 170, 185, 189
Hopkins, Harry: 170
House bills
  H.R. 7553: 142
  H.R. 7601: 142–43
  H.R. 7872: 142–43
House Committee on Military Affairs: 13–14, 45, 95, 99, 140
House Economy Committee: 98
House Subcommittee on Military Appropriations: 88, 95
Howard, F. L.: 131–32
Howell Commission: 148, 166
Hughes, Charles Evans: 60
Hunsaker, Jerome: 41

Hurley, Patrick J.: 72–76, 78, 85–91, 93–94, 99

Ickes, Harold L.: 101–2
Illustrated London News: 15
Indiana: 15–16
Ingalls, David S.: 75–76, 93
Inter-Allied Munitions Council: 1

Jahncke, Ernest L.: 72, 74
James, W. Frank: 68
Japan: 27, 136, 139
JL-12: 32
Johnson, Louis: 170
Joint Aeronautical Board: 64–66, 68–69
Joint Army and Navy Board: 17, 73–75, 91
Joint Commission on Aerial Coastal Defense: 69
Joint Planning Commission: 90
Junkers Ju-83: 162
Junkers Ju-87 Stuka: 162

Kelly Field, Tex.: 14
Kelly, O. G.: 27
Kenney, George C.: 161–62
Kerwin, A. R.: 131–32
Keystone B-3A: 158
Keystone LB: 158–59
Kilbourne, Charles E.: 102–5, 135, 137–38, 140, 142, 146–49, 166
Kilner, W. G.: 100
King, William H.: 14, 69
Knerr, Hugh J.: 158–59, 168
Knox, Frank: 178
Kuhn, J. E.: 63
Kuter, Laurence S.: 174
Kybertown, Pa.: 131

LaGuardia, Fiorello H.: 12
Lahm, Frank P.: 19, 176
Lampert Committee: 35, 37–38, 42, 45
Lampert, Florian: 35
Langley Field, Va.: 77, 93, 150, 158
Lansdowne, Zachary: 39
Lassiter Board: 19, 20, 31, 36–37, 64, 90, 134, 136
Lassiter, William: 7
LePere (aircraft): 27
LeMay, Curtis E.: 176, 188–89
Liddell Hart, Basil H.: 95
Lindbergh, Charles A.: 144
Lockheed XP-38: 162
Lodge, Henry Cabot Jr.: 173
Loening amphibian aircraft: 59
Lovett, Robert A.: 178–79, 189

Lufbery, Raoul: 2
Luke Field, Honolulu: 14
LWF Owl (aircraft): 33

MacArthur, Douglas: 43–44, 78, 88–89, 91, 93–96, 133–35, 138, 140–41, 150, 161, 165–66, 168
    MacArthur–Collins controversy: 95–96
    MacArthur–Pratt Agreement: 71, 78, 90, 96–97, 149
    proposal to abolish military aviation: 91–98
Macready, J. A.: 27
Maginot Line: 172
Mahan, Alfred T.: 62, 74, 192
Maitland, Lester J.: 59
Manufacturers' Aircraft Association: 35
March Field, Calif.: 150
March, Peyton C.: 9, 12, 37
Marine Corps: 36, 45, 65, 91
Marshall, George C.: 170–71, 174, 192
Martin 146: 164
Martin B-10 (XB-10): 63, 159
Martin B-18: 173
Martin MB-2: 15, 158
Martin XB-17: 163
Martin, Charles H.: 99
Martin, Frederick L.: 27
Martin, James Vernon: 34
Mascoutin: 92
Massachusetts Institute of Technology: 41, 144
Materiel Division: 163
Maughan, Russell L.: 27
McAdoo, William G.: 3
McCook Field, Ohio: 32, 34
McSwain, John J.: 95, 142
Menoher Board: 9–12
    airmen's reaction: 11–12
    findings: 10, 12
    members: 10
Menoher, Charles T.: 6, 8, 12, 14, 17–18, 20
    description: 6
    on separate air service: 8, 12
    resignation: 17–18
    testimony before Frear committee: 8
Middletown, Pa.: 15
Milling, Thomas D.: 16, 45, 192
Mine Force: 77
Miraflores locks: 72
Mitchel Field, N.Y.: 27
Mitchell court-martial: 42–45
    defense: 42
    findings: 44
    members of the court: 43
    proceedings: 43–44
    scene: 42
Mitchell, William "Billy": 2–5, 8, 10–11, 13, 17, 35–38, 41–45, 64, 69, 74, 88, 190–92
    flamboyance: 4–5
    vision for airpower: 2–3
Mitchell, William D.: 71–73
Moffat, Jay Pierrepont: 97–98
Moffett, William A.: 35, 64, 66, 100
Montgomery, Ala.: 15
Morgan, J. P.: 60, 84
Morgenthau, Henry: 170
Morin Bill: 45
Morin, John M.: 45
Morrow Board: 143
Morrow, Dwight W.: 40–42, 59–60
Mount Shasta: 100

National Broadcasting Company: 92
National Crime Commission: 60
National Defense Act of 1920: 14
Naval Affairs Committee: 140
Naval Air Operating Policy: 77
Navy Bureau of Aeronautics: 100
Navy five-year plan: 31, 62, 65, 75
Nelson, John M.: 35
New Bill: 10–13, 15
New Jersey: 32
New Orleans (aircraft): 28
New York Stock Exhange: 185
New, Harry S.: 9
Nolan, Dennis E.: 30
Northrop A-17: 162–63

O'Donnell, Emmett "Rosie": 178
O-38E: 132
O-39: 131
Office of the Assistant Secretary of War for Air: 189
Office of the Chief of the Air Corps: 100
Office of the Secretary of the Navy: 90
Office of the Secretary of War: 90
Ogden, H.: 28
Oglala: 77
Olds, Robert: 148, 168
Ostfriesland: 16, 158, 190

P-35 pursuit: 162
P-36: 162, 173
Pan American Airways: 144
Panama: 29, 33, 63, 71, 76, 77, 163, 164–67
Paranaque Field, Manila: 14
Parker, James S.: 41

Patchogue, N.Y.: 131
Patrick, Mason M.: 18, 20, 28, 34–36, 42, 45, 59, 62–63, 65–66, 134
    character: 18
    coastal defense missions: 19
    proposals for the Air Service: 19
    relations with Mitchell: 18
Patterson Field, Ohio: 160
Payne, Frederick H.: 76, 96
Pearl Harbor, Hawaii: 66, 68, 73, 75, 77, 173
Pearson, Drew: 92
Pedro Miguel locks, Panama: 72
Perkins, Randolph: 38–39
Pershing, John J.: 1, 6, 12–13, 16–18, 28, 30–31, 33, 48
Philippines: 29, 33, 86, 178
PN-9 (seaplane): 39
Power, Thomas S.: 176
Pratt and Whitney R-1860-11 engine: 159
Pratt, R. S.: 75
Pratt, William V.: 76–78, 90–91, 149, 168
Project A: 163
Public Works Administration: 101–2
Pulitzer Trophy: 59
Putt, Donald L.: 176
PW-8: 32
PW-9: 32

Quesada, Elwood R.: 176

Randolph, William M.: 176
Rawlings, Edwin W.: 176
Reardon, J. D.: 66
Reed, David A.: 69
Reid, Frank: 42–44
Reid, W. N.: 132
Republican Campaign Textbook of 1924: 29
Rex (Italian liner): 168
Richardson, H. C.: 41
Rickenbacker, Edward V. "Eddie": 2, 133, 172, 190
Rockwell Field, Calif.: 63
Rodgers, John: 39
Roop, J. Clawson: 88, 91
Roosevelt, Franklin D.: 98–102, 132–33, 170–74, 186
round-the-world flight: 27
Royal Air Force (RAF): 179

San Antonio, Tex.: 15, 168, 177
Saratoga: 71–72
Schneider Cup: 59

Schroeder, R. W.: 27
SE-5 pursuit: 15
Seattle (aircraft): 27
Second Aviation Objective: 174
Shenandoah: 39
Signal Corps: 36
Simonds, George S.: 67–68, 71, 73, 75, 77, 91, 94, 138
Sims, William S.: 60, 69–70, 76
Site Selection Board: 176
Sladen, Fred W.: 43
Smith, Alfred E.: 68
Smith, Lowell H.: 27–28
Snow, William J.: 10
Southwest Pacific Air Forces: 161
Spaatz, Carl A.: 1, 4, 45, 94, 192
Spanish–American War: 76
Stark, Harold R.: 170
Stettinius, Edward R.: 1
Stimson, Henry L.: 87, 98, 172, 178–79,
Stutz Motor Car Company: 44, 144
Subcommittee on Army Appropriations: 73
Summerall, Charles P.: 43–44, 67–68, 70, 73, 75, 84–85, 88

Taylor, Karl: 144
Thomas-Morse MB-3A: 32–33
Tinker, Clifford A.: 132
Tower, Les: 165
training bases
    Chanute Field, Ill.: 177
    Kelly Field, Tex.: 176
    Randolph Field, Tex.: 176
Transcontinental Air Transport: 144
Tyner, George P.: 169

Utah: 168

Vinson, Carl: 41
Virginia: 32

Wade, L.: 28
Wainwright, J. M.: 45
Walker, Kenneth W.: 174
Walsh, Raycroft: 35
War Department: 5–6, 13–14, 19, 39, 61–62, 65, 76, 89, 94, 98–100, 105, 133, 142–44, 162, 167, 170–71, 174, 178, 187
War Department Major Project Number 4: 30
War Department Training Regulation 440-15: 166–67

War Plans Division: 36–37, 65–66, 73, 85, 91, 94, 102–6, 166–67, 170
Warner, Edward: 41
Washington Conference for the Limitation of Naval Armaments: 17
Washington Herald: 37
Webster, Robert M.: 148
Weeks, John W.: 17, 19–20, 30, 37–38, 64, 90
West Coast maneuvers (1934): 160
Westover, Oscar M.: 136–38, 150–51, 166, 169
White, Herbert A.: 42
White, Thomas D.: 99
Wienecke, Otto: 131–32
Wilbur, Curtis D.: 31, 64
Williams, John S.: 29
Wilson, Donald: 148
Wilson, Hugh R.: 170
Wilson, Woodrow: 3, 8
Winged Defense: 38–39, 41

Winship, Blanton: 43
Wolfe, K. B.: 192
Wood, William R.: 95
Woodring, Harry H.: 169, 171
World War I: 1, 4–5, 9, 20, 29, 41, 43–44, 64, 105, 132, 176
World War II: 162, 171, 189
Wright Field, Ohio: 163–64
Wright R-1820-G5 Cyclone engine: 164
Wright, Orville: 144

XB-17 (later B-17): 164
XB-907: 159
XFM-1 (Airacuda): 162
XO-36: 159
XP-39: 162
XP-40: 162

Yale Aviation Unit: 60
YB-9 (later B-9): 159